Adventures in English Syntax

For anyone who wants to become a more effective writer, a more perceptive reader, and a more precise thinker, an understanding of English sentence structure is indispensable. This book shows you how to begin. Using clear and engaging examples from English, it introduces the basic concepts of syntactic structure to readers with no background in linguistics. Starting with simple, familiar phrases, and progressing to more complex sentences, it builds on what we already intuitively know, to provide a step-by-step account of why we understand these examples as we do. It then shows how that understanding can be applied to writing, helping us to avoid some of the common hallmarks of 'bad writing', such as ambiguity, redundancy, and vagueness. A unique and valuable resource, this book will enrich your understanding of English in ways that will make you a more effective user of the language.

ROBERT FREIDIN is Emeritus Professor of Linguistics at Princeton University, and author of *Syntax: Basic Concepts and Applications* (Cambridge University Press, 2012).

Adventures in English Syntax

Robert Freidin

Princeton University

Cambridge
UNIVERSITY PRESS

University Printing House, Cambridge CB2 8BS, United Kingdom

One Liberty Plaza, 20th Floor, New York, NY 10006, USA

477 Williamstown Road, Port Melbourne, VIC 3207, Australia

314–321, 3rd Floor, Plot 3, Splendor Forum, Jasola District Centre,
New Delhi – 110025, India

79 Anson Road, #06–04/06, Singapore 079906

Cambridge University Press is part of the University of Cambridge.

It furthers the University's mission by disseminating knowledge in the pursuit of
education, learning, and research at the highest international levels of excellence.

www.cambridge.org
Information on this title: www.cambridge.org/9781108487726
DOI: 10.1017/9781108767774

© Robert Freidin 2020

First published 2020

Printed in the United Kingdom by TJ International Ltd, Padstow Cornwall

A catalogue record for this publication is available from the British Library.

Library of Congress Cataloging-in-Publication Data
Names: Freidin, Robert, author.
Title: Adventures in English syntax / Robert Freidin.
Description: 1. | New York : Cambridge University Press, 2019. | Includes
  bibliographical references and index.
Identifiers: LCCN 2019038243 (print) | LCCN 2019038244 (ebook) |
  ISBN 9781108487726 (hardback) | ISBN 9781108737807 (paperback) |
  ISBN 9781108767774 (epub)
Subjects: LCSH: English language–Syntax.
Classification: LCC PE1361 .F74 2019 (print) | LCC PE1361 (ebook) |
  DDC 425–dc23
LC record available at https://lccn.loc.gov/2019038243
LC ebook record available at https://lccn.loc.gov/2019038244

ISBN 978-1-108-48772-6 Hardback
ISBN 978-1-108-73780-7 Paperback

Contents

Preface

The seed for this book was planted more than 55 years ago when my 10th grade English teacher, Harriet Perl, taught us the elements of English sentence structure: prepositional phrases and relative clauses; finite vs. infinitival and gerundive clauses; compound vs. complex sentences (and thus the difference between coordination and subordination). For me, this was a revelation – leading to a 50-year career in linguistics as a syntactician. My high school understanding of English sentence structure allowed me to engage with my own writing at a fundamental level where I could view my sentences as syntactic structures that connected to other syntactic structures, and thus to different sentences for expressing the same thoughts – providing a basis for comparison/evaluation. From the 10th grade on, I had an intellectual tool for crafting inevitably imperfect first drafts into prose that presented my thoughts clearly. The process of writing became a way to clarify my thinking on the topic I was writing about – what Francis Bacon had in mind when he wrote in "Of Studies" (1625) that *writing [makes] an exact man*. Externalizing thoughts in black and white is perhaps the best way to discover what is unclear, illogical, or based on questionable assumptions – if you are paying attention. And as a result, writing is never surprise-free. It ceases to be a chore, and becomes instead fun and interesting – if you enjoy exploring your thoughts and how best to express them.

On the usefulness of understanding the elements of sentence structure, Henry Watson Fowler, author of one of the most important and most celebrated commentaries on the English language in the twentieth century, wrote in 1906:

... sentence analysis – the taking of a sentence to pieces and determining the exact relation of each piece to the rest – has a very practical value for every one who would either write without blunders or be sure of a writer's meaning.[1]

---

[1] From the first paragraph of the preface to *Sentence Analysis for the Lower Forms of Public Schools* (Oxford,1906). Fowler's celebrated commentary is *A Dictionary of Modern English Usage* (Oxford, 1926).

Fowler is making the point here that an understanding of sentence structure is useful to both writers <u>and</u> readers. And being *sure of a writer's meaning* applies to what you write (does your syntax clearly express what you intend to say?) as well as to what you read (what is the meaning conveyed by the syntax of the sentences you are reading?, a question that applies equally to what you write). The writer Lee Child makes this point more generally as a question:

How can you write – or even just read – and not be attentive to language and how it's put together?[2]

– a question that applies to all of us.

How the elements of sentence structure fit together constitutes the SYNTAX of a language. And while the study of syntax has been an important and lively subfield in linguistics for more than sixty years, beginning with Noam Chomsky's famous 1957 monograph *Syntactic Structures*, what has been learned from linguistics about the syntactic structure of English is almost never discussed in books about writing.[3] Moreover, the subject of syntax seems to have had virtually no place in the teaching of English in elementary or secondary education since the early 1960s,[4] or even college writing programs. Consider, for example, how *Grammar Alive!: A Guide for Teachers* (2003) describes this situation:

At the start of this new millennium, throughout much of the K-12 English curriculum, grammar is a broken subject. If you find yourself just not knowing what to do about grammar – how to teach it, how to apply it, how to learn what you yourself were never taught – you are not alone. Grammar is often ignored, broken off altogether from the teaching of literature, rhetoric, drama, composition, and creative writing. Grammar is the skunk at the garden party of the language arts.[5]

Grammar Alive! was published as an attempt to repair this situation, and although it proposes as one goal that

Every student will complete school with the ability to analyze the grammatical structure of sentences within English texts, using grammatical terminology correctly and

---

[2] Quoted in *Reacher Said Nothing: Lee Child and the Making of <u>Make Me</u>* by Andy Martin (Bantam Books, 2015), p. 64).

[3] With the notable exception of Steven Pinker's *The Sense of Style: The Thinking Person's Guide to Writing in the 21st Century* (2014), which devotes a chapter to the analysis of sentence structure.

[4] Martha Kolln & Craig Hancock (2005), "The Story of English Grammar in United States Schools", *English Teaching: Practice and Critique*, 4.3: 11–31.

[5] By Brock Haussamen with Amy Benjamin, Martha Kolln, Rebecca S. Wheeler, and members of the Assembly for the Teaching of English Grammar, a group in National Council of Teachers of English formed in the late 1980s.

demonstrating knowledge of how sentence-level grammatical structure contributes to the coherence of paragraphs and texts,

the syntactic analysis in the book employs outmoded late nineteenth-century technology (Reed–Kellogg diagrams[6]) for representing sentence structure.

Like *Grammar Alive!*, one goal of this book is to provide readers with an understanding of how basic English sentence structure contributes to both interpretation of sentences and *the coherence of paragraphs*. And while the analysis of sentence structure in the chapters that follow comes from contemporary linguistics, reading this book requires no prior knowledge of either linguistics or traditional grammar. The book's analyses of key examples will provide you with an understanding of how English sentences are put together that you can use to improve both your writing and your comprehension of complicated syntax in the texts you are reading. This understanding serves as a solid basis for evaluating criticism of the English language in the form of prescriptive 'rules of grammar' (about not splitting infinitives or ending sentences with prepositions) and prescriptions for good style like avoiding the passive voice – based mostly on false characterizations of English syntax. Plus, focusing on the details of sentence structure in great literature is one way to reveal and appreciate the artistry of its language – demonstrated in Chapter 6.

Each chapter of this book is titled with an English expression that is then analyzed in detail. The first three chapters and the first part of the fourth concern the syntactic structure of English expressions that are not complete sentences, but nonetheless illustrate fundamental properties of syntax that generalize to sentences. The remainder of the book is about sentences, as the chapter titles show.

The very short Chapter 1 concerns the ambiguity of the words that title a famous children's book by Dr. Seuss, starting with the latter two *fish* (singular or plural?) and extending to how the 4 modifier-noun pairs of the title relate to one another. It demonstrates how our understanding of a tiny piece of English syntax, consisting of 8 words (2 numbers and 2 colors plus 4 instances of the same word *fish*), is determined by an intricate computation that we perform automatically and unconsciously.

Chapter 2 continues the investigation of ambiguity in English syntax, where in this case a single string of words corresponds to more than one syntactic structure. Chapter 2 focuses on nouns and their modifiers in coordinate structures formed with the conjunction *and*. The chapter ends with a

---

[6] Reed & Kellogg (1887). See more recently Martha Kolln, Loretta Gray, and Joseph Salvatore, *Understanding English Grammar*, 10th edition (Pearson, 2016). For an example along with some discussion, see Chapter 4, footnote 1.

demonstration of how using multiple conjunctions in a coordinate construction also creates ambiguities that result from differences in syntactic structure. This chapter shows how such ambiguities arising from the use of conjunctions can be eliminated.

Chapter 3 further develops the theme of ambiguity in coordinate structures through a detailed analysis of the title of the introductory linguistics course at Princeton University. This leads to the question of the interpretation of the two nouns the title coordinates: *language* and *linguistics* – and their relation. The chapter concludes with a discussion of both the usefulness of coordination in writing and also how the use of the conjunction *and* invites not only ambiguity, but also redundancy and vagueness – all hallmarks of poor writing. Surprisingly, the misuse of *and* – a persistent problem in students' writing – is not discussed in books on grammar or writing, from the first prescriptive grammars of the eighteenth century to the books on writing of the previous and present centuries.

Chapter 4 begins with an ambiguity in the interpretation of prepositional phrase modifiers in complex noun phrases – those that contain multiple nouns, another ambiguity grounded in syntactic structure. This ambiguity extends to clauses that modify nouns (relative clauses), leading to the syntactic analysis of clauses via relative clauses, which can be finite or non-finite (infinitival). Infinitival relative clauses in English sometimes require ending the clause with a preposition, contrary to the prescriptive rule. The chapter concludes with a discussion of how various prescriptive prohibitions against certain grammatical structures (ending a clause with a preposition, 'splitting' an infinitive, and using *which* in restrictive relative clauses) distorts our natural understanding of English syntax.

The first half of Chapter 5 focuses on the phenomenon of DISPLACEMENT – in this case, involving the syntactic subject of a clause that is interpreted as if it occupied another syntactic position. The chapter begins with the structure and interpretation of infinitival clauses, and then expands the discussion to displacement of clauses, displacement with passive voice, and displacement in complex noun phrases built on a noun that corresponds to a verb (for example, the nouns *indictment* and *indicting*, which correspond to the verb *indict*). The second part of the chapter considers the utility of displacement, including a brief history of the criticism of the passive voice, which is shown to be essentially unfounded because every example of a 'bad' passive sentence cited in these criticisms turns out to be problematic for other reasons. This leads to a consideration of the role of displacement in discourse, which in writing concerns of the structure of paragraphs. The chapter concludes with a very useful structural analysis of the paragraph.

Chapter 6 employs the syntax discussed in the previous chapters in an extended analysis of the opening sentence in Jane Austen's *Pride and*

Prejudice, an analysis which reveals something about the artistry of sentence structure by comparing it to the millions (!) of variant sentences she could have written.

The title of Chapter 7 returns to the theme of ambiguity in syntax, focusing here on the syntax of questions. The ambiguity of the title concerns which of the two verbs the adverb modifies, where each of the two possible interpretations corresponds to a distinct syntactic structure. The title, which is itself a question, also involves what appears to be a displacement of the finite auxiliary *does* in front of the subject. The chapter analyzes the syntactic structure of questions – both direct and indirect – and extends this analysis to the displacement of *wh*-elements (for example, *who* and *what*) in both interrogative constructions (for example, *who have they invited?*) and non-interrogative constructions (relative clauses, cleft and pseudo-cleft constructions).

Chapter 8 examines the phenomenon of ellipsis, where certain parts of sentences in coordinate and subordinate clauses are understood but not pronounced or written. The focus and title of this chapter is an example from Henry Fowler's discussion of problematic passive constructions. The chapter begins with Fowler's analysis of the example and continues with a more detailed syntactic analysis of the title that reveals the syntactic complexity of this example and, in the process, uncovers something surprising about how ellipsis works in English.

To the extent that this book demonstrates the utility of understanding the elements of English sentence structure for writing and reading, it offers readers an intellectual tool for controlling and ultimately improving their own use of language. In this way, having some knowledge of modern linguistics (the syntactic analysis of English) might contribute to improving a person's effective use of language. This intriguing conjecture comes from the late Paul Campbell Jr., who spent his career as an investment banker on Wall Street. *Imagine*, Paul would say, *if such knowledge could improve your use of language just a few percent each year, what that would mean over a lifetime.* This book is an attempt to demonstrate that Campbell's Conjecture may be valid.

This is primarily a book about English sentence structure, a topic that connects naturally to questions of composition, including criticism of English usage. It also connects to the study of syntax in linguistics, which Chomsky defined more than sixty years ago in the first sentence of the first chapter of *Syntactic Structures*:

Syntax is the study of the principles and processes by which sentences are constructed in particular languages.

– what has come to be known as *generative grammar*. But although some of these processes and principles are briefly mentioned in the book, the primary focus remains the sentence structure that results from their application to the English lexicon.[7] To the extent that an understanding of the insights into sentence structure of English gained from the study of syntax is useful for writing and reading, this book demonstrates the general usefulness of generative grammar.

In terms of just writing well, understanding how a sentence is constructed contributes to one of the prerequisites: *Good writing requires a certain confidence*.[8] In addition to having the confidence that you have something to say and that you know what you are talking about – which no book on writing will give you, there is also the confidence that you can express your ideas in clear prose – which is what understanding the workings of English syntax can provide.

When I began writing this book, the plan was to start with the words in the Dr. Seuss title, which is at first sight deceptively simple, and proceed to incrementally more complex examples, ultimately to complex sentences, questions, and finally to ellipsis. Along the way, writing each chapter turned into an unexpected adventure: discovering new connections within familiar material in syntax, and exploring unfamiliar areas (like the history of prescriptive grammar, and literary criticism via syntactic analysis) – hence the title *Adventures in English Syntax*. My hope is that you, the reader of this book, will also experience these chapters as adventures, and that the understanding gained from them will equip you for your own adventures with the sentences you write and read.

---

[7] See Freidin (2012) for an introduction to these principles and processes, and how they apply in the analysis of languages.

[8] Krantz (1997), p. 2.

Acknowledgments

For their help along the way, I would like to thank Helen Barton, Noam Chomsky, Michael T. Davis, Adam Elga, Harvey E. Finkel, Walter Frank, Adam Freidin, Lisa Green, Robert C. Gunning, Adam Hooper, Marvin Israel, David Jenkins, Laura Kalin, Joshua Katz, Samuel Jay Keyser, Jeffrey Kingsley, Hisa Kitahara, Howard Lasnik, John Logan, Alberto Bruzos Moro, Carlos P. Otero, A. Carlos Quícoli, Ian Roberts, Matthew Seal, Charlotte Singer, Lawrence Solan, Jon Sprouse, Yuri Suzuki, Edward Tenner, Heinrich van Staden, Vinithan Sethumadhavan, Yuval Widgerson, and Ronnie Wilbur.

one fish two fish: thus begins the title of a famous Dr. Seuss children's book, which continues *red fish blue fish*, a title familiar to millions. In a 2001 *Publisher's Weekly* list of books that have sold more than a million copies, the book was listed at #13 with 6,314,391;[1] and six years later, it ranked in the National Education Association online survey for Teachers' Top 100 Books for Children at #80.[2] So the chances are that you recognize the title because you have read the book as a child, or have had the book read to you before you could read, or have read the book to a child. But you may not remember how many fish the title describes.

On the left side of the cover Dr. Seuss draws 5 fish: one white fish on the top, two green fish under it, one red fish under them, and one blue fish under the red fish. On the right side of the cover, we read the 2 words that describe each of these drawings. These words and drawings are repeated on the first page of the book but with the words appearing down the middle of the page and the words in front of the drawings (except for the drawing of *two fish*). On the first page the first three fish change color to yellow, the first yellow fish with red fins and tail. Furthermore, on the first page Dr. Seuss punctuates the title as a sentence by capitalizing *one* as *One* and putting a period after *blue fish*. With the illustrations, it is easy to take for granted how the interpretation of the words in the title works.

Consider the title as it appears on the first page, where the color of the words matches the color of objects they describe.

(a)   One fish two fish red fish blue fish.

This title consists of eight words: the noun *fish* repeated 4 times, the numbers *one* and *two*, and the colors *red* and *blue*, where each noun is modified by a number or a color. The noun together with its modifier constitutes a syntactic unit, as illustrated in (b), which brackets the 4 units.

---

[1] vol. 248, issue 51, December 17.
[2] www.nea.org/grants/teachers-top-100-books-for-children.html

(b)

#1   #2   #3   #4

[One fish] [two fish] [red fish] [blue fish]

The number *One* indicates a single fish, while *two* indicates multiple fish – in this case, exactly 2. Thus the noun *fish* in the first syntactic unit is interpreted as SINGULAR, while in the second unit, *fish*, having the same pronunciation (in linguistics, PHONETIC FORM) and spelling, is interpreted as PLURAL. Given Dr. Seuss's drawing of one red and one blue fish, the two instances of *fish* in the 3rd and 4th syntactic units are also interpreted as singular. We can distinguish the singular/plural distinction graphically by representing the plural in boldface, as shown in (c).

(c)   [One fish] [two **fish**] [red fish] [blue fish]

Furthermore, each syntactic unit describes different fish.

Untethering the title from its illustration opens the gateway to other interpretations, revealing something of the magic of language.

1.1   How an 8-word title can have many interpretations

Consider first the possible interpretations for just *red fish blue fish*. Because the noun *fish* in the English LEXICON (roughly, the collection of words used in a language) can be interpreted as either singular or plural, this part of the title can represent 4 distinct interpretations, as illustrated graphically in (d), where the plural interpretation of *fish* is indicated with boldface.

(d)   1. [red fish] [blue fish]
         2. [red fish] [blue **fish**]
         3. [red **fish**] [blue fish]
         4. [red **fish**] [blue **fish**]

Without a drawing to illustrate which interpretation is intended, all 4 interpretations are equally possible.

In contrast, the first part of the title, *one fish two fish*, might at first glance appear to have only one interpretation, where the two syntactic units designate distinct sets of fish. Thus *one* plus *two* equals 3 fish. However, there is another possible interpretation of *two fish* where this includes the *one fish*. Imagine that Dr. Seuss had drawn a name tag *Mary* on the first fish, and then drawn *Mary* again with another fish *Harry* to represent *two fish*. Under this representation, *one fish two fish* would represent only 2 fish, *Mary* and *Harry*. The same situation can happen without name tags, when for example someone pointing at a single fish in a tank says *one fish* and then pointing to a second fish and says *two fish*, including the first. So the interpretation of these two syntactic units can be either distinct or inclusive, which is another source of ambiguity with this title.

Putting the two parts of the title back together allows for a further compounding of the ambiguities inherent in each part. Let's suppose that all the fish described are either red or blue, in which case the title could be rendered as either (e) or (f), where only the *fish* modified by *two* is interpreted as plural and the other instances of *fish* are singular.

(e)   [One fish] [two **fish**] [red fish] [blue fish]

(f)   [One fish] [two **fish**] [red fish] [blue fish]

If the 4 syntactic units in these representations of the title are interpreted as distinct, this yields 5 fish: $1 + 2 + 1 + 1$ (2 red fish + 3 blue fish) in (e) and $1 + 2 + 1 + 1$ (3 red fish + 2 blue fish) in (f).

Alternatively, the unit *blue fish* in (e) could be interpreted as describing *two fish* and the unit *red fish* could be describing *one fish*. Under this interpretation (*two blue fish* and *one red fish*), there are only 3 fish – and the representation in (e) would actually be (g), where the syntactic unit *blue fish* contains the plural, and to show the identities between *one fish* and *red fish* and between *two fish* and *blue fish*, the corresponding syntactic units carry identical subscripts *a* and *b*.

(g)   [One fish]$_a$ [two **fish**]$_b$ [red fish]$_a$ [blue **fish**]$_b$

Thus $1 + 2 = 3$ fish. And similarly for *two red fish* and *one blue fish* in (f), yielding $2 + 1 = 3$ fish.

In between the 5-fish and 3-fish interpretations lurk several 4-fish interpretations. These interpretations can be derived in more than one way. For one, the interpretation represented in (g) can be modified as (h), where *one fish* and *red fish* are 2 separate fish and thus these syntactic units do not bear an identical subscript.

(h)   [One fish] [two **fish**]$_b$ [red fish] [blue **fish**]$_b$

(h) represents one 4-fish interpretation: 2 red fish and 2 blue fish ($1 + 2 + 1$). The same unlinking strategy applies to *two fish* and *blue fish* in (g), yielding (i).

(i)   [One fish]$_a$ [two **fish**] [red fish]$_a$ [blue fish]

(i) represents a different situation where there is only 1 red fish and 3 blue fish ($1 + 2 + 1$). Two additional 4-fish interpretations result from flipping the colors of *one fish* and *two fish* in (h) and (i), yielding (j.1) and (j.2) where there are again 2 blue fish and 2 red fish ($1 + 2 + 1$), but in a different configuration.

(j)   1. [One fish] [two **fish**]_b [red **fish**]_b [blue fish]
             2. [One fish]_a [two **fish**] [red **fish**] [blue fish]_a

(j.1) represents the interpretation of two red fish and two blue fish ($1 + 2 + 1$), whereas (j.2) yields one blue fish and three red fish ($1 + 2 + 1$). In each of these interpretations one pair of syntactic units describe the same fish (plural in (j.1), singular in (j.2)), while the other two units describe different fish. However, it probably seems more natural to understand the four syntactic units as either paired or distinct.

The other way to understand the Dr. Seuss title as 4-fish is to apply the inclusive interpretation to *two fish* as discussed above, where *two fish* includes the *one fish*, and both *red fish* and *blue fish* designate two other fish. Under this interpretation 4 fish can be matched to the 4 syntactic units as follows, where R designates the color red, and B the color blue:

(k)   syntactic units: 1   2   3   4
             fish: R_a $(R_a + B)$ R   B

The subscript *a* on the first fish functions essentially like a name tag. Without the identical subscript, R and R_a designate different fish, as do the two instances of B in (k). (k) represents two red fish and two blue fish. Because the color of the first two fish in *one fish, two fish* is open to interpretation, the colors assigned the first two units could be switched, yielding again two red fish and two blue fish. Moreover, the first two fish could be the same color, either red or blue. If both are blue, then we have 3 blue fish and 1 red fish, but if both are red, then 3 red fish and 1 blue fish. And as we know from the Dr. Seuss illustrations, the fish described by *one fish two fish* could be colors other than red or blue.

The inclusive interpretation of *one fish two fish* also provides another way to calculate 3-fish with the title. Just assume *red fish* describes the *one fish*. This produces a modification of (k) as (l), where the representation of the third syntactic unit bears the same subscript as the first:

(l)   syntactic units: 1   2   3   4
             fish: R_a $(R_a + B)$ R_a B

Now there is only 1 red fish along with 2 blue fish ($1 + 1 + 1 = 3$).

And from (l) it is simple to find the 2-fish interpretation, simply by interpreting *blue fish* as a description of the second fish in *two fish* – yielding (m):

(m)   syntactic units: 1   2   3   4
             fish: R_a $(R_a + B_b)$ R_a B_b

Which illustrates how Dr. Seuss could have illustrated his cover with just his single red fish and single blue fish.

If 2 is the smallest number of fish that the title can describe, what is the largest number – that is, can we get beyond the 5-fish representations? To see how this is done, reconsider one of the 5-fish representations (repeated below), where all 4 syntactic units represent different fish.

(e)   [One fish] [two **fish**] [red fish] [blue fish]

Fish in both *red fish* and *blue fish* is, under this interpretation, singular. If instead, one of these *fish* is interpreted as plural, yielding either (n) or (o), then the title would be understood as at least one additional fish.

(n)   [One fish] [two **fish**] [red **fish**] [blue fish]
(o)   [One fish] [two **fish**] [red fish] [blue **fish**]

(n) represents the situation where there are at least 3 red fish and 3 blue fish ($1 + 2 + 2 + 1 = 6$), while (o) represents 2 red fish and at least 4 blue fish ($1 + 2 + 1 + 2 = 6$). And if *fish* in both *red fish* and *blue fish* is plural, as in (p), then the title would represent at least 7 fish.

(p)   [One fish] [two **fish**] [red **fish**] [blue **fish**]

So just in terms of how many fish the title could represent, these 8 words are 6-ways ambiguous – putting aside the assignment of other colors to *one fish two fish*.

1.2   Syntax and punctuation

Given the multiple interpretations for this title, we might wonder whether adding some internal punctuation could uniquely identify one or more of them, as happens in title of Lynne Truss's well known 2003 book on punctuation: *Eats, Shoots & Leaves: The Zero Tolerance Approach to Punctuation*. The main title, the back cover of the paperback edition tells us, concerns a panda with a sense of humor who reads English. Having read *eats, shoots and leaves* as part of a description of pandas in a wildlife manual, the panda enters a cafe, orders and consumes a sandwich, fires a gun in the air and then heads for the door. When confronted by a confused waiter, the panda tosses *a badly punctuated* wildlife manual over his shoulder, telling the waiter to look up the entry for *panda*.[3]

As a description of pandas, the comma after *eats* is a mistake if the writer intended to say that the diet of pandas consists of shoots and leaves – in which case, *shoots* and *leaves* are both nouns. With the comma, both *shoots* and *leaves* can only be interpreted as verbs describing actions, because a comma

---

[3] Different versions of this panda joke with the same punch line occur in Ursula Le Guin's 1998 book on story writing, *Steering the Craft* (p. 35), and also in volume 111 of *The Illustrated Weekly of India* (September 30, 1990). Le Guin's discussion occurs at the end of a chapter titled *Punctuation*, and although she tells the panda story *to illustrate the importance of the presence or the absence of the comma*, she does not put a comma after *eats* as Truss does.

can never be used to separate a verb (*eats*) from the noun that functions as its object (*shoots*) – for example, #*reads, novels* (where # marks what is impossible in written English). Given that both *shoots* and *leaves* can be interpreted as either nouns or verbs, the 4 words of the punch line to the panda joke could be legitimately interpreted in three different ways and illegitimately in a fourth, as shown in (q), where * marks an impossible interpretation.

(q)

	Eats	*shoots*	*and*	*leaves*
1.	V	N	&	N
2.	V	V	&	V
3.	V	N	&	V
4.	*V	V	&	N

In (q.1) the two nouns are joined together by the conjunction *and* to form a syntactic unit, a COORDINATE STRUCTURE in which each noun constitutes one CONJUNCT, where this unit is interpreted as the object of the verb *eats*. In (q.2), while the conjunction overtly connects the last two verbs, all three verbs are on a par, so that the title could be rewritten by replacing the comma with another *and*, yielding *Eats and shoots and leaves* with no ambiguity. In this way, (q.2) constitutes a coordinate structure with three conjuncts, each one a verb – the panda's interpretation. With (q.3), the verb *eats* forms a syntactic unit with its object, the noun *shoots*. This syntactic unit (traditionally called a PREDICATE) constitutes the left-hand conjunct of a coordinate structure containing the single verb *leaves* as the right-hand conjunct. The single verb *leaves* also functions as a predicate, so in (q.3) *and* coordinates two predicates. In contrast, (q.1) constitutes a single predicate.

This contrast can be represented graphically by bracketing the syntactic units in (q.1) and (q.3) as illustrated in (r).

(r)

	Eats	*shoots*	*and*	*leaves*
1.	[V	[N	&	N]]
2.	[[V	N]	&	V]

In (r.1 (= q.1)), the coordinate structure that conjoins two nouns constitutes a subpart of the predicate, whereas in (r.2 (= q.3)) the predicate consisting of the first verb and the only noun constitutes a conjunct in the larger coordinate structure. As for the impossibility of (q.4), this follows from the fact that conjuncts in a coordinate structure must be the same type: for example, both nouns as in (r.1) or both predicates as in (r.2); but a noun can never form a coordinate structure with a verb as would have to be the case with (q.4).

Truss's title illustrates how the placement of a comma after *eats* forces the interpretation of *shoots* as a verb, thereby arriving at a unique interpretation out of 4 possible interpretations of the 4 words it contains. This raises the question of whether the other two legitimate interpretations represented in (r) can be distinguished in terms of internal punctuation. In (r.1) where *shoots and leaves* is a coordination of nouns, no internal punctuation is possible. But in (r.2) where *and* coordinates two predicates (*eats shoots* and *leaves*) some punctuation mark between the first predicate and *and* might be plausible. Consider the choices in (s).

(s)
1. *Eats shoots, and leaves*
2. *Eats shoots; and leaves*
3. *Eats shoots: and leaves*
4. *Eats shoots – and leaves*

Grammatically, the comma in (s.1) makes as much sense as in the coordination of *these bankers* and *those politicians* punctuated as *these bankers, and those politicians* (or in a coordination of two verbs as in *eats, and departs* – that is, no sense at all. Whether the semicolon in (s.2) or the colon in (s.3) make more sense, depends what we understand these two punctuation marks to indicate. Lynne Truss's engaging chapter about them surveys a wide range of opinion on their use and abuse. Regarding the colon, she endorses Henry Fowler's colorful description of its function: *that of delivering the goods that have been invoiced in the preceding words; it is a substitute for such verbal harbingers as viz., scil., that is to say, i.e., etc.*[4] And therefore, (s.3) fails to express the intended reading (r.2), where *shoots* is a noun and *leaves* is a verb.

The function of the semicolon, in contrast to the colon, is similar to that of the comma in some coordinate structures. Truss's title coordinates three verbs, an interpretation which could have been expressed by substituting another *and* for the comma, yielding *Eats and shoots and leaves* and showing how some commas stand in for the conjunction *and*. But when the conjuncts in such coordinate structures themselves contain commas – as in *Bloomington, Indiana and Cambridge, Massachusetts and Princeton, New Jersey* – replacing the first *and* with a comma risks confusing the new comma, which is interpreted as 'and', with the ones that come before and after, which clearly do not mean 'and'. A general strategy of punctuation is to use the semicolon instead of the comma in such cases: *Bloomington, Indiana; Cambridge, Massachusetts and Princeton, New Jersey* – a strategy that generalizes to other instances where conjuncts contain commas. Furthermore, when two sentences are joined together with *and* where the two sentential conjuncts are complex and contain commas, the first conjunct is punctuated with a semicolon to indicate the point of separation between the two sentences. Consider for example, George Orwell's discussion of *operators or false verbal limbs* in "Politics and the English Language," which begins with a complaint: *These save the trouble of*

---

[4] *A Dictionary of Modern English Usage* (Oxford, 1926), p. 569. *viz* stands for the Latin *videlicet*, meaning literally 'one may see'; *scil* for the Latin *scilicet*, meaning literally 'one may know'. *i.e.* is an abbreviation for the Latin *id est*, meaning 'in other words'.

picking out appropriate verbs and nouns, and at the same time pad each sentence with extra syllables which give it an appearance of symmetry; and ends with the following compound sentence, where the conjunction (in bold-face) joins two sentences that could otherwise stand alone:

Simple conjunctions and prepositions are replaced by such phrases as *with respect to, having regard to, the fact that, by dint of, in view of, in the interests of, on the hypothesis that*; **and** the ends of sentences are saved by anticlimax by such resounding commonplaces as *greatly to be desired, cannot be left out of account, a development to be expected in the near future, deserving of serious consideration, brought to a satisfactory conclusion*, and so on and so forth.

Because the two sentential conjuncts conjoined by *and* contain commas, the semicolon is used before the *and* to mark the boundary of the first conjunct in a way that distinguishes it from boundaries established by the commas inside it. Otherwise, a comma in this position could easily be lost among the other commas in the sentence. The same use of the semicolon also occurs in the sentence above that precedes the example from Orwell.

In addition, the semicolon can be used to link two independent but related sentences in the absence of a conjunction, as illustrated in the following sentences from the first page of Noam Chomsky's *Language and Thought* (Moyer Bell, 1993).

When I was a graduate student forty years ago, it took no great effort to master the theoretical content of linguistics and psychology; what was then at all understood occupies very little of today's curricula.

Specialization is no proof of progress; it has often meant displacement of penetrating insights in favor of technical manipulation of little interest.

But neither of these functions justify the use of the semicolon between *shoots* and *leaves* in Truss's title (s.2). Which leaves the dash in (s.4) as the only plausible way to punctuate this 4-word sentence to render unambiguously the interpretation (r.2), where *shoots* is a noun and *leaves* is a verb.

Returning to the 4 syntactic units in the Dr. Seuss title, under the interpretation where each unit designates a distinct group of fish, the 4 units function as 4 conjuncts in a coordinate structure. This interpretation could be represented unambiguously by making this explicit: inserting *and*s between the 4 units, as in (t).

(t)   *One fish and two fish and red fish and blue fish.*

However, (t) no longer describes Dr. Seuss's illustration of 5 fish because *fish* in *red fish* and in *blue fish* would most plausibly be interpreted as plural, yielding the at-least-7-fish interpretation. To match the Dr. Seuss illustration, the coordinate structure would have to read *One fish and two fish and a red fish and a blue fish*.

The unambiguous interpretation of the coordinate structure of (t) can also be achieved with punctuation by replacing the first two *and*s with commas, as in (u), or all three *and*s with commas, as in (v).

(u)   *One fish, two fish, red fish and blue fish.*

(v)   *One fish, two fish, red fish, blue fish.*

In (t) and (u) the compact rhythm of Dr. Seuss's title is lost; but reappears in (v), which constitutes an ASYNDETIC coordination, a coordinate structure without any coordinating conjunctions. Truss's title could also be expressed unambiguously as an asyndetic coordination: *Eats, shoots, leaves*.

Asyndetic coordinate structures are primarily stylistic devices in writing; and it's doubtful that they occur in casual speech (or casual writing such as texting). Consider the following four examples highlighted in boldface in (w).[5]

(w)   1. *Although the Inventors* [of the United States] *were hostile to the idea of democracy and believed profoundly in the sacredness of property and the necessary dignity of those who owned it, they did not like the idea of* **king, duke, marquess, earl**.
            2. *Look for independent sources of information beyond* **official pronouncements, the mass media, the formal educational system**.
            3. *It's satisfying to see that sentences shrink, snap into place, and ultimately emerge in a more polished form:* **clear, economical, sharp**.
            4. **Wee, sleeket, cowran, tim'rous** *beastie*

The coordinate structure highlighted in (w.1) coordinates 4 nouns; and functions as the object of the preposition *of*. (w.1) tells us that the founders of the United States did not like the idea of any of these titles equally. The coordinate structure highlighted in (w.2) coordinates 3 syntactic units that are larger than single nouns. This syntactic unit functions as the object of the preposition *beyond*. (w.2) advises us to look beyond the sources of information highlighted in (w.2), which, it is implied, are not the whole story. (w.3) illustrates an asyndetic coordination of adjectives defining *a more polished form* (recall Fowler's characterization of the function of the colon). In (w.1), (w.2), and (w.3) these asyndetic coordinate structures come at the end of the sentence, giving the sentence a bit more tang than the usual syndetic coordinate structure

---

[5] (w.2) comes from Gore Vidal's essay on the Adams family (*New York Review of Books*, March 1976, reprinted in *United States: Essays 1952–1992* (Random House, 1993)). (w.2) occurs as the first sentence of a one paragraph statement by Howard Zinn, author of the best-selling *A People's History of the United States*, in *Take My Advice: Letters to the Next Generation from People Who Know a Thing or Two*, edited by James L. Harmon (Simon & Schuster, 2002), p. 35. (w.3) comes from *Reading Like a Writer* by Francine Prose (HarperCollins, 2006), p. 2. (w.4) is the first line of the Robert Burns poem "To a Mouse".

where the final conjunct is preceded by the coordinating conjunction *and*. In contrast, the 4 adjectives highlighted in (w.4) that describe the *beastie* that is the mouse form a coordinate structure that precedes a noun. Asyndetic coordination of adjectives in front of a noun is perhaps the more usual form – sometimes without commas as in *rich invigorating satisfying flavor* said of a wine.

There is yet another way of punctuating coordinate structures with more than two conjuncts, where the final conjunct is preceded by a coordinating conjunction and the penultimate conjunct is followed by a comma – called a 'serial' comma (or Oxford comma, because the editorial style sheet of Oxford University Press insists on the use of the serial comma). Punctuated with the Oxford comma, Truss's title would read *Eats, Shoots, and Leaves*. While mandatory for Oxford, it is not according to Truss. In demonstrating when an Oxford comma is useful, Truss cites one of her own sentences (on p. 7) which credits an unnamed author with the idea that *punctuation marks are the traffic signals of language: they tell us to slow down, notice this, take a detour, and stop*. She reasons that without the final comma after *detour*, the coordinate structure might be misread as 3 instructions, the last being a compound of 2, instead of 4 separate instructions. Consider another situation where you and a friend have invited 3 people for dinner: Judy, Fred, Helen. Now compare the situation where these three people are independent and therefore 3 invitations were issued, as opposed to the situation where Fred and Helen are a couple. The former situation would be expressed using the Oxford comma straightforwardly as *Judy, Fred, and Helen*, while the latter might be rendered as *Judy, and Fred and Helen*, which applies the Oxford comma to the first conjunct *Judy* (or alternatively by flipping the two conjuncts as *Fred and Helen, and Judy*). These are subtle points; ultimately, a matter of personal taste.[6]

---

[6] A matter of taste normally, but apparently not in legal matters. In February of 2018, Oakhurst Dairy settled a suit filed by company drivers concerning unpaid overtime for $5,000,000. The dispute centered on a piece of syntax in Maine's overtime law, which required that workers be paid 1.5 times their hourly wage for each hour exceeding 40 hours per week. The suit concerned *the handling – in one way or another – of certain, expressly enumerated food products* (quoting from the appeals court decision that ruled in favor of the drivers (https://cases.justia.com/federal/appellate-courts/ca1/16-1901/16-1901-2017-03-13.pdf?ts=1489437006). The piece of syntax in dispute, which is not a full sentence even though it is punctuated as one, formulates one exemption to the protection of the overtime law as:

> *The canning, processing, preserving, freezing, drying, marketing, storing, packing for shipment or distribution of:*
>
> *(1) Agricultural produce;*
> *(2) Meat and fish products; and*
> *(3) Perishable foods.*

The issue is whether the coordinate structure in the first part before the colon contains 8 conjuncts or 9. That is, does it exempt *distribution* as a separate and equal activity?

The Oxford comma, nonetheless, does not help with disambiguating Dr. Seuss's title. *one fish, two fish, red fish, and blue fish* would be interpreted unambiguously as synonymous with the syndetic coordination in (u) or the asyndetic coordination in (v). The usages of the semicolon, discussed above, would not apply. That leaves the colon, which can be used to punctuate the title in a way that uniquely identifies one of the several ways of interpreting the title without internal punctuation. If we separate *one fish two fish* from *red fish blue fish* with a colon after *two fish* (as in (x)), then the 3-fish interpretation emerges if *two fish* does not include *one fish*, or the 2-fish interpretation emerges if it does.

(x)   *One fish, two fish: red fish, blue fish.*

The colon tells us that the 1 and 2 fish invoiced in words preceding the colon are red and blue respectively, thereby delivering additional information about what those words describe. But while the colon induces either the 3-fish or 2-fish interpretation, it does not help with the ambiguity involving color – whether *one fish* is red and *two fish* are blue, or conversely. While punctuation can be helpful in computing the syntactic structure of written language, there is much more to syntactic structure than what punctuation expresses.

One problem with the syntax of the exemption is that, as formulated, it is ambiguous. The object of the preposition *for* could be either *shipment* or *shipment or distribution*. On the latter interpretation, *distribution* (like *shipment*) is subordinated to *packing* (as part of the compound object of the prepositional phrase that modifies *packing*) and therefore not a separate activity excluded by the exemption. However, this interpretation is strange given that *shipment* and *distribution* are pretty close to being synonyms. Nonetheless, all of the activities excluded are formulated as gerunds (see Chapter 5) while *shipment* and *distribution* are different forms (derived nominals – see Chapters 3 and 5). If instead of *distribution*, the law had said *distributing*, it is plausible that the appeals court would have upheld the lower court's ruling against the suit regardless of the missing Oxford comma.

Inserting the Oxford comma to produce *packing for shipment, or distribution* would make it clear that *distribution* is a separate activity from *packing* – even though they have different morphological forms – and therefore, excluded under the overtime law. The punctuation also shows that coordinate structure involves the disjunction of the 9 conjuncts – so interpreted as 'canning or processing or preserving . . .'. But if *or* coordinates only *shipment* and *distribution* as the conjoined object of *for*, then there is no visible conjunction that applies to the list. And if the coordination is intended as a disjunction of terms, then it should have been formulated as *the canning, processing, preserving, freezing, drying, marketing, storing, **or** packing for shipment or distribution*, where the 8th conjunct is preceded by *or*. Had the appeals court focused on this syntactic detail, it is again plausible that it would not have reversed the judgment of the lower court. Otherwise, the list of 8 conjuncts would have to be interpreted as asyndetic coordination, where the missing conjunction is *and* not *or*.

What this shows is that while the use of the Oxford comma in the formulation of the Maine overtime law could have eliminated the ambiguity its absence created, there are additional syntactic factors that could be cited to argue for one interpretation over the other, which the appellate court did.

Coda

In this chapter we have seen how a careful examination of the titles of two well-known books, one 8 words long and the other 4 words long, demonstrates that the interpretation of language involves the computation of its syntactic structure beyond the mere order of words. This computation operates on syntactic units, which could be single words or multiple words grouped together. In written language these units can sometimes be marked by punctuation internal to a sentence that aids in the computation of its syntactic structure. In this way, punctuation provides a lesson in syntax.

The previous chapter showed how the insertion of the conjunction *and* in the Dr. Seuss title eliminates what would otherwise be a surprisingly massive amount of ambiguity – and similarly on a much lesser scale for the title of Lynne Truss's book on punctuation. This chapter will focus instead on how coordinating conjunctions like *and* and *or* can be a syntactic source of ambiguity, and what this ambiguity reveals about syntactic structure.

The title of this chapter consists of a string of 4 words: 1 adjective (*exceptional*), 1 conjunction (*and*), and 2 plural nouns (*students, teachers*). The adjective participates in a modification relation, as in *exceptional students* where the adjective modifies the noun. The conjunction participates in a coordination relation, as in *students and teachers* where *and* coordinates the two nouns, the two conjuncts of the coordinate structure: *students* the left conjunct and *teachers* the right conjunct. The ambiguity of the title results from the two distinct possibilities for interpreting what the adjective modifies. Imagine the adjective as a spotlight with two settings, dim and bright. On the dim setting, the spotlight illuminates only *students*; while on the bright setting, it illuminates both *students* and *teachers*. Thus the scope of the illumination from the spotlight can be narrow, illuminating only the closest object; or it can be wide, illuminating both objects in the coordinate structure. The difference in illumination yields different interpretations.

As will be shown below, this difference follows straightforwardly from the two syntactic structures that can be assigned to the title.

2.1   Syntactic structure in coordinate constructions

On one reading, the chapter title has the same interpretation as *teachers and exceptional students*, where *exceptional* can only be interpreted as modifying *students*. In this unambiguous narrow-scope interpretation of the adjective, the right conjunct is a distinct syntactic unit consisting of the adjective joined together with the noun, while the left conjunct is a syntactic unit consisting of the single noun *teachers*. This analysis can be represented by bracketing words to identify the way they function as syntactic units within the whole expression.

(a)   [[*teachers*] *and* [*exceptional students*]]

This syntactic structure can be represented equivalently but more graphically as a *tree* structure (also called a TREE DIAGRAM), where the lines constitute *branches* which join together at nodes to form unique syntactic units.

(b)

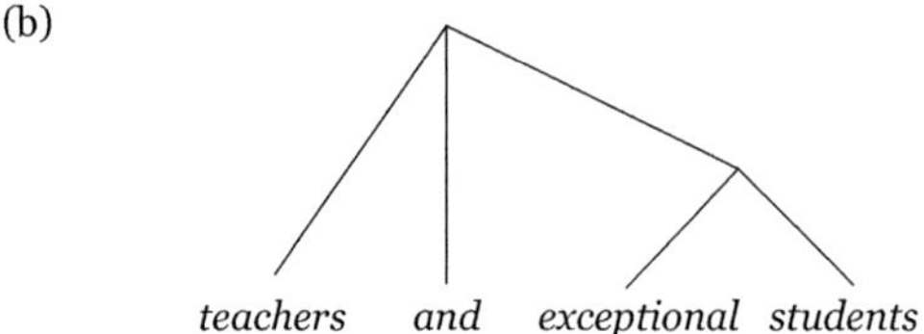

Both representations (a) and (b) show the hierarchical arrangement of syntactic units, where words in a linguistic expression group together to form syntactic subparts of the whole. This HIERARCHICAL STRUCTURE contributes significantly to interpretation beyond the contribution of the individual words in the linguistic expression.

In this coordinate structure, the linear order of the two conjuncts can be reversed without affecting the interpretation, simply by switching the position of the two conjuncts. Switching the linear order of the conjuncts in (a–b) yields a syntactic representation (c), which has the same hierarchical structure as (b) because both contain *exceptional students* as a distinct syntactic unit which is joined to *and* and *teachers* in the same way, but a different linear order (the one of the chapter title).

(c)

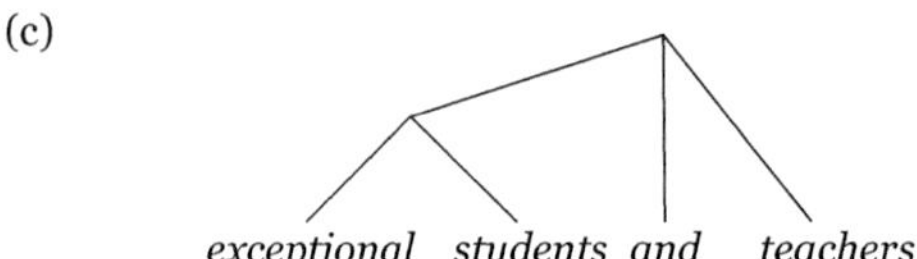

That (b) and (c) have the same interpretation follows from having the same hierarchical structure. The difference in linear order in this case contributes nothing to the interpretation of the two expressions.

On the other interpretation of the chapter title, where *exceptional* modifies both *students* and *teachers*, the two nouns form a coordinate structure that does not include the adjective, and the adjective forms a syntactic unit with the whole coordinate structure (not just the left-hand conjunct). This is illustrated in (d).

(d)

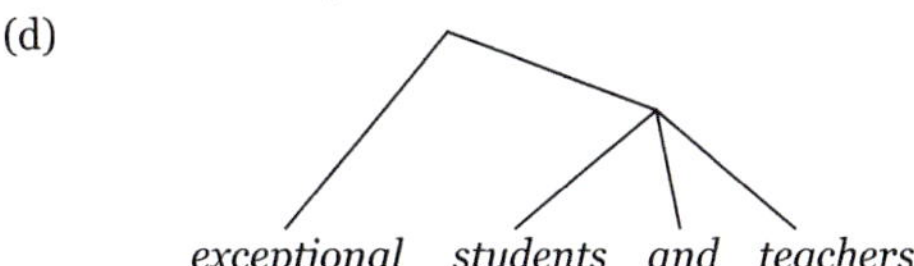

Thus the adjective modifies the coordinate structure, hence the two conjuncts it contains. This yields the wide-scope interpretation.

(c) and (d) share the same linear order of words, but differ in their hierarchical structures. This difference in hierarchical structure determines the different interpretations. Moreover, the linear order of words represented in (d) can be changed by switching the two conjuncts, yielding *teachers and students*, where the hierarchical structure and thus the interpretation remains the same. And of course, the linear order of *exceptional teachers and students* also corresponds to a different hierarchical structure in which *exceptional* forms a distinct syntactic unit with *teachers*, yielding the narrow-scope reading for the adjective. This shows again how (1) a single linear order can correspond to two distinct hierarchical structures, each with a different interpretation, and (2) a single hierarchical structure can correspond to two different linear orders, each having the same interpretation.

Given this syntactic analysis, the hierarchical structure of adjectives in coordinate structures directly reflects the spotlight interpretation of adjectives. However, the end of this section will demonstrate how this spotlight metaphor fails to account for the interpretation of slightly more complicated examples.

These narrow-/wide-scope readings can be distinguished by painting the adjective blue when it is interpreted as having narrow scope (the dim spotlight setting), and red in boldface when it is interpreted as having wide scope (the bright spotlight setting).

(e)   1. *exceptional* *students and teachers*
           2. ***exceptional*** *students and teachers*

Each color corresponds to a distinct hierarchical structure that has an unambiguous interpretation. As shown above, the narrow-scope reading (e.1) can be expressed unambiguously by reversing the order of the conjuncts, yielding *teachers and exceptional students*, while the wide-scope reading can only be expressed unambiguously by repeating the adjective in the second conjunct, yielding *exceptional students and exceptional teachers*.

The same scope ambiguity involving coordinations of nouns arises with modifiers of nouns that follow the noun, for example *teachers from Romania*. The noun *teachers* is modified by the syntactic unit *from Romania*, consisting of a preposition *from* and a noun *Romania*, which form a PREPOSITIONAL PHRASE [P + N], where the noun *Romania* constitutes the object of the preposition *from*. Combining prepositional phrase modification with a coordinate structure as in *students and teachers from Romania* yields the same kind of scope ambiguity that occurs with adjectives. This is illustrated in (f), where (f.1) represents the narrow-scope reading of the prepositional phrase *from Romania* and (f.2) the wide-scope reading.

(f)   1.   *students and teachers from Romania*
           2.   *students and teachers **from Romania***

The interpretation represented in (f.1) corresponds to the hierarchical structure given in (g.1), while the interpretation in (f.2) corresponds to the structure in (g.2).

(g)   1.

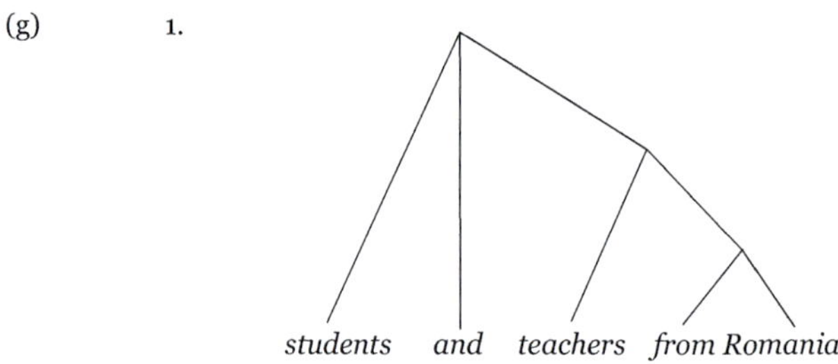

           2.

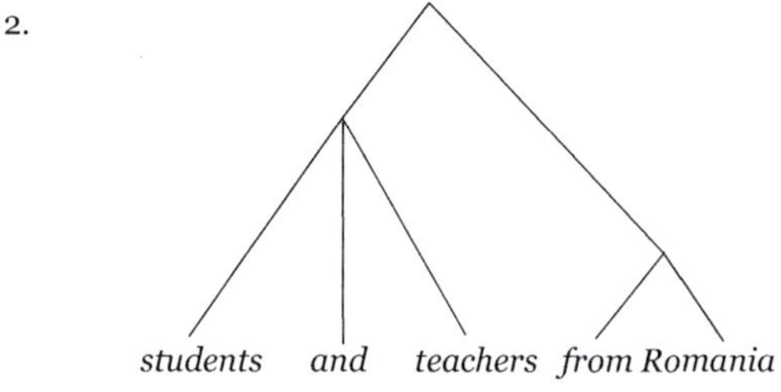

The narrow-scope reading (f.1)/(g.1) can be expressed unambiguously by switching the conjuncts as in *teachers from Romania and students*, where the hierarchical structure of the syntactic units remains the same. One way the wide-scope reading (f.2)/(g.2) can be expressed unambiguously is by repeating the prepositional phrase after *students* as in *students from Romania and teachers from Romania*.

   With one modifier in front of the coordinated nouns and another following them (as in *exceptional students and teachers from Romania*), a four-way ambiguity results because all four interpretations (2 x 2) are possible, as illustrated in (h).

(h)   1.   *exceptional* students and teachers *from Romania*   N–N
             2.   ***exceptional*** students and teachers *from Romania*   W–N
             3.   *exceptional* students and teachers ***from Romania***   N–W
             4.   ***exceptional*** students and teachers ***from Romania***   W–W

Syntactically, this single linear order can be rendered with 4 distinct hierarchical structures, each with a different interpretation.

On the narrow-scope interpretation of both modifiers (h.1), switching the two conjuncts of the coordinate structure yields an alternative linear order with no change in hierarchical structure and therefore the same interpretation. Thus (h.1′) is synonymous with (h.1).

(h)   1′.   *teachers from Romania and exceptional students*   (N–N)

However, when one or both modifiers is interpreted with wide scope, switching conjuncts does not yield an unambiguous linear order. Instead, expressing wide-scope modification unambiguously requires repeating the modifier in both conjuncts. Therefore, (h.2–h.4) could be rendered unambiguously as (h.2′–h.4′).

(h)   2′.   *exceptional teachers from Romania and exceptional students*   (W–N)
             3′.   *teachers from Romania and exceptional students from Romania*   (N–W)
             4′.   *exceptional students from Romania and exceptional teachers*   (W–W)
                   from Romania

In terms of hierarchical structure, all the modifiers in (h.1′–h.4′) constitute narrow-scope modifiers.

While all four readings are possible given that four distinct hierarchical structures can be assigned to the same linear string of words, it may actually be easier to process the modifiers as having the same scope (either W–W or N–N) than as having different scopes. This illustrates how natural language syntax produces some structures that are difficult to process, a point that will come up again at the end of this chapter and in the discussion of relative clauses in Chapter 4.

For the three readings that involve at least one narrow-scope modifier there is only one hierarchical structure that corresponds to each reading. However, for the reading where both modifiers take wide scope, two different hierarchical structures are possible. The difference depends on whether the coordinate structure combines with the prepositional phrase to form a syntactic unit before it combines with the adjective (as illustrated in (i.1) – or conversely (as in (i.2))).

(i)   1.

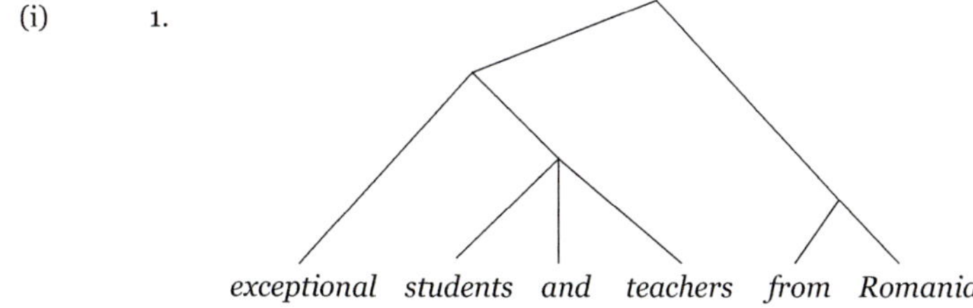

2.

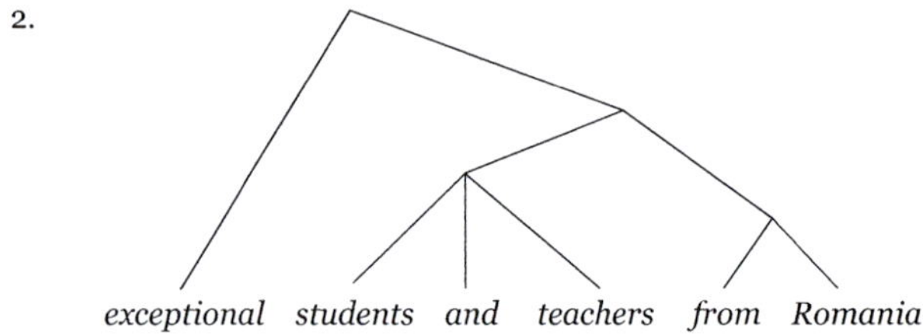

Given the first hierarchical structure, *exceptional students and teachers* constitutes a unique syntactic unit that does not occur in the second; whereas in the second hierarchical structure *students and teachers from Romania* constitutes a unique syntactic unit that does not occur in the first. Nonetheless, the differences in hierarchical structure do not seem to result in easily detectible different interpretations. Therefore, while certain ambiguities result from differences in hierarchical structure, not all differences in hierarchical structure necessarily yield clear differences in interpretation.

The prepositional phrase modifier *from Romania* in the previous examples is essentially synonymous with the adjective *Romanian*. Like *exceptional*, *Romanian* will have both a wide- and narrow-scope interpretation when it occurs in front of a coordinate structure, as in *Romanian students and teachers*. But when *exceptional*, which also has both a wide- and a narrow-scope interpretation as part of a coordinate structure, is combined with *Romanian*, the result *exceptional Romanian students and teachers* is not 4-ways ambiguous.

Instead, there are three possible interpretations, given below in (j.1–j.3), each paired with a synonymous but unambiguous paraphrase.

(j)   1. a. *exceptional Romanian students and teachers*   N–N
            b. *teachers and exceptional Romanian students*
         2. a. ***exceptional** Romanian students and teachers*   W–N
            b. *exceptional teachers and exceptional Romanian students*
         3. a. ***exceptional Romanian** students and teachers*   W–W
            b. *exceptional Romanian students and exceptional Romanian*
               teachers

The interpretation in which *Romanian* has wide scope and *exceptional* has narrow scope, as illustrated in (k), is not possible for this linear order even though this interpretation can be legitimately paraphrased as (l).

(k)   **exceptional **Romanian** students and teachers*   N–W
(l)   *Romanian teachers and exceptional Romanian students*

In (l) neither instance of *Romanian* takes scope over both conjuncts of the coordinate structure, whereas for the interpretation represented in (k), the single instance of *Romanian* would have to take scope over both conjuncts.

The question is why (k) is an impossible interpretation for *exceptional Romanian students and teachers*.

The answer emerges straightforwardly from considering what the syntactic structure of (k) would have to be. Given that *Romanian* would have to take scope over both conjuncts, the syntactic analysis requires that this adjective forms a syntactic unit with the coordinate structure *students and teachers*, as illustrated in (m).

(m)

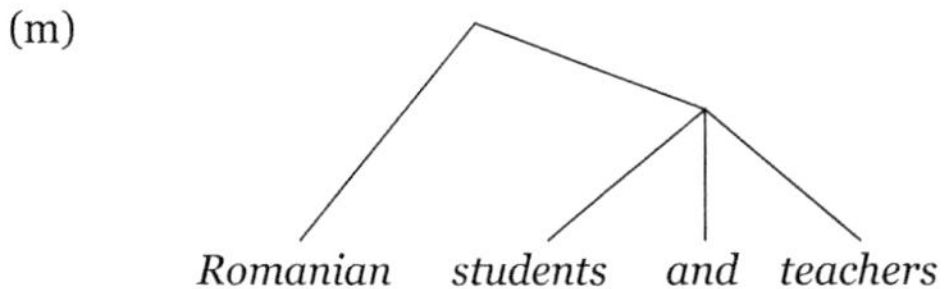

But if *exceptional* in (k) is interpreted with narrow scope over just *students*, then this adjective should form a syntactic unit with just that noun – which it can't because it is separated from *students* by *Romanian*, which forms a syntactic unit with the entire coordinate structure. The hierarchical structure in which *exceptional* is interpreted as having narrow scope therefore conflicts with the necessary hierarchical structure in which *Romanian* is interpreted as having wide scope. Thus it follows from hierarchical syntactic structure that the reading in (k) is impossible because there is no syntactic structure for that linear order of words that supports it.

In contrast, the spotlight analysis of modifiers mentioned above doesn't explain why (k) is an impossible interpretation. A dim spotlight should illuminate the nearest conjunct even though it is separated from that conjunct by a bright spotlight, just as it does when the intervening spotlight is another dim spotlight. In this way, the spotlight metaphor, which works for all the other examples discussed above, fails for this specific case. If adjectival scope were just a matter of dim versus bright spotlight settings, then (k) should have been a possible interpretation, which it isn't.

These kinds of scope ambiguities with coordinated nouns show up in other venues besides books about English syntax. Consider, for example, the title of a Dr. Seuss book even more famous than the one discussed in the first chapter, listed as #4 on both lists cited in Chapter 1, and having sold over 8.1 million copies: *Green Eggs and Ham*. While the Dr. Seuss illustrations, starting with the cover of the book, make it clear that both the eggs and the ham are green, the title as a piece of English syntax on its own also has a narrow-scope interpretation of the adjective, synonymous with *ham and green eggs*.

These scope ambiguities also figured in a life-and-death court decision, where the California Supreme Court reversed a death sentence and the U.S. Supreme Court reinstated it based on differing interpretations of the instruction to the jury at the sentencing phrase of the initial trial, where the court instructed that the jury *must not be swayed by mere sentiment, conjecture, sympathy, passion, prejudice, public opinion or public feeling*. There are two ways to interpret the instruction: either *mere* has narrow scope, modifying only *sentiment*, or it has wide scope, modifying each coordinated noun – hence *mere sentiment, mere conjecture, mere sympathy, mere passion, mere prejudice, mere public opinion*, and *mere public feeling*.

On the narrow-scope reading, the instruction tells the jury not to be swayed by sympathy. Here is what the majority decision of the California Supreme Court says in *People v. Brown* (1985):[1]

At the penalty phase, we agree with defendant's objection to instructions that the jury must not be swayed by sympathy or consequences in choosing a sentence. Prior authority of this court flatly prohibits the giving of such antisympathy instructions at a capital penalty trial. (People v. Lanphear (1984) 36 Cal. 3d 163, 166 [203 Cal. Rptr. 122, 680 P.2d 1081]; People v. Easley (1983) 34 Cal. 3d 858, 876 [196 Cal. Rptr. 309, 671 P.2d 813].) We are persuaded that their inclusion in this case was prejudicial on the issue whether defendant should live or die. The penalty judgment must therefore be reversed.

The U.S. Supreme Court disagreed:[2]

(b) The California Supreme Court improperly focused solely on the word "sympathy" in the instruction. A reasonable juror would be unlikely to single out the word "sympathy" from the other nouns accompanying it, and would most likely interpret the admonition to avoid basing a decision on "mere sympathy" as a directive to ignore only the sort of sympathy that was not rooted in the aggravating and mitigating evidence introduced during the penalty phase. Pp. 479 U. S. 541–543.

The two courts differ on their interpretation of the instructions to the jury. The California Supreme Court apparently assumed the narrow-scope interpretation of *mere*, while the U.S. Supreme Court assumed the wide-scope interpretation. However, the charge that the California court *improperly focused solely on the word "sympathy" in the instruction* is clearly mistaken, simply on syntactic grounds. There is more to discuss here when we consider coordinate structures more generally in the next chapter.[3]

---

[1] https://law.justia.com/cases/california/supreme-court/3d/40/512.html

[2] https://supreme.justia.com/cases/federal/us/479/538/. This retrieves the syllabus; to retrieve the dissenting opinions as well, click on "Case".

[3] For a more detailed discussion of the case, see Lawrence M. Solan, *The Language of Judges* (University of Chicago Press, 1993).

2.2   Ambiguities with multiple coordination

The ambiguities that arise in coordinate structures containing the conjunction *and* also arise with the conjunction *or* – for example, *exceptional students or teachers*. And in an expression that combines both conjunctions, as in *John and Mary or Susan*, ambiguity also arises, which, like the ambiguity discussed above, derives from hierarchical structure. Thus *John and Mary or Susan* can have one of two possible syntactic structures, each linked to one of the two possible readings for this expression.

(n)   1.   [[*John*] *and* [*Mary or Susan*]]
           2.   [[*John and Mary*] *or* [*Susan*]]

In both (n.1) and (n.2), *John* is the left conjunct of *and*, and *Susan* is the right conjunct of *or*. The difference concerns simultaneously the right conjunct of *and* and the left conjunct of *or*, illustrated in table A.

Table A

	right conjunct of *and*	left conjunct of *or*
n.1	*Mary or Susan*	*Mary*
n.2	*Mary*	*John and Mary*

Thus either the coordination with *and* is a conjunct of the coordination with *or*, or conversely. This is an example of LAYERED COORDINATION, where the interpretation of one conjunction is subordinated with respect to the interpretation of the other.

The hierarchical structures in (n) can be realized in three other linear orders. (n.1) for example can be mapped onto two distinct linear orders either by switching the order of the conjuncts of *and* or by switching the conjuncts of *or*, as shown in (o).

(o)   [[*John*] *and* [*Mary or Susan*]] <–> [[*Mary or Susan*] *and* [*John*]]

                         ^
                         |
                         v

    [[*John*] *and* [*Susan or Mary*]]

Both of these new linearizations in (o) can be mapped onto the same fourth linear order, as illustrated in (p).

(p)   [[*John*] and [*Mary or Susan*]] <–> [[*Mary or Susan*] and [*John*]]

[[*John*] and [*Susan or Mary*]] <–> [[*Susan or Mary*] and [*John*]]

Because they have the same hierarchical structure, all of these linearizations have the same interpretation. (p) illustrates again how a single hierarchical structure can correspond to multiple linear orders. The same analysis can be applied to the other hierarchical structure in (n.2), yielding another 4 linear orders for the same hierarchical structure.

Whether these expressions can be disambiguated by employing punctuation is not obvious. For example, could (n.1) be rendered unambiguously by inserting a comma between *John* and *and* or between *and* and *Mary*? It seems that none of the books that attempt to give rules for English punctuation (including Lynne Truss's *Eats, Shoots & Leaves* and Karen Gordon's *The Well-tempered Sentence: A Punctuation Handbook for the Innocent, the Eager, and the Doomed*) consider these constructions. Furthermore, it is not clear that punctuation could solve the problem of more complicated examples – consider the 5-way ambiguity of *John and Mary or Susan and Bill*, which would require multiple commas.

The better alternative is to use the modifiers *both* and *either*, where (n.1) translates as *both John and either Mary or Susan* and (n.2) translates as *either both John and Mary or Susan*. Syntactically these translations have essentially the hierarchical structures given in (n) but with the addition of the modifiers so that the linear order of the words in each expression is now different.

(q)   1. [*both* [[*John*] and [*either* [*Mary or Susan*]]]]
      2. [*either* [*both* [*John and Mary*]] or [*Susan*]]]

Again, the linear order of each example in (q) has three additional possible linearizations, all unambiguous and all with the same interpretation. (q.1) for example can be rendered also as given in (r).

(r)   1. *both John and either Susan or Mary*
      2. *both either Mary or Susan and John*
      3. *both either Susan or Mary and John*

Note that the examples where *both* and *either* are adjacent (r.2–3) may appear less felicitous than the examples where these modifiers are not adjacent. Consider also the apparent contrast between (q.2) and the alternatives *either Susan or both John and Mary* and *either Susan or both Mary and John*, which are apparently easier to comprehend.

Using *both* and *either* to disambiguate an expression that combines three conjunctions (as in the above-mentioned *John and Mary or Susan and Bill*) yields a contrast between *both either both John and Mary or Susan and Bill* and *both Bill and either Susan or both John and Mary*, both of which can be analyzed as sharing the same hierarchical structure. This contrast is pretty extreme. The former is close to unreadable gibberish at first glance, while the latter is a lot clearer. Furthermore, it's possible to eliminate a *both* in the latter and just have *Bill and either Susan or both John and Mary*. This example with three conjunctions illustrates how some linearizations of a single hierarchical structure may be more difficult to process (parse) than others.

The *Cambridge Grammar of the English Language* (p. 1305) makes a distinction between binary coordination (with only two conjuncts) versus multiple coordination (with more than two conjuncts). It notes that while *either* may take more than two conjuncts, *both* is limited to only two – citing the following two examples as evidence, where the asterisk marks the example as deviant.

(s)   1.   *I [*both locked the doors and set the alarm and informed the police*].
           2.   *I'll* [*either call out or bang on the door or blow my whistle*].

While it is correct that *both* cannot apply to all three conjuncts, the underlined syntactic units in (s.1), it is nonetheless possible to assign the coordinate structure in brackets a different syntactic structure that is not deviant.

(t)   *I* [[*both* [*locked the doors*] *and* [*set the alarm*]] *and* (*also*) [*informed the police*]]

(t) demonstrates that layered coordination applies to multiple instances of *and*.

Coda

The few examples of English examined here reveal that syntax has two dimensions, one visible in writing, and the other invisible. There is a visible horizontal dimension where words are strung together (like beads on a string) in a linear order to form linguistic expressions of a language. And beyond this there is an invisible vertical dimension where words join together to form syntactic units, which in turn form larger syntactic units by joining together with other syntactic units (including a single word) – the hierarchical structure. Beyond the meaning of the words themselves, hierarchical structure contributes substantially to the full interpretation of linguistic expressions.

The interplay between these two dimensions, linear order and hierarchical structure as discussed above, shows how a single hierarchical structure can correspond to several different linear orders, and how a single linear order may correspond to multiple hierarchical structures. In the former case, the different linear orders have exactly the same interpretation – they are synonymous; whereas in the latter case, the single linear order can have different interpretations determined solely on the basis of the different hierarchical structures – it is ambiguous. However, it seems to be possible that some differences in hierarchical structure may not correspond to distinctly different interpretations.

Understanding English syntax, this interplay between linear order and hierarchical structure, is a useful tool for controlling and crafting the sentences we write, and for interpreting the sentences that we read (including the ones we write).

The title of the introductory course in Linguistics at Princeton University is easy to take for granted. I taught *Introduction to Language and Linguistics* for over two decades before I realized on the first day of class in the fall of 2006 that the title is structurally ambiguous. This realization fueled that first lecture, which became my introductory lecture for the course in subsequent years. What follows is based on that lecture. The question this ambiguity poses is: what is the interpretation of the course title?

3.1   Ambiguity in the interpretation of conjuncts

The ambiguity of the title, which contains 3 nouns (*introduction, language, and linguistics*), 1 preposition (*to*), and 1 conjunction (*and*), hinges on whether the coordinate structure *Language and Linguistics* or just the noun *Language* is interpreted as the object of the preposition *to*. Under both interpretations, *Linguistics* functions as the right conjunct of the coordinate construction; however on one, the left conjunct is *Language*, while on the other, the left conjunct is *Introduction to Language*. Painting the conjunction red and its conjuncts blue renders two distinct pictures of the title.

(a)   1. *Introduction to Language and Linguistics*
          2. *Introduction to Language and Linguistics*

These two distinct interpretations correspond to two different hierarchical structures, as shown in (b) and more graphically in (c).

(b)   1. [*Introduction* [*to* [*Language and Linguistics*]]]
          2. [[*Introduction* [*to* [*Language*]]] *and Linguistics*]

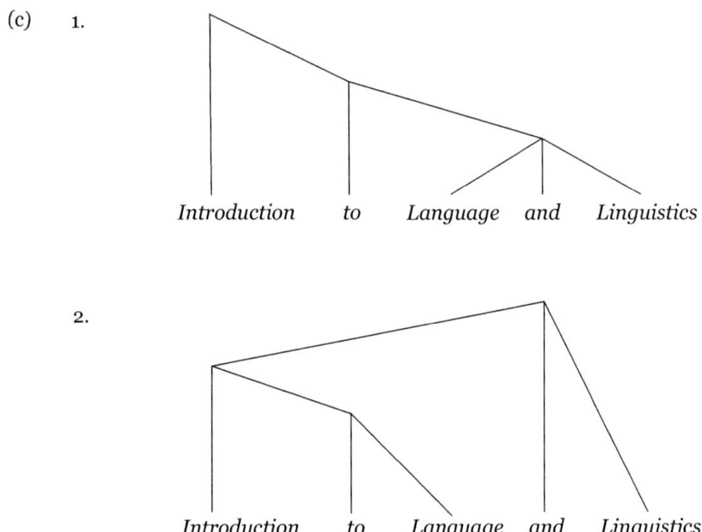

In (b.1/c.1) *Language and Linguistics* constitutes a syntactic unit, but not in (b.2/c.2); whereas in (b.2/c.2) *Introduction to Language* forms a syntactic unit that does not occur in (b.1/c.1). Given the syntactic structure (b.1/c.1), the course title can be paraphrased unambiguously as *Introduction to both Language and Linguistics*, which raises the question of how the two terms are to be distinguished (see below). In contrast, (b.2/c.2) can be paraphrased unambiguously by switching the two conjuncts yielding *Linguistics and Introduction to Language*, an awful title for an introductory linguistics course because the relation between the two conjuncts is even less clear than in the other paraphrase.

No matter which syntactic structure we assign to the course title, our interpretation depends crucially on our understanding of what the words *language* and *linguistics*, capitalized or not, actually mean. In effect we need to answer the more basic questions: 'what is language?' and 'what is linguistics?' – the answers to which will clarify the relation between these two terms that are linked by the conjunction *and*.

As will become clear in what follows, it is somewhat easier to answer the second question than the first. According to the website of the Linguistic Society of America (www.linguisticsociety.org/what-linguistics), the professional association of linguists in the United States, *linguistics, in a nutshell, is the scientific study of language* – a definition that is repeated in the *Oxford English Dictionary* (online) and David Crystal's *Dictionary of Linguistics and Phonetics* (6th edition, 2008). Putting aside the issue of how this study is scientific (but see below for further discussion), defining *linguistics* as 'the study of language' now raises the first question more urgently: what is language? – to which we will return in a bit.

Unfortunately, substituting *the study of language* for *linguistics* in the course title turns out to be distinctly unhelpful, yielding (d) as paraphrases for (b).

(d)   1. *Introduction to both Language and the Study of Language* (= (b.1))
             2. *The Study of Language and Introduction to Language* (= (b.2))

The problem remains even if the study of language is designated as *scientific*. With (d.2), the first conjunct alone could serve as a reasonable title for an introductory linguistics course, whereas the addition of the second conjunct adds almost nothing of substance, and perhaps also some confusion as to how the two conjuncts should be distinguished. The second conjunct of (d.2) modified by the indefinite article *an* serves as the title for a well-established textbook for introductory courses in linguistics with an eleventh edition in 2018[1] In contrast, the coordination of *Language* and *the Study of Language* as a syntactic unit in (d.1) raises the problem of distinguishing the two conjuncts in a meaningful way given that the Study of Language entails Language as the object of study in the context of an introductory university course.

One way that might avoid the dilemma that the various coordinations of *Language* and *Linguistics* poses for a coherent interpretation of the Princeton course title is to consider a somewhat different interpretation of *linguistics* as a field of study and branch of human knowledge[2] in the same way that *mathematics* names a field of study as well as the phenomena under investigation. Thus just as the field of mathematics studies mathematics, the field of linguistics studies the phenomenon of language. However, this interpretation does not resolve the problem of the course title because an introduction to a field of study is simultaneously an introduction to the subject matter of that field. No introductory mathematics course would ever be titled *Introduction to*

---

[1] *An Introduction to Language* by Victoria Fromkin, Robert Rodman & Nina Hyams (Cengage Learning, 2018).

[2] Curiously, this interpretation of *linguistics* does not occur in any of the major dictionaries of English (American Heritage, Webster's, Collins, or Oxford Online), although the Oxford definition – *the scientific study of language and its structure* – comes close by adding an addendum that states *Also: this as a subject of educational study and examination* (see p. 47 for further discussion).

Mathematics and Mathematics, even as a joke – even though it is possible to distinguish the two interpretations of *mathematics*; perhaps unsurprisingly, the phrase itself gets zero hits on a Google search.

Whether we interpret *linguistics* in the course title as 'the study of language' or 'the field that studies language', deciphering the meaning of the Princeton course title ultimately requires an answer to the deceptively simple question *what is language?*. Answering this question, which serves as the title and topic of the first of Noam Chomsky's 2013 Dewey Lectures at Columbia University (subsequently published as a book in 2016 under the title *What Kind of Creatures Are We?*), is essential for understanding human nature because, as one leading researcher in human evolution has written, *language is perhaps the single most remarkable thing about our modern selves.*[3] Even so, language, as Chomsky remarks at the beginning of his lecture, *has been studied intensively and productively for 2,500 years, but with no clear answer to the question of what language is.*

In the history of ideas, the notion that language is central to human nature comes into focus in the seventeenth century in the work of the French philosopher, scientist, and mathematician René Descartes. The notion is developed in the modern period by Chomsky, starting with his 1967 Beckman Lectures delivered at the University of California at Berkeley titled *Language and Mind*, published the following year and now in its third edition (Cambridge University Press [2009a]). Chomsky begins the first lecture (Linguistic Contributions to the Study of Mind: Past) with the question *What contribution can the study of language make to our understanding of human nature?* and comments at the beginning of the third lecture (subtitled *future*):

It is quite natural to expect that a concern for language will remain central to the study of human nature, as it has been in the past. Anyone concerned with the study of human nature and human capacities must somehow come to grips with the fact that all normal humans acquire language, whereas acquisition of even its barest rudiments is quite beyond the capacities of an otherwise intelligent ape – a fact that was emphasized, quite correctly, in Cartesian philosophy.

This explains how and why language is a central part of human nature: all normal humans acquire it – pretty much regardless of level of intelligence. It is therefore a property of the species, one that is, on substantial evidence, unique to humans.[4]

But this doesn't get very far in explaining what language is. An answer to this fundamental question requires some concrete specification of what it is

---

[3] Ian Tattersall, *Masters of the Planet* (Palgrave Macmillan, 2012), p. ix – quoted in Chomsky's lecture.

[4] See Robert Berwick & Noam Chomsky, *Why Only Us: Language and Evolution* (MIT Press, 2016) for discussion.

that all normal humans acquire. Part of the problem is that the noun *language* is not concrete, in marked contrast to the count noun *language* (as in *one language or two languages*). This difference raises the question of the relation between the nonconcrete noun *language* and the countable noun *language*. The plural count noun *languages* directs our attention to how one language differs from the next, rather than what different languages might share in common. The nonconcrete and noncount noun *language* instead focuses on the properties that all languages share. However we spell this out, it remains a simple fact that every person possesses a capacity for language that allows them to acquire a language. So one way to begin answering the fundamental question is to give a precise characterization of what a language is.

3.2   What a language is: the lexicon

For a precise characterization, let us start with an example of what we call the English language: the title of Princeton University's introductory linguistics course (and the title of this chapter). The five words of the title belong to the vocabulary of English, what in linguistics is called a LEXICON – in this case the English lexicon. Each word has a phonetic form, a phonetic label that specifies its pronunciation, which can be represented in writing as a sequence of letters in the English alphabet. Each word also has a semantic interpretation that constitutes its meaning. The pronunciations of the five words in the title are relatively straightforward, as are the semantic interpretations of the noun *introduction*, the preposition *to*, and the conjunction *and*. The semantic interpretations of the nouns *language* and *linguistics* are more complicated, as discussed above. So a precise characterization of a language must involve the specification of a lexicon.

3.2.1   *The mental lexicon*

Given that a language is something that virtually every human acquires and that a lexicon is one essential part of the specification of a language, the lexicon must exist in the mind of the speaker – as a form of information that constitutes in part the speaker's knowledge of the language. Thus a language contains a mental lexicon, which is internal to each individual speaker.

Having identified the mental lexicon as an object of inquiry merely identifies the tip of an enormous linguistic iceberg that is easily identified by two questions: what information is contained in a speaker's lexicon, and how it is organized?

While it may seem tempting to answer these questions by equating a mental lexicon of English with a dictionary of English, which is intended to be an external representation of the English lexicon, there are several problems.

A dictionary of English is organized in terms of spelling, the orthographic representation of pronunciation (that is, in terms of letters of the English alphabet). We call the entries in the dictionary 'words', easily identified orthographically as a series of connected letters bounded before and aft by a space (or followed by a punctuation mark). Thus lexical items in the dictionary are equated with words commonly understood in terms of spelling. However, speakers acquire a language (and therefore a mental lexicon) well before they learn to read, so it's a virtual certainty that their lexicons are not organized orthographically.[5] Whether items in the mental lexicon actually correspond to words in a dictionary will depend on identifying 'words' in some other way, which is a difficult problem.

Another problem with the dictionary's representation of the English lexicon is its reliance on defining a word in terms of other words, which, if we then define the words of the definition and keep repeating this process, leads inevitably either to circularity or possibly a dead end. As a thought experiment, try defining a couple of nouns (for example, *book* and *computer*) and then try verbs like *expect* and *persuade*, which are a harder problem.

Some modern dictionaries, for example the 4th edition of *The American Heritage Dictionary of the English Language* (2000), tend towards the encyclopedia by including entries for famous people (Charlie Chaplin (along with his photograph) and Julia Child (along with a portrait of her)), photographs of objects, maps, and diagrams. This suggests that the interpretation of items in the mental lexicon could easily be connected to images rather than words. It also ably demonstrates how the interpretation of words connects to knowledge of the world and also beliefs – which will differ from speaker to speaker.[6] Nonetheless, there is enough shared understanding of the interpretation of lexical items that we can comprehend the meaning of linguistic expressions produced by other speakers of 'our language'. And in many instances, it is probably the case that we share the same interpretations of lexical items. For example, in *We expect you to persuade him to attend the meeting*, it seems improbable that speakers would understand the verbs *expect*, *persuade*, and *attend* differently. However the mental lexicon connects to a speaker's knowledge and beliefs, that lexicon, which is itself part of our knowledge of the world, must be identifiable separately from the rest if we are to achieve a precise characterization of what a language is.

---

[5] Nonetheless, the orthographic definition of *word* is useful for talking about language, and in some cases identifies what must be items in the mental lexicon – for example, the preposition *to* and the conjunction *and* in the course title under discussion.

[6] For example, how a speaker interprets the words *language* and *linguistics* depends on what the speaker knows about the topics they designate. A reader of this chapter will most likely come to a different understanding of these words than the one they started with, unless they already have a certain background in linguistics.

3.2.2   Some structure in the mental lexicon

This precise characterization of what a language is will in turn require a more precise description of what constitutes an item in the mental lexicon and how these items are organized. Some insight can be gained by taking a closer look at one word in the title of the Princeton University course: *introduction*. The word is interpreted as singular in number, as opposed to *introductions*, which is interpreted as plural. In the case of the plural form we can identify two pieces (called *morphemes*), [*introduction* + *s*], where −*s* is an inflectional suffix that is interpreted 'plural'. Under this analysis, the root morpheme *introduction* is interpreted as neither singular nor plural − in other words, the root itself carries no information about number. In contrast, the singular form of the word *introduction* has no visible inflectional suffix that indicates singular in number (that is, with phonetic content). But given that the singular and plural forms of the word must surely share the same root, the morphological analysis of the singular form of the word would have to include an unpronounced (phonetically null) singular suffix that contrasts with the phonetically realized suffix −*s*. That is, the singular form *introduction* has a morphological structure [*introduction* + ø], where ø represents the phonetically empty singular suffix.

The morphological structure of nouns with regular plural forms raises a nontrivial question about the content and organization of the mental lexicon. Are the lexical entries for these nouns actually just the nominal root uninflected for number, in which case the regular plural suffix −*s* and the regular singular suffix ø would have to also be independent items in the lexicon? Or alternatively, are the singular and plural forms part of the same entry in the mental lexicon? If entries for nouns with regular plural inflection are just the nominal root, then items in the lexicon do not always correspond to words in the dictionary. Thus it appears that the language we speak (and which we mostly take for granted) is actually stranger than we realize − a familiar lesson in the natural sciences (in physics for example with the theory of relativity, quantum mechanics, and string theory).

In contrast to *introduction*, which can be pluralized as *introductions*, the nouns *language* and *linguistics* in the title are inherently singular, as demonstrated by the deviance of the finite plural form of the verb *be* (indicated with an asterisk) in the questions in (e).

(e)   1. *What is/*are language?*
           2. *What is/*are linguistics?*

The deviance results from the failure of agreement (in number) between the noun and the finite verb. Neither *language* (as opposed to the countable *a language*) nor *linguistics* has a plural form, which follows from their semantic property as noncount nouns. In English noncount nouns are treated grammatically, as opposed to semantically, as singular.

While dictionaries generally treat singular and plural forms of count nouns as members of a single entry, they present other related words as separate entries. Thus the 4th edition of *The American Heritage Dictionary of the English Language* (2000) lists as separate entries the noun *introduction*, the related verb *introduce*, and the related adjective *introductory*. The relationship between the three words is visible in their orthographic representations (all contain the spelling *introduc*) but not in their pronunciations – the letter c in *introduce* is pronounced like the first sound in the word *sing*, whereas the same letter in *introduction* and *introductory* is pronounced most like (but not exactly like) the first sound in the word *king*. Pronunciation aside, the three words can be related in terms of their internal structure (in linguistics, their *morphological structure*), where, for example, the word *introduction* can be analyzed as the combination of the verbal form *introduce* plus a suffix *–tion* (pronounced like the word *shun*), which turns the verb into a noun. In the morphological analysis of the adjective *introductory*, the verbal root *introduce* is joined with the nominalizing suffix *–tion* forming a noun which is then joined with the suffix *–ory* forming an adjective. Thus the adjective would have the hierarchical structure given in (f), where the e in the verbal root is deleted from the spelling as is the ion from the nominalizing suffix *–tion*.

(f)

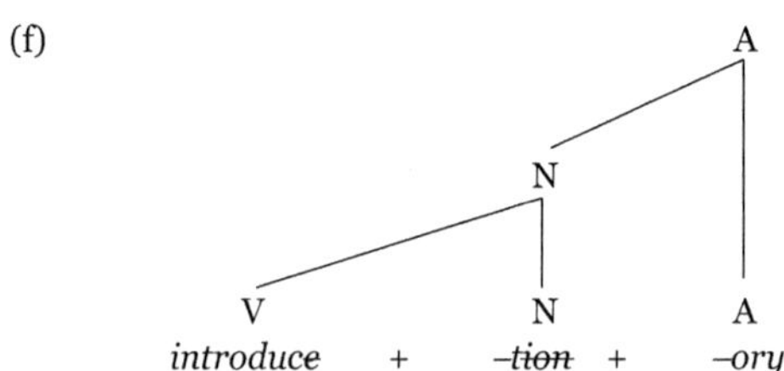

In addition to hierarchical structure, (f) represents the inherent syntactic categories of the root and the two suffixes as labels (V for verb, N for noun, and A for adjective). The label N of the suffix *–tion* becomes the label of the construction that combines the verbal element with the suffix. The label A of the suffix *–ory* becomes the label of the construction that combines the nominalization (with its internal structure) and that suffix. A suffix whose label becomes the label of the morphological unit created by adding this suffix is called derivational, in contrast to an inflectional suffix (for example, the English plural *–s*), which has no category label to project.

In terms of semantics, an inflectional suffix adds a discrete bit of information like number (singular vs. plural) to the interpretation of the root it combines with, whereas a derivational suffix fundamentally changes the interpretation of the root. For example, the 4th edition of *The American Heritage Dictionary of the English Language* lists four presumably distinct definitions for the noun *introduction*. The one relevant to the Princeton course title is listed as number 4, which reads: *something spoken, written, or otherwise presented in beginning or introducing something, especially: ... c. A basic introductory text or course of study.* In the context of the course title, the interpretation of *introduction* as 'a basic introductory course of study' might be sufficient. Even so, this definition requires a definition of *introductory*, which the dictionary defines in two ways: *of, relating to, or constituting an introduction* and *serving to introduce.* The circularity of the first definition of the adjective with respect to the definition of *introduction* is clear. The second definition of the adjective shifts the precise definition of the adjective to the definition of the verb *introduce*, for which there are six definitions, two with two subparts. The relevant definition of the verb reads: *to provide (someone) with beginning knowledge or first experience of something.* The questions for the interpretation of the nominalization *introduction* are what the suffix *–tion* specifically contributes to interpretation and how it changes the interpretation of the verbal root, a change that does not appear to be systematic when we consider other nominalizations with the same suffix (for example, *production, hallucination, adulation, articulation, compensation, participation*).

However, the semantic contribution of some derivational suffixes is systematic to the extent that it can be represented as a general formula. Consider the words *introducer* and *introducible*, which American Heritage lists as part of the entry for the verb *introduce*. The semantic contribution of the nominal suffix *–er* is captured in the formula 'someone/something that Vs' where V stands for verb, and stands in for a large number of English verbs – thus an introducer is someone who introduces, but not on the interpretation of *introduce* that applies in the interpretation of *introduction*. Likewise, the semantic contribution of the adjectival suffix *–ible* (alternatively and more usually *–able*) is expressed as the formula 'able to be Ved', where in the case of *introducible* the interpretation is 'able to be introduced', but again not on the interpretation of the verbal root that forms *introduction*.

How all the information about lexical items discussed above is represented and organized in the mental lexicon of a speaker remains an open and difficult question. However, it should be clear that information about the morphological structure of lexical items as discussed above (and which is not represented in dictionaries), as well as about the pronunciation and interpretation of these items, is part of a speaker's (mostly unconscious) understanding of the items in the mental lexicon and would therefore be part of lexical representations.

3.3   What a language is: the computational procedure

In addition to a mental lexicon, a language acquired by a speaker must have a means of combining items from the lexicon to form linguistic expressions that have a pronunciation (which we can characterize broadly as some form of externalization: speech, writing, or signing in the case of sign languages) and an interpretation. The interpretation of a linguistic expression is determined in part by the interpretations of the individual lexical items it contains, but also by the way the expression is structured – as illustrated by the examples in the previous chapter as well as by the Princeton course title under discussion in this chapter. We can think of the structures assigned to the lexical items in a linguistic expression as the output of a computational procedure that combines lexical items into structured expressions. For example, the structure of the expression *an introduction to linguistics* given as a tree diagram in (g) could be derived from a simple computational procedure that combines pairs of syntactic units, starting with the pair of lexical items *to* and *linguistics* and yielding a new syntactic unit {*to*, *linguistics*}, represented with braces (curly brackets) and a comma to indicate that the two lexical elements contained in them are unordered.[7]

(g)

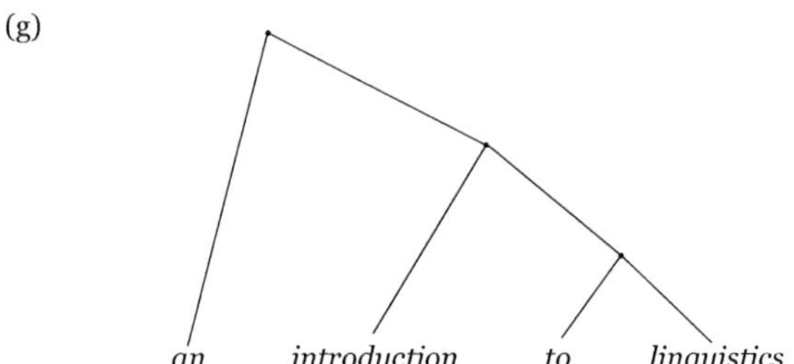

---

[7] Thus {*to, linguistics*} is equivalent to {*linguistics, to*}. The square bracket representation without a comma [*to linguistics*] indicates a specific linear order. The reason for making these distinctions will become clear when we briefly consider the differences in word order between English and Japanese in the next few pages.

This procedure then reapplies to the new unit produced plus *introduction*, creating the new unit {*introduction*, {*to*, *linguistics*}} that is further combined with the article *an*, yielding {*an*, {*introduction*, {*to*, *linguistics*}}}, which is an equivalent representation for the hierarchical structure of the example expressed in (g).[8]

In linguistics, the computational procedure that combines two syntactic units to form a new syntactic unit is called MERGE. The operation Merge creates a syntactic relation between the formerly separate syntactic units as SISTER constituents in the new syntactic unit constructed. For example, in the syntactic unit {*to*, *linguistics*} the preposition *to* is a sister of the noun *linguistics*, and that noun is also a sister of the preposition. Thus the sister relation is symmetric. In the syntactic unit {*introduction*, {*to*, *linguistics*}}, the constituent units *introduction* and {*to*, *linguistics*} are sisters. In this way, hierarchical structure can be expressed in terms of sister relations among syntactic units.

In its simplest formulation, all Merge does is determine the hierarchical structure of syntactic units within a linguistic expression, but not their linear order. Think of the output of Merge as a three-dimensional object without a fixed linear order (much like a kinetic sculpture called a mobile), where a pair of syntactic units merged together can rotate 360°. When a mobile is flattened into two dimensions, the objects that it contains assume a fixed linear order; likewise for hierarchical structures created by Merge. For example, the syntactic unit {*to*, *linguistics*}, which technically has no linear order (even though to express it in writing we have to impose a linear order on the two lexical constituents), can potentially be linearized as [*to linguistics*] or [*linguistics to*]. Under the interpretation that the noun is the object of the preposition, the first linearization is legitimate in English while the second is not. However, in Japanese the reverse is true, demonstrating how the same hierarchical structure can have different linear orders in different languages.

Consider a slightly more complicated pair of English/Japanese examples in (h), which could be titles of an introductory book on linguistics.

---

[8] If you are wondering why the article *an* doesn't form a syntactic unit with *introduction* and then that unit combines with the prepositional phrase *to linguistics*, consider the linguistic expression *nontechnical introductions to linguistics*. The natural interpretation is 'introductions to linguistics that are nontechnical', where *nontechnical* applies to *introductions to linguistics*. The alternative, 'nontechnical introductions that are to (or about) linguistics', is distinctly odd. Now consider *a nontechnical introduction to linguistics*. Again, most naturally the adjective *nontechnical* applies to *introduction to linguistics*, in which case the syntactic structure of this expression would be: [*a* [*nontechnical* [*introduction* [*to linguistics*]]]]. In this case, the article *a* forms a syntactic unit with one containing *introduction to linguistics*, so there is empirical motivation for this structure when the adjective occurs. The simplest analysis for (g), where there is no adjective, should be the same minus the adjective – unless there is a strong reason to assume otherwise.

(h)   1. *invitation to linguistics*
          2. *genngogaku eno syotai*

In Japanese *genngogaku* is how you pronounce 'linguistics'. *Eno* corresponds to the English preposition *to*, and *syotai* corresponds to the English noun *invitation*, the Japanese word that would be used to paraphrase *introduction* in *introduction to linguistics* because the Japanese word *nyumon* 'introduction' would not be used in the title of an introductory linguistics course. While the order of words in Japanese seems radically different from the word order of English, the hierarchical structure of the two expressions is nonetheless identical, as illustrated in (i).

(i)   1.

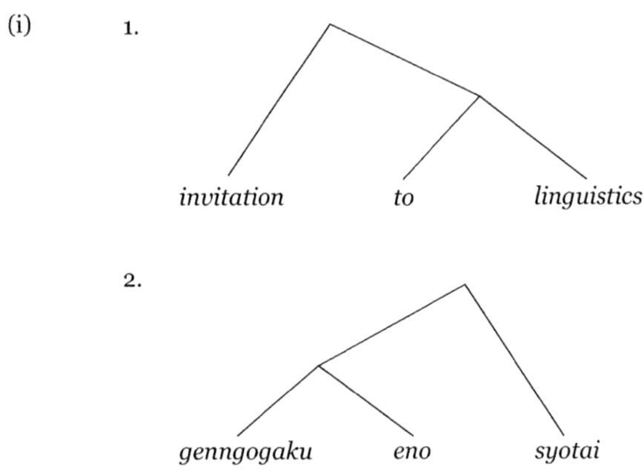

          2.

Given this hierarchical structure, there are actually 2 additional ways for (i.1) to linearize, which are of course impossible – illustrated for English in (j).

(j)   1. **invitation linguistics to*
          2. **to linguistics invitation*

Likewise, (i.2) shows the only legitimate way to linearize this expression in Japanese.

   Why (i.1) linearizes as it does in English depends in part on the hierarchical structure of the expression, where the first principle of linearization would be that sister syntactic units must be adjacent – that is, one sister must immediately precede the other. The relation 'precede' that determines linear order is, unlike the sister relation that determines hierarchical structure, asymmetric: if a sister syntactic unit A precedes its sister B, then B cannot also precede

A. Linearization also depends on the syntactic relation between sisters in a syntactic unit.

Consider again {*to, linguistics*} where a preposition P is merged with a noun N, P and N being syntactic category labels of these lexical items. Following traditional grammar, we say that N is the object of P where P + N forms a PREPOSITIONAL PHRASE – that is, a syntactic unit labeled P that contains a preposition. This generalizes the labeling analysis of morphological structure discussed above. When P merges with N, the label of P is 'projected' as the label of the new syntactic unit created. The label of this new syntactic unit identifies the HEAD of the phrase created. In both the English and Japanese examples, P is the head of the phrase containing the P and N, but the linear order differs. In English, the head P precedes its object N, whereas in Japanese, the head P follows its object.

In the larger structure where the noun *invitation* merges with a prepositional phrase, it is the noun that projects its label to the syntactic unit constructed – which identifies the noun as the head of the larger phrase, a NOUN PHRASE. The prepositional phrase *to linguistics* modifies the noun *invitation* that functions as the head of the noun phrase *invitation to linguistics*. The full syntactic structure of (h.1) would be (k), where for clarity the vertical branches of the tree diagram identify the projections of a head.

(k)

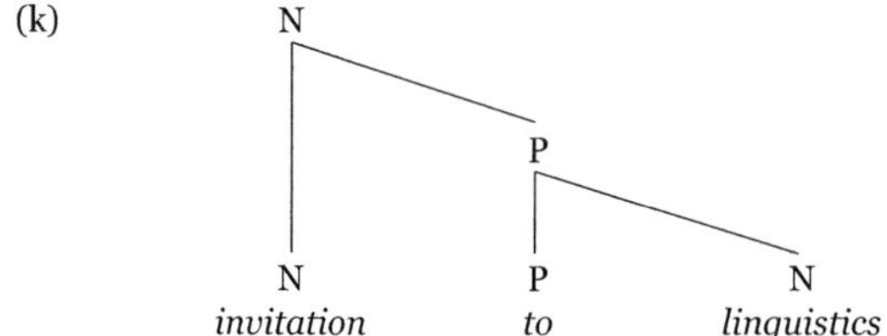

(k) illustrates that in English syntactic units are generally linearized as head-initial (with of course qualifications when we consider the full range of syntactic structures in English), in contrast to Japanese, where linearization is head-final. Thus there appears to be a linearization parameter across languages where a head of certain syntactic units occurs either in initial position or final position.

Where this headedness parameter generalizes across syntactic categories (as it does for P and N in both English and Japanese), this explains why there is only one way to linearize the hierarchical structures in (i). The two impossible linearizations for English in (j) both involve one head-initial and one head-final order for N and P. And while the Japanese word order in (i.2) maintains the same headedness for N and P, it's the opposite order that occurs in English. The setting of the headedness parameter for N and P in English limits linearization to one possible outcome.

What this simple comparison of English and Japanese shows is that interpretation depends on the semantic content of lexical items and their hierarchical structure in an expression (identical for the two languages), not on their (different) linear order or pronunciation, which are the two properties required for the externalization of language.

The externalization of language requires that language interfaces with the motor cortex of the brain, which controls the production of speech, writing, and signing. In order for externalized language to be understood, it must first be perceived through the ears, the eyes, or in the case of braille, through the fingertips – and therefore it interfaces with the sensory cortex of the brain. Internal language in the mind of the speaker interfaces with the cognitive components of the brain related to thought and understanding. Given that there are no formal (that is, explicit) models for what a thought is – in contrast to the formal models for language that have been developed over the past sixty years, the relation between language and thought remains pretty much a mystery. Unquestionably, language interfaces with cognition – which, apparently, is primarily concerned with the covert properties of linguistic expressions (hierarchical structure and the semantic content of lexical items it contains), but not with the properties specific to externalized language: linearization and the phonetic labeling of lexical items (both overt).

Our simple comparison of English and Japanese shows how languages involve three computational procedures: one for creating hierarchical structures with lexical items (Merge), one for the labeling of hierarchical structures (LABEL), and one for linearizing hierarchical structures for externalization of linguistic expressions (LINEARIZE). These three basic operations – to which a fourth will be added in the last chapter when we explore ellipsis constructions – constitute the computational system for any human language, a system of operations that interacts with a lexicon to produce the linguistic expressions in a language. From this perspective, a language can be defined simply as a mental lexicon plus a computational system, also in the mind of a speaker. The lexicon incorporates the idiosyncratic properties of a language that distinguish one language from another (including dialects or idiolects of the 'same language'), the phonetic labels of lexical items and word order being the most obvious. In contrast, the basic operations of the computational system are part of all human languages.

Just as the mental lexicon constitutes the knowledge of individual speakers, a language (which includes the computational system) also constitutes a form of knowledge. What a speaker knows when she or he knows a language is a lexicon connected to a computational system that together account for the linguistic expressions in the language (in linguistics called a GRAMMAR).

A speaker of a language 'knows' the linguistic expressions of the language indirectly through an internal grammar. One reason for this is that the set of linguistic expressions (for example, sentences) in a language is unbounded. Imagine the longest sentence of English that exists in print (or was ever spoken); it is child's play to make this sentence longer, ad infinitum. In contrast, the lexicon and the computational system are both finite, containing a finite number of lexical items and a finite number of basic operations, respectively.

The unbounded character of languages derives from Merge, an operation that can reapply to its own output indefinitely – a *recursive* operation. Given the recursive property of Merge, the use of any language will produce novel utterances – that is, utterances that are new to the experience of the speaker. Moreover, the production of utterances in a language is a matter of choice by the speaker, not any kind of automatic response to some external stimulus, linguistic or otherwise – in other words, a product of 'free will' as far as we can determine. This contrasts with the interpretation of linguistic utterances, which involves the internalization of linguistic expressions and is virtually a reflex in the mind of the speaker because there is no choice of whether or not to interpret linguistic expressions that we see or hear; the mind automatically assigns an interpretation.

Normal language use is also generally coherent and appropriate to the situation. These properties, appropriateness to the situation and coherence, like freedom from stimulus control (which is part of free will), cannot be explained in terms of the computational system for human language and are fundamentally difficult to characterize precisely. They, along with the unboundedness of language and the production of novel utterances, constitute what Chomsky calls *the creative aspect of language use*, referring to normal language use among all speakers.[9] Part of the problem is that coherence and appropriateness involve a speaker's (or pair of speakers') knowledge and beliefs, emotional states, and ways of reasoning that inevitably vary from speaker to speaker. Thus a general formulation for these properties will be excessively difficult if not impossible.

Therefore it makes sense to distinguish between knowledge of a language and language use, under the assumption that with a language, knowledge of its lexicon and the computational system underlies linguistic behavior. Exactly how knowledge is translated into behavior remains a difficult question – in any domain, not just for language.

3.4   What is language?

The definition of a language as a lexicon combined with a computational system provides a solid basis for attempting to answer the question of

---

[9] Noam Chomsky, *Cartesian Linguistics: A Chapter in the History of Rationalist Thought*, 3rd edition (Cambridge, UK: Cambridge University Press 2009).

what language is. As touched on above, the interpretation of the noncount noun *language* encompasses what languages share in common. This would include the computational system, which applies generally across languages, and also those properties of the lexicon that can be identified as common to the lexicons of all human languages (possibly, for example, syntactic categories like noun, verb, and adjective). From this perspective, the noncount noun *language* would be synonymous with the universal properties of languages.

Another less prosaic way of coming to terms with what language is would be to consider again the fact that every human acquires a language and then ask what makes it possible for a child to acquire a computational system and lexicon that together constitute the language this child will come to speak. If there is no way to get to hierarchical structure and labeling (the covert properties of the language) solely on the basis of the overt properties of linguistic data (phonetic labels of words, their linear order in linguistic expressions, and the intonation patterns of these expressions), then a child acquiring a first language must bring to the task some innate mental apparatus that compensates for the limitations of the initial linguistic data. If so, then the major portion of the computational system for human languages, Merge and Label at least, must exist in the mind of the child at birth, part of the child's genetic heritage as a human and therefore universal across the species. This apparatus would be part of an innate language faculty that provides a biological basis for the ability to acquire and use a language. So another way of interpreting the noncount noun *language* is as a synonym for this innate (hence biological) faculty.

3.5   What is linguistics?

From this biological perspective, the study of language is first and foremost the study of the language faculty in the mind of the speaker – in particular, how that faculty determines the form and function of the grammars of the seemingly diverse languages that humans acquire. In this way, linguistics constitutes a subfield in the study of human biology (called biolinguistics), which itself is a subfield of the biological sciences.

Almost three decades ago, Noam Chomsky summarized how linguistics should be construed as the scientific study of language in these words:[10]

For about 30 years, the study of language – or more accurately, one substantial component of it – has been conducted within a framework that understands linguistics

---

[10] This is the first paragraph in a chapter titled "On the Nature, Use and Acquisition of Language" in a 1987 monograph, *Generative Grammar: Its Basis, Development and Prospects*, published as a special issue of *Studies in English Linguistics and Literature* (Kyoto University of Foreign Studies). See also Chapter 5 (Section 5.6) for additional discussion of this paragraph.

to be a part of psychology, ultimately human biology. This approach attempts to reintroduce into the study of language several concerns that have been central to Western thought for thousands of years, and that have deep roots in other traditions as well: questions about the nature and origin of knowledge in particular. This approach has also been concerned to assimilate the study of language into the main body of the natural sciences. This meant, in the first place, abandoning dogmas that are entirely foreign to the natural sciences and that have no place in rational inquiry, the dogmas of the several varieties of behaviorism, for example, which seek to impose a priori limits on possible theory construction, a conception that would properly be dismissed as entirely irrational in the natural sciences. It means a frank adherence to mentalism, where we can understand talk about the mind to be talk about the brain at an abstract level at which, so we try to demonstrate, principles can be formulated that enter into successful and insightful explanation of linguistic (and other) phenomena that are provided by observation and experiment. Mentalism, in this sense, has no taint of mysticism and carries no dubious ontological burden. Rather, mentalism falls strictly within the standard practice of the natural sciences and in fact, is nothing other than the approach of the natural sciences applied to this particular domain. This conclusion, which is the opposite of what is often assumed, becomes understandable and clear if we consider specific topics in the natural sciences: for example, 19th century chemistry, which sought to explain phenomena in terms of such abstract notions as elements, the periodic table, valence, benzene rings, and so on – that is, in terms of abstract properties of then unknown, perhaps still unknown physical mechanisms. This abstract inquiry served as an essential preliminary and guide for the subsequent inquiry into physical mechanisms. Mentalistic inquiry in the brain sciences is quite similar in approach and character to the abstract inquiry into properties of the chemical elements, and we may expect that this abstract inquiry too will serve as an essential preliminary and guide for the emerging brain sciences today; the logic is quite similar.

This amazing paragraph ties together the central themes of language-as-a-form-of-human-knowledge and linguistics-as-the-scientific-study-of-language. The former connects linguistics to an intellectual history that has its origins in ancient Greece with the philosopher Plato's work on the nature and origin of knowledge (epistemology). The latter concerns the program of research in modern generative grammar, founded in the 1950s in Chomsky's earliest work, which attempts to formulate abstract principles *that enter into successful and insightful explanation of linguistic (and other) phenomena that are provided by observation and experiment*, comparable in character to the abstract concepts of nineteenth-century chemistry that *served as an essential preliminary and guide for the subsequent inquiry into physical mechanisms*.

One crucial feature of the ongoing effort of the past sixty years to assimilate linguistics *into the main body of the natural sciences* has been a focus on the formal (in the sense of 'explicit') analysis of natural languages with the goal of constructing a computational theory of language. This formal analysis, as discussed above and in the previous chapters, is primarily concerned with the assignment of structure to linguistic expressions by general mechanisms and the principles that constrain both the operation of these mechanisms and their output. For example, consider as a general constraint on the labeling of syntactic units created by Merge that labels are limited to the features of the lexical items contained in that unit. As a result, labels like *Sentence* are not possible (see the next chapter for further discussion). Linearization, as discussed above, is constrained by the correspondence between hierarchical structure and adjacency, where sisters in hierarchical structure must be adjacent in linear order. Merge can be constrained by limiting the operation to pairs of syntactic units, making the operation strictly binary. All of these constraints contribute to what could be characterized as a theory of minimal computation, which postulates only as much structure as necessary (a version of Ockham's Razor, which generally governs theorizing in the natural sciences).

3.5.1   *A puzzle in linguistics: the syntactic structure of coordination*

Strictly binary Merge forces us to reconsider the hierarchical structure of coordinate constructions. As represented in (c) at the beginning of this chapter (and in the previous chapter), coordinate constructions would have to involve the merger of three syntactic units in a single operation, which may be prohibited in principle. Under binary Merge, the coordination of *Language* and *Linguistics* in the course title would have to involve the merger of the conjunction *and* with one of the nouns as a first step, followed by merger with the other noun. This results in two distinct possible derived hierarchical structures, given in (l) where *and* and *Linguistics* form a syntactic unit in (l.1), while *and* and *Language* form a syntactic unit in (l.2).

(l)   1. { *Language* { *and, Linguistics* } }
           2. { { *Language, and* } *Linguistics* }

(l.1) can be linearized in 4 ways, two of which are not possible for English (**Language Linguistics and* and **and Linguistics Language*). The other two yield different linearizations for the same hierarchical structure.

(m)   1. [*Language* [*and Linguistics*]]
           2. [[*Linguistics and*] *Language*]

In (m.1) *and* is linearized to the left of *Linguistics* and in (m.2) it is linearized to the right.

   One interesting question that now arises is whether both linear structures in (m) are equally plausible. What might bear on an answer is the fact that (l.2) also has the same two legitimate linearizations as (m.1) but with different hierarchical structures, given in (n).

(n)   1. [*Linguistics* [*and Language*]] ≈ (m.2)
           2. [[*Language and*] *Linguistics*] ≈ (m.1)

Thus (m.1) and (n.2) have the same linearization but different hierarchical structures, and similarly for (m.2) and (n.1). Unless there is empirical motivation for postulating the two distinct hierarchical structures for a single linear order, we might reasonably assume that considerations of minimal computation would restrict derivations to a single hierarchical structure.

To see how this might be achieved, we need to pay attention to the details of the analyses of the examples under investigation. A comparison of one pair of examples that share the same linear order but have distinct hierarchical structures ((m.1) and (n.2), for example) shows that the conjunction *and* linearizes to the left of its sister *linguistics* in (m.1) but to the right of its sister *language* in (n.2). The same observation holds for the remaining pair of structures. If the conjunction *and* can linearize in only one direction, then the distinct linearizations in (m) and (n) will each have only a single hierarchical structure. For example, if (m.1) is the correct hierarchical structure for that linearization (which seems more natural in terms of prosodic intonation), then the alternative hierarchical structure of (n.2) will be ruled out by a specific linearization constraint on *and* – in contrast to some constructions where linearization appears to be unconstrained.[11]

Given this analysis of the hierarchical and linear structure of coordinate constructions, all that is left for a complete analysis of the Princeton University introductory linguistics course title is the labeling of the syntactic units that contain more than one lexical item. Part of this analysis has already been spelled out in (k) above. What remains is the labeling in coordinate structures, starting with the merger of a conjunction with a noun. If conjunctions have a syntactic category label, then there are two possibilities for labeling the merger of noun and conjunction: either N or Conj. Identifying the resulting syntactic unit of this merger as Conj seems to serve little purpose because the entire coordinate structure functions syntactically in all essentials exactly like noun phrases that do not contain conjunctions. Furthermore, a coordination of nouns that occurs as the subject of a finite sentence always triggers plural agreement on finite present tense verbs, as in (o), providing strong empirical evidence that both conjuncts are computed as the head of the subject noun phrase.

(o)   *Linguistics and philosophy intersect/*intersects in interesting ways.*

---

[11] Consider the analysis of adverbs for the virtually synonymous pair *quickly left the room* vs. *left the room quickly*. The latter example would have a hierarchical structure [[*left* [*the room*]] *quickly*]. If the hierarchical structure of the former example is [*quickly* [*left* [*the room*]]], then it would appear that manner adverbs like *quickly* can linearize in either order and the synonymy of the pair follows from their having the same hierarchical structure. Note that if the adverb forms a unique syntactic unit with the verb as [*quickly left*], then the alternative linear order [*left quickly*] would yield the deviant **left quickly the room*. In contrast to manner adverbs, if *and* can only linearize to the left, then (m.2) and (n.2) are not possible linearizations. The question that remains is why, for example in *Language and Linguistics*, the unit *and Linguistics* cannot linearize to the left of *Language*, yielding the deviant **and Linguistics Language*.

This contrasts with subject noun phrases which contain more than one noun but where one noun is clearly subordinate to the other, as illustrated in (p).

(p)   1. *Reviews of that book {have/*has} been universally laudatory.*
     2. *One review of those books {has/*have} been extremely laudatory.*
     3. *One review of that book {has/*have} been extremely laudatory.*

In (p.1) the plural *reviews* determines agreement with the finite present tense verb, the plural form *have*, not the singular form *has*. Similarly in (p.2), the singular *review* determines agreement. (p.3) shows that unlike coordinate structures (see (o)), two singular nouns in these structures do not render the subject plural in number. The dual headedness of coordinate structures is a special property of these constructions.

One consequence of postulating binary hierarchical structure for coordinate constructions is that the synonymy of these constructions with different linear orders cannot be accounted for on the basis of identical hierarchical structure. Therefore synonymy would not always depend on having the same hierarchical structure.[12]

From these labeling considerations, the syntactic structure for the first interpretation of the Princeton course title, distinguished as (b.1) and repeated below), would be represented as (q).

(b)   1. [*Introduction* [*to* [*Language and Linguistics*]]]

(q)

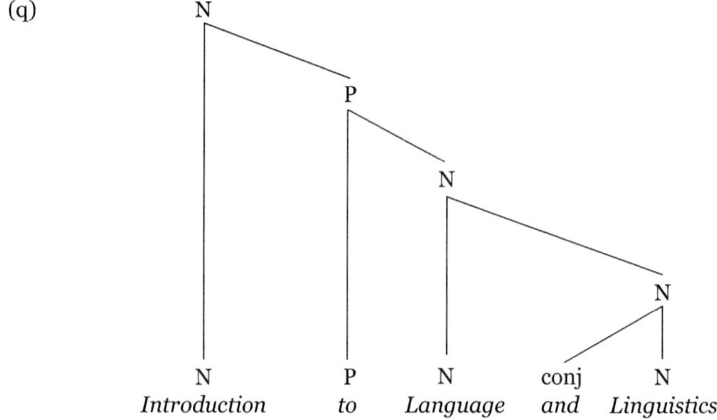

The full syntactic structure of the other possible interpretation of the Princeton course title is left as an exercise for the reader.

---

[12] Recall the examples in the previous chapter where the adjective *Romanian* is substituted for the prepositional phrase *from Romania*.

3.6   On the use and misuse of *and*

As illustrated in this chapter and the previous one, the conjunction *and* can be a source of inadvertent ambiguity. But it is also a useful tool for concision in writing – especially unnecessary repetition, which surely falls within the scope of Strunk & White's famous dictum *omit needless words*[13] (although coordinate structures do not play a role in their discussion). For example, although (r.1) is a perfectly acceptable sentence of English that conjoins two clauses *John sold books to Mary* and *John sold books to Fred*, the repetition of *John sold books* in the second conjunct is unnecessary because (r.2), which eliminates the repetition by coordinating the two prepositional phrases *to Mary* and *to Fred*, is synonymous with (r.1).

(r)   1. *John sold books to Mary and John sold books to Fred.*
            2. *John sold books to Mary and to Fred.*

A related sentence *John sold books to Mary and Fred*, which eliminates the repetition of *to* in the second conjunct of (r.2), could be synonymous with both (r.1) and (r.2), but could also be interpreted as John's selling books to Mary and Fred together rather than separately, an ambiguity that is best avoided unless the context indicates which interpretation is intended.

Syntactically the conjunction *and* connects two syntactic units, which we have been calling *conjuncts*, following traditional grammar. Purely in terms of syntactic structure the two conjuncts usually bear the same syntactic label (parallelism); thus nouns are conjoined with other nouns, and similarly with verbs, adjectives, adverbs, and prepositions – and this applies as well to phrases headed by nouns, verbs, adjectives, adverbs, and prepositions. This parallelism requirement accounts for the impossible interpretation of *eats shoots and leaves* where the first two words are interpreted as verbs and the last word is interpreted as a noun, as discussed in the first chapter. A failure of parallelism in coordinate structures also creates problems in writing. Consider for example the third sentence from the first paragraph of this chapter as it appeared in a previous draft: *The realization fueled that first lecture and also in the following years I taught the course.* The coordinate structure *that first lecture and also in the following years I taught the course* conjoins a noun phrase *that first lecture* with a prepositional phrase *in the following years I taught the course.* What is missing in the second conjunct is an explicit reference to first lectures as in *that first lecture and also **the first lecture** in the following years I taught the course.* It is worth comparing the revision of this sentence to the one used in the opening paragraph to this chapter: *This*

---

[13] *The Elements of Style*, II. Elementary Principles of Composition.

realization fueled that first lecture, which became my introductory lecture for the course in subsequent years. I leave it to the reader to decide whether there is a clear preference for one over the other and what the reason(s) for this preference might be.

The use of *and* (and therefore of coordination) also invites another type of redundancy involving the interpretative relation between the two conjuncts. Syntactically it is possible to coordinate words where the interpretation of one conjunct includes the interpretation of the other – for example, *dogs and canines*, where *canines* includes *dogs* so that the relation between the conjuncts is part/whole. Expressions like *dogs and canines* are fine syntactically but distinctly peculiar – especially compared to *dogs and other canines* where the two conjuncts are now disjoint in interpretation. In addition to part/whole problems, the use of *and* can also yield a coordination of synonyms, as in *shut and close the door*, an extreme example to be sure – but it's often surprising what people can write when they aren't paying attention.

Unlike syntactically ill-formed coordinate structures, which we don't normally find in speech and writing, examples of redundant coordinate structures can be found in writing (even by quite skilled writers). In fact, there are several examples in this chapter. Two examples occur in the definition of *linguistics* in the Oxford online dictionary of English, which defines the term as *the scientific study of language and its structure,* with the addendum *Also: this as a subject of educational study and examination.* Given that the structure of language is part of language, the study of language would include the study of its structure. The second example coordinates *study* and *examination*, virtual synonyms if these nouns are related to the verbs *study* and *examine*, where the latter is not a synonym for *test*.[14] This latter example also involves a scope ambiguity for the adjective *educational* of the sort discussed in Chapter 2. In this case, context does not help in choosing one interpretation over the other. Regarding the wide-scope reading, the interpretation 'educational examination' is a bit peculiar, especially compared to 'educational study' – what's the distinction? The unambiguous rendering of the narrow-scope reading as *examination and educational study* is equally peculiar.

A fourth fascinating example occurs in George Orwell's famous and celebrated essay "Politics and the English Language", whose purpose is *the defense of the English language* – a rather bizarre notion given the perspective developed in this chapter. In it Orwell writes that his defense of the language

---

[14] Note the amusing ambiguity of this sentence, where *the latter* could refer equally to *examination* or *examine*. In one case, *test* is interpreted as a noun and in the other, a verb. Of course, when I formulated this sentence I had only one interpretation in mind and only noticed the other on rereading the sentence. Since both interpretations are equally valid, this ambiguous sentence remains.

has nothing to do with correct grammar and syntax, which are of no importance so long as one makes one's meaning clear. The culprit here is *grammar and syntax*, where on our understanding of the term *grammar, syntax* is a part of *grammar*. If, as is probably likely, Orwell means by *correct grammar* such issues as subject/verb agreement in finite clauses – which is a subpart of syntax (more precisely MORPHOSYNTAX, the intersection of syntax and morphology), then the part/whole relation goes the other way. A further problem with Orwell's formulation concerns (once again) the scope ambiguity of an adjective (*correct*) as a modifier of one or both conjuncts in the coordinate structure – that is, either *correct grammar and correct syntax* or *syntax and correct grammar*. However, the most egregious problem with Orwell's formulation concerns the claim that syntax, correct or not, is *of no importance as long as one makes one's meaning clear.* As should be obvious from the discussion of the first three chapters of this book, because meaning crucially depends on syntactic structure, making one's meaning clear will depend on the syntax one uses to express it.

The relation between conjuncts of a coordinate structure can also be an issue with *or*. The instruction to the California jury (discussed in the previous chapter) that its members *must not be swayed by mere sentiment, conjecture, sympathy, passion, prejudice, public opinion or public feeling* is a salient example. First, the elements of the list are not separate-but-equal in the context of the instruction. For example, *sympathy* is a form of *sentiment*, so the two terms are in a part/whole relation, which is inappropriate for coordinate structures. There is also the question of whether *passion* and *public feeling* also fall under the umbrella of *sentiment*. Clearly the court would not want a jury weighing a death sentence to be swayed by *conjecture, passion, prejudice, public opinion,* or *public feeling*. Therefore, it would seem that *mere* should not qualify these terms in the instruction – which would argue for the narrowscope reading of *mere*. But then, the instruction tells the jury not to be swayed by *sympathy*, which would constitute the antisympathy instruction that the California Supreme court objected to in its decision to reverse the death penalty. But the wide-scope reading of *mere* is also problematic because it would allow for the possibility that the jury could be swayed by some form of *conjecture, prejudice, public opinion,* or *public feeling* – a point that was made in one of the dissenting opinions to the U.S. Supreme Court's decision. The problem with the instruction to the jury was not only ambiguity of the scope of the adjective *mere*, but also the overlapping and/or unequal relations between the conjuncts.

Another problem with conjunct relations occurs at the conclusion of the chapter in Steven Pinker's *The Language Instinct: How the Mind Creates Language* (1994) where he criticizes the pronouncements of writers he calls *language mavens* – self-appointed guardians of correct use of the English language (including Orwell among many others), where Pinker writes: *Overcoming one's natural egocentrism and trying to anticipate the knowledge state of a generic reader at every stage of exposition is one of the most important tasks in writing well.* In this case the two conjuncts, *overcoming one's natural egocentrism* and *trying to anticipate the knowledge state of a generic reader at every stage of exposition*, are syntactically complex – in contrast to the coordinations of nouns that we have been discussing. Nonetheless it is possible to evaluate the two conjuncts in simpler terms by reducing them to a coordination of just the heads of the phrases that constitute the conjuncts – in this case, *overcoming* and *trying* (or perhaps *anticipating*, which is the relevant activity in the second conjunct). From this perspective, the relation between the two activities does not appear to be separate and also of equivalent importance (for example, *running and swimming*). Rather, the second conjunct specifies a way to realize the goal expressed in the first. Roughly speaking, anticipating the knowledge state of a generic reader is a means for overcoming the natural egocentric perspective every writer starts with. The relation between the two conjuncts is more specific than simple coordination; it is actually more like cause and effect, where in this case the general goal of overcoming the writer's natural egocentric perspective is achieved by the writer trying to imagine the mind of a general reader who does not possess the special knowledge the writer has. All this can be captured simply by changing one word in Pinker's sentence: substitute the preposition *by* for the conjunction *and*. The result, *Overcoming one's natural egocentrism **by** trying to anticipate the knowledge state of a generic reader at every stage of exposition is one of the most important tasks in writing well*, explicitly expresses the relation between the former conjuncts, making the revision a stronger sentence.

This revision also eliminates a potential grammatical error of the original: the main verb *is* does not agree in number with the subject, which coordinates two gerundive nominals *overcoming* and *trying*, thus two distinct tasks not one. Subordinating the second nominal to the first by using a preposition rather than a conjunction makes the subject singular in number, justifying *is*. The singular *is* in the original sentence suggests that the writer understood the subject as singular and therefore did not notice that the use of *and* changed the formulation to a plural subject.

A similar example of this use of *and* occurs in the last sentence of the quotation from Henry Fowler's book on sentence analysis that appears in the preface of this book:

But sentence analysis – the taking of a sentence to pieces and determining the exact relation of each piece to the rest – has a very practical value for every one who would either write without blunders or be sure of a writer's meaning.

Here Fowler's definition of *sentence analysis* consists of two parts: *the taking of a sentence to pieces* and *determining the exact relation of each piece to the rest* – expressed as two conjuncts of a coordinate structure. However, the two conjuncts are not really separate and equal because the determination of the relation of each part of a sentence to the rest results in *the taking of a sentence to pieces*. This can be expressed with greater clarity by substituting *by* for *and*:

*But sentence analysis – the taking of a sentence to pieces **by** determining the exact relation of each piece to the rest – has a very practical value for every one who would either write without blunders or be sure of a writer's meaning.*

In this case too, *and* masks the cause-and-effect relation between the two conjuncts.

The same problem occurs in the second sentence in the Gore Vidal quotation from Chapter 1, repeated and extended below.

Although the Inventors were hostile to the idea of democracy and believed profoundly in the sacredness of property and the necessary dignity of those who owned it, they did not like the idea of king, duke, marquess, earl. Such a system of hereditary nobility was liable to produce aristocrats who tended to mix in politics (like the egregious Lord North) instead of good politically responsible burghers.

The subordinate clause that begins this second sentence contains two instances of *and* and therefore two coordinate constructions. The two conjuncts of the first are *were hostile to the idea of democracy* and *believed profoundly in the sacredness of property and the necessary dignity of those who owned it*. Thus the second conjunct contains a coordinate structure, *the sacredness of property and the necessary dignity of those who owned it*, that functions as the object of the complex verbal expression *believe in*. This second coordination conjoins *the sacredness of property* with *the necessary dignity of those who owned it*, the two conjuncts being separate and equally significant (though it seems reasonable that the *necessary dignity* of property owners derives from *the sacredness of property*). However, in the first coordination the second conjunct actually explains why the Inventors of the United States were *hostile to the idea of democracy*. The relation between the two conjuncts is cause-and-effect, where second can be subordinated to the first by substituting *because* for *and*, and thereby making the relation explicit.

*Although the Inventors were hostile to the idea of democracy **because they** believed profoundly in the sacredness of property and the necessary dignity of those who owned it, they did not like the idea of king, duke, marquess, earl.*

The result is a stronger sentence, one that eliminates one of the three coordinate structures in the original.

The amazing paragraph from Chomsky quoted above (pages 40–41) provides yet another example where the conjunction *and* fails to express the more explicit relation between two conjuncts. Talking about the approach that attempts *to assimilate the study of language into the main body of the natural sciences*, Chomsky writes *This meant, in the first place, abandoning dogmas that are entirely foreign to the natural sciences and that have no place in rational inquiry...* The two conjuncts are *that are entirely foreign to the natural sciences* and *that have no place in rational inquiry*, both modifiers of the noun *dogmas*. The contrast expressed in this coordinate structure is between being *entirely foreign to the natural sciences* and having *no place in rational inquiry*. The connection between *the natural sciences* and *rational inquiry* is that, above all, the natural sciences are fields committed to rational inquiry. The conjunction *and* does not capture the more precise relation between the two conjuncts, but the substitution of *because* for *and* does – and furthermore shows that one of the conjuncts is actually in a subordinate relation with respect to the other. Revised in this way, the sentence would read: *This meant, in the first place, abandoning dogmas that are entirely foreign to the natural sciences **because** they have no place in rational inquiry ...* To the extent that *and* masks the subordinate relation between the conjuncts, coordinate constructions invite vagueness, another characteristic of weak writing.

Chomsky too is a highly skilled writer, both of technical material as well as work directed to a general reader. So all this discussion really shows is how easy it is for even highly skilled writers to occasionally misuse *and*, where misuse occurs when a more precise version of the sentence is possible without using *and*. This suggests that one way of improving your writing is by reducing the use of *and*s – where a sentence can often be made stronger by eliminating a coordinate structure. But this is not a recommendation for the wholesale elimination of *and*s from writing; rather, a suggestion that because *and* (and *or*) can introduce problems in written text, it would be useful to put *question coordinate structures!* at the top of your list for editing first drafts.

Coda

Language, like the air we breathe, surrounds our lives and fills us with an essential ingredient for living. Because it is so familiar, a constant companion (even in dreams), we mostly take it for granted. But when we pay careful attention to it, especially how it is put together, the familiar becomes strange and full of wonder. This was my own experience with the title of the Princeton University introductory linguistics course.

Starting with the realization that the string of words representing the title could have two distinct syntactic structures (two different hierarchical structures) and thus two different interpretations leads immediately to a question:

which interpretation (and thus which syntactic structure) is the one that describes the course? In terms of syntactic structure the question translates as: what is the left conjunct of the coordinate structure – *language* or *introduction to language*? The answer crucially depends on the relation between the left conjunct and *linguistics*, the right conjunct. This leads to an investigation of the meaning of both *language* and *linguistics* (as well as *introduction*), which turns out to be more complicated than you might have expected.

An answer begins to emerge from a definition of *a language* (as opposed to *language* with no article). *A language* is defined as a lexicon plus a computational system that combines words in the lexicon into structured expressions of the language. From this perspective, a language constitutes a system of knowledge in the mind of the speaker.

Roughly, the lexicon in the mind of a speaker (the mental lexicon) specifies the pronunciation (the phonetic label) and the interpretation of the words of a language. An investigation of the interpretation of the 3 nouns in the course title demonstrates the inadequacy of physical dictionaries as a model of this mental lexicon. This investigation also demonstrates how the interpretation of words – the 3 nouns in the title – is inexorably tied to our knowledge of the world. It is a virtual certainty that someone who has not read this chapter (or taken a linguistics course or read about modern linguistics) will not interpret *language* and *linguistics* as the chapter does.

The computational system contains the mechanisms that derive the structured expressions of languages from the contents of the lexicon. One mechanism Merge applies to the elements of the lexicon, creating syntactic units which specify the hierarchical syntactic structure of linguistic expressions (titles of books and courses, and of course sentences). In addition, there is a mechanism Linearize that creates a linear order of the words for these hierarchical structures. The distinction between the two mechanisms now underpins the demonstration in the previous chapter of how hierarchical structure, but not linear order, determines interpretation. This is further supported in this chapter by the comparison of word order in English and Japanese, where expressions containing words with corresponding interpretations have different linear orders but the same hierarchical structure, yielding the same interpretation. And finally, the computational system contains a mechanism for labeling syntactic units (Label), which distinguishes, for example, between a subject *the striped fish* and a predicate *swam lazily upstream* in the sentence *the striped fish swam lazily upstream* by labeling the subject as N and the predicate as V.

The definition of a language as a mental lexicon plus a computational system in the mind of the speaker provides a solid basis for defining *language*. From this perspective, language is what languages share in common: general properties of the computational system and the lexicon, properties that appear to be universal for humans. To the extent that such properties cannot be specified solely in terms of what is overt in speech (primarily phonetic form), they would otherwise have to constitute an innate faculty of language, which guides the acquisition of a language and determines both its essential nature and its use.

Under this definition of language, *linguistics* becomes the study of the faculty of language, a part of human biology. Therefore, linguistics is concerned with the essential nature of language (and languages) – including how they vary, the acquisition of languages by individuals, the origin of language in the species, and how knowledge of a language is put to use.

The use of the conjunction *and* in the course title is what creates the ambiguity of the title. This reveals that *and* can be easily misused in writing to create unintended ambiguity. The chapter also considers how it can create both redundancy (in the form of overlapping conjuncts) and vagueness (when the relation between conjuncts is actually stronger than simple coordination). In this way, the misuse of *and* produces three hallmarks of poor writing: ambiguity, redundancy, and vagueness. With this understanding, one simple way of improving the clarity of your writing is to edit out such *and*s.

As with the previous three chapters, the title of this chapter has more than one interpretation. This ambiguity results from the interpretation of the prepositional phrase *by two philosophers* as a modifier of a noun. On one interpretation, the prepositional phrase modifies *book* as in *a book by two philosophers*, while on the other interpretation it modifies *review* as in *a review by two philosophers*. This can be pictorially represented by coloring *review* red and *book* blue and matching the color of *by two philosophers* to the noun it modifies, as illustrated in (a).

(a)　　　1.　*a review of a book by two philosophers*
　　　　　2.　*a review of a book by two philosophers*

In the first case, the prepositional phrase is adjacent to the noun it modifies, whereas in the second, it is separated from that noun by another prepositional phrase *of a* book, which also modifies *review*. This complexity results from having multiple prepositional phrase modifiers within a noun phrase. Furthermore, there is no interpretation of the title where the prepositional phrase *by two philosophers* modifies both *review* and *book* at the same time, and no interpretation where it modifies neither. As with the modification relations between noun/adjective and noun/prepositional phrase discussed in Chapter 2, the interpretation of this modification relation is also totally determined by hierarchical structure.

4.1　　The syntactic structure of complex noun phrases

This section begins with the syntax of the chapter title, specifically the syntax of prepositional phrase modifiers. In the case of the prepositional phrase *by two philosophers*, there is a potential lexical ambiguity in the interpretation of the preposition *by*: it could be interpreted as locative in the sense of 'near by' or 'along side of' instead of agentive, where the object of *by* is interpreted as the agent of an action. Thus for example in *a review by two philosophers* we interpret the two philosophers as agents of an action as in *two philosophers reviewed the book*. The agentive *by* implicates larger syntactic units, predicates and clauses, as will be spelled out in Section 4.1.2.

4.1.1   *The syntax of prepositional phrase modifiers*

The same ambiguity in the chapter title holds for *reviews of books by philosophers*, which simplifies the chapter title by eliminating two indefinite articles and the number *two* – thereby reducing the hierarchical structure of the example to the bare essentials needed to explicate the syntactic nature of the ambiguity. The revised example consists of just 5 words: 3 nouns and 2 prepositions, where each preposition functions as the head (recall Section 3.3 of Chapter 3) of a distinct prepositional phrase (thus 2 in total). Under both interpretations of this complex noun phrase, *by philosophers* alone constitutes one prepositional phrase. Where *by philosophers* is interpreted as modifying *books*, the noun and the prepositional phrase form a unique syntactic unit *books by philosophers*, which itself functions as the object of the preposition *of*. Thus the prepositional phrase headed by *of* contains the prepositional phrase headed by *by*, and it is this larger prepositional phrase that is interpreted as modifying the noun *reviews*. This yields a hierarchical structure given in (b).

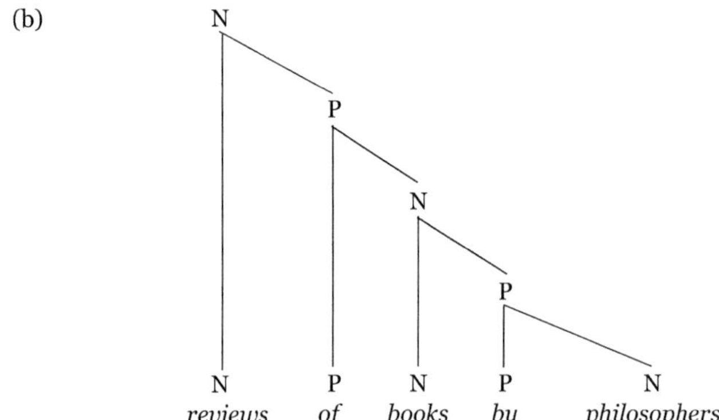

In (b), the prepositional phrase *by philosophers*, as a sister of the noun *books*, modifies *books*. Likewise, the larger prepositional phrase *of books by philosophers*, as a sister to the noun *reviews*, modifies *reviews*.

On the other interpretation, *by philosophers* does not modify *books*, but instead modifies *reviews*. Therefore, that prepositional phrase cannot be in a sister relation with *books*, and instead must be in a more direct hierarchical relation with *reviews*. This is illustrated in the other possible hierarchical structure, given in (c).

(c)

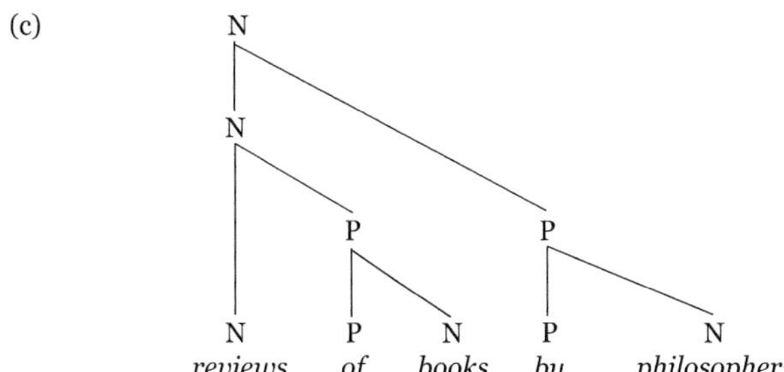

In (c) *by philosophers* is not a sister of the noun *reviews*, but nonetheless is interpreted as modifying that noun because that prepositional phrase is hierarchically a sister of a larger syntactic unit *reviews of books*, which is labeled N by *reviews*.

Both hierarchical structures result straightforwardly from the application of Merge. Given that Merge applies only once to the prepositional phrase *by philosophers* it establishes a modification relation with either *books* or *reviews*, but not both at the same time. Also, given that all the elements in a linguistic expression must collaborate in a single hierarchical structure to be interpretable, there is no way for *by philosophers* not to form a sister relation with one of the other two nouns. In this way, the interpretive properties of this linguistic expression follow from Merge as the primary structure-building operation of the computational system for human language.[1]

---

[1] At this point, we can compare the representation of syntactic structure that results with Merge plus linearization to the Reed–Kellogg diagrams mentioned in the Preface. The 10th edition of *Understanding English Grammar* presents the following diagram for the sentence *my sister manages the flower shop in the new brick building near the park on Center Street.*

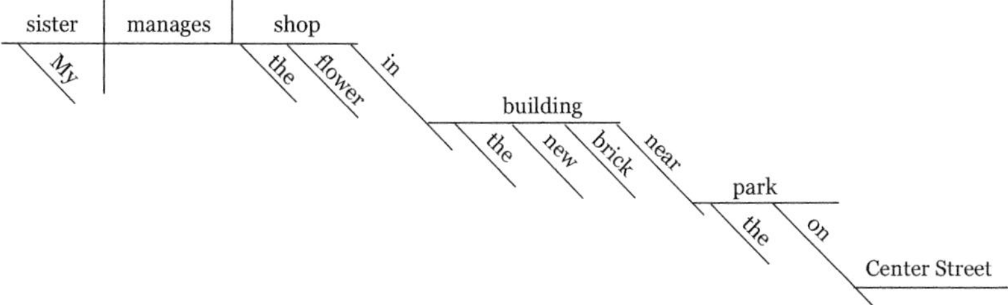

Unlike a standard tree diagram, Reed–Kellogg does not label the parts of speech, nor does it specify the exact linear order of modifiers, represented on diagonal lines attached to a horizontal line under the word they modify. Thus for *building* it doesn't show that the first three modifiers

Note further that there is no way to punctuate these complex noun phrases in a way that distinguishes between the two possible interpretations.

4.1.2   *From prepositional phrase to clausal modifiers*

The linguistic expression *reviews of books by philosophers* is not only ambiguous, but also virtually synonymous on its two interpretations with the significantly more complicated expression *reviews of books written by philosophers*. In the latter, the prepositional phrase *by philosophers* forms a syntactic unit with *written*, a form of the verb *write*. Under one interpretation, the books are written by philosophers; whereas under the other, it is the reviews that are written by philosophers.

The 3-word modifier *written by philosophers*, consisting of a verb, a preposition, and a noun, has a simple hierarchical structure with the labeling given in (d).

(d)

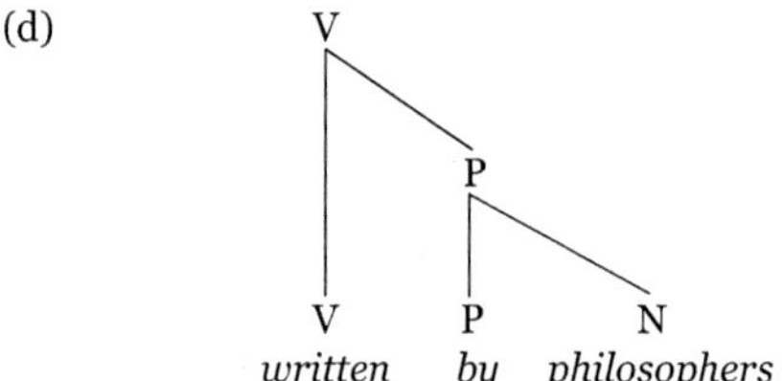

occur before the word, while *near* (and what it attaches to) follows. Compared to a standard tree diagram, these diagrams are rather opaque, leaving out important details.

Understanding English Grammar notes that noun phrases containing multiple prepositional phrases "are sometimes open to ambiguity"; but given basic English syntax, they are always open to ambiguity because there are always multiple ways these prepositional phrases can form syntactic units within the noun phrase. In the example cited, *on Center Street* could be interpreted as modifying *building* or even *shop*, rather than *park*. In addition, *on Center Street* could modify the verb *manages*, indicating where the sister manages a flower shop. In this case, the syntactic differences don't result in significant interpretive differences. If the shop is on Center Street, then the building which houses it must be too – and similarly if the building is on Center Street, then the shop that it houses must be too. And if the management of the flower shop occurs on Center Street, then it would follow that the shop and the building that houses it are also on Center Street.

One syntactic ambiguity that makes an interpretive difference concerns whether *on Center Street* modifies *park* or *building*. If *building*, then *near the park* and *on Center Street* are independent prepositional phrases – in which case the ambiguity could be eliminated by reversing their linear order (*in the building on Center Street near the park*), provided that *near the park* would not be interpreted as modifying *Center Street* (which raises the question of whether it's natural to talk about parts of a single street, one near the park and the other not – an interpretation that would be forced if *on Center Street* with this linear order modifies *shop* rather than *building*).

Structurally this modifier is a verb phrase that contains a prepositional phrase as a constituent. The preposition *by* is the head of the prepositional phrase and the verb *written* is the head of the verb phrase. Given that the preposition is the agentive *by* – thereby designating *philosophers* as the writers, *written* is the only form of the verb *write* that can combine with the prepositional phrase, as illustrated by the deviance of the examples in (e).

(e)   1. *writes by philosophers*
        2. *(to / will / can) write by philosophers*
        3. *is writing by philosophers*

Thus the agentive prepositional phrase cannot be legitimately combined with a finite form of the verb (e.1), or with the bare form to the verb that occurs with either infinitival *to* or modal auxiliaries – informally called 'helping verbs' – like *will* and *can* (e.2), or with the progressive participle that accompanies the progressive auxiliary *be* (e.3). Furthermore, as the deviance of *has written by philosophers* shows, *written* in (d) cannot be interpreted as the perfective participle that accompanies the perfective auxiliary *have*.[2]

The verb form *written* in (d) is interpreted only as the passive participle that combines with some form of the passive auxiliary *be* as in *those books were written by philosophers*. The presence of the agentive preposition *by* requires the co-occurrence of the passive participle form of the verb, constituting a HEAD-TO-HEAD DEPENDENCY. Notice that while agentive *by* requires the passive participle form of the verb in *written by philosophers* (d), the passive participle does not require the agentive *by* because this verb form could just as well combine with a prepositional phrase headed by some other preposition (as in *written on a computer*) or with no prepositional phrase at all (as in *written quickly*).

---

[2] Basically, the progressive auxiliary *be* indicates ongoing action, while the perfective auxiliary *have* indicates completed action. These actions can be located in the past, present, or future – as in (1).

(1)   a. *Philosophers were writing books.*   (past)
           Philosophers are writing books.   (present)
           Philosophers will be writing books.   (future)
        b. *That philosopher had written books.*   (past)
           That philosopher has written books.   (present)
           That philosopher will have written books. (future)

The perfective and progressive auxiliaries can be combined, as in (2).

(2)   *Philosophers had been writing books for centuries.*   (past)
        Philosophers have been writing books for centuries.   (present)
        Philosophers will have been writing books for centuries.   (future)

With the operation Merge introduced in Chapter 3, the syntactic unit (d) labeled V and headed by the verbal form *written* can form a syntactic unit with *books*, corresponding to the interpretation 'books written by philosophers' as in (f).

(f)

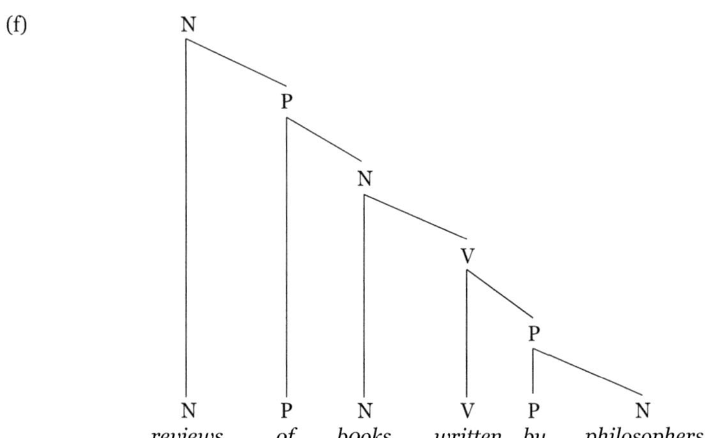

Alternatively, the syntactic unit (d) can be merged with the syntactic unit *reviews of books*, yielding a structure (g) that corresponds to the interpretation 'reviews written by philosophers'.

(g)

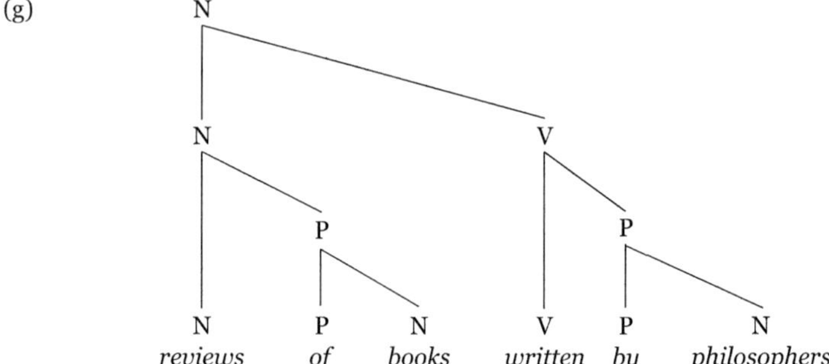

Thus the hierarchical structure (f) corresponds to (b), while the hierarchical structure (g) corresponds to (c), where the only difference is that the modifying phrase in (b–c) is the prepositional phrase *by philosophers* while in (f–g) the modifying phrase is a verb phrase containing that prepositional phrase and headed by the verb form *written*.

Underlying the synonymy of (b & f) is the fact that *books by philosophers* is synonymous with *books written by philosophers*. For the purposes of this discussion, synonymy can be characterized as a relation between two linguistic expressions that have different phonetic forms but share the same interpretation. How we account for synonymy in general (and this pair of expressions in particular) depends on whether we consider synonymous pairs from the perspective of internalizing external language (that is, phonetic form) or from the perspective of externalizing internal language (what can be called COGNITIVE FORM). Starting with phonetic form, there must be a process that converts *books by philosophers* into its interpretation 'books written by philosophers', thereby accounting for the shared interpretation of the pair of expressions. However this process works exactly, it goes far beyond the computational power of the computational system proposed in Chapter 3 to characterize knowledge of a language. Alternatively, starting with cognitive form, the two expressions would have the same syntactic structure with the same lexical elements. The externalization of this structure would in the case of *books by philosophers* involve the deletion of the phonetic features of *written*.

DELETION is another operation of the computational system, one that is motivated independently by ELLIPSIS phenomena (the main topic of Chapter 8), as illustrated in (h.2) – another way of expressing (h.1).

(h)   1. *Mary has written a book and John has written a book too.*
         2. *Mary has written a book and John has too.*
         3. Mary has written a book and John has ~~written a book~~ too.

The ellipsis in (h.2) results from the deletion of the phonetic features of *written a book*, represented in (h.3) with a strikethrough of the words that are part of the interpretation of the second conjunct, but not pronounced (or written).

(h.2) is an instance of verb phrase ellipsis, where a phonetically identical syntactic unit in a second conjunct of a coordinate construction can be deleted from the phonetic form of a linguistic expression. This deletion is possible, but not required given that (h.1) is another way of externalizing the same cognitive representation, because the unpronounced syntactic unit exists in the first conjunct – which renders the deletion 'recoverable' from the phonetic material in that first conjunct.

In contrast, the optionality of *written* with respect to *books by philosophers* would not be a recoverable deletion in the same way that deletion in ellipsis constructions is. Rather this absence of *written* is recoverable to the extent that it appears to be the only verb possible for relating *books by philosophers* to *books* V*ed by philosophers*, where *–ed* represents the suffix of the passive participle and V represents the verbal root of the participle. While there are many other verbs that could be substituted for *written* – for example {*read, edited, published, criticized, praised*, etc.}, none of the expressions [V*ed by philosophers*] formed with these verbs is synonymous with the expression missing the verb. Thus *books by philosophers* has a single interpretation that does not involve any of these other verbs. This interpretation is no doubt connected to interpretation of *book* as an object that is written. A similar analysis will apply to *reviews*, which in the context of *reviews of books* is synonymous with the compound noun *book reviews*.[3]

Not only is *books by philosophers* synonymous with *books written by philosophers*, this pair of expressions is also synonymous with *books which were written by philosophers*. In this longer expression, the modifier of *books* contains both a pronoun *which* that stands in for the noun *books* (the Antecedent of the relative pronoun) and a finite auxiliary verb *were*. This modifier *which were written by philosophers*, standardly called a Relative Clause (a clause that modifies a noun), contains the hierarchical structure of *written by philosophers*, given in (d), as a subpart. A relative clause is one form of Subordinate Clause – roughly, a clause that forms a subpart of a sentence. This relative clause can be transformed into a non-subordinate (or Main) clause simply by replacing the relative pronoun *which*[4] with the noun phrase *these books*, yielding *these books were written by philosophers*, a simple sentence containing a single clause. Thus the syntactic analysis of the relative clause will reveal the analysis of clauses in general, including other forms of subordinate clauses.

4.2   The syntactic analysis of (relative) clauses

Both the relative clause and the simple sentence into which it can be transformed contain the verb phrase (d) (*written by philosophers*) as a subpart. In

---

[3] In terms of morphological structure, this compound noun consists of two nominal roots *book-* and *review-* that join together to form a unit which is then inflected with the plural affix for number: [[*book + review*] + -*s*]. Recall the analysis of plural nouns in Chapter 3, where the root of a noun is uninflected for number. Note further that the first root of the compound cannot be independently inflected for number, as illustrated by the deviance of **books review* and **books reviews*.

[4] The relative pronoun *which* should not to be confused with the interrogative *which* as in *which books will you read?*, where *which* modifies the noun *books*. See Chapter 7 for further discussion of the syntax of questions.

addition, they both contain the phrase *were written by philosophers*, which would have the hierarchical structure given in (i).

(i)

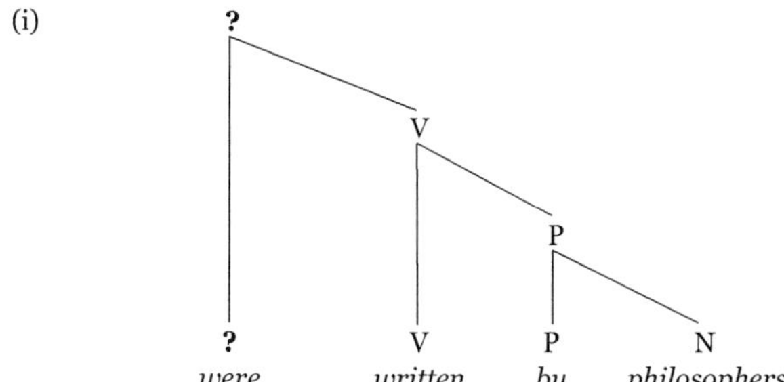

The finite auxiliary *were* is labeled with **?** to indicate that its actual label remains to be identified. In both the simple sentence and the relative clause, (i) provides a structural analysis of the predicate of a sentence/clause as the combination of a verb phrase with a finite auxiliary element.

This provides a simple and straightforward way to identify predicates, without worrying about defining them in terms of meaning (semantic content and semantic function): a predicate is a syntactic unit headed by a finite verbal element, which includes any verbal element that expresses past, present, or future tense. In addition to *books which were written by philosophers*, where the past tense *were* heads the predicate, there are also (j.1) and (j.2).

(j)   1. *books which are written by philosophers*
      2. *books which will be written by philosophers*

In (j.1) the predicate is headed by the present tense *are* and in (j.2) the relative clause is headed by the modal auxiliary *will*, which in English expresses the future tense. Completing the syntactic analysis of the predicate rendered in (i) now requires specifying the syntactic label of the element designated as **?**. The solution crucially involves head-to-head dependencies mentioned in the previous section.

Just as the agentive *by* requires the passive participle form *written*, this verbal form requires that the verb phrase it heads be merged with some form of the passive auxiliary *be* – for example, *is **being** written, has **been** written,* or *will **be** written.* In linguistics these head-to-head dependencies are characterized as SELECTION, where the head of a syntactic unit *selects* (now a technical term with the sense of 'determine') the lexical item that the unit can legitimately merge with. Thus the passive participle *written* selects some form of the passive auxiliary *be*.

If that form is the progressive participle *being*, for example, then *being* selects a form of the progressive auxiliary *be*. Similarly, the perfective participle *been* selects a form of the perfective auxiliary *have* as in *has been written*, and the bare form of the passive auxiliary *be* selects a modal auxiliary (*will, can, could, shall, should, may, might,* and *must*) as in *will be written*. In (i) *by* selects *written*, and *written* selects *were* as the form of the passive auxiliary *be*. This identifies *were* as the head of *were written by philosophers*, in which case the syntactic label of *were* labels the whole construction.

Under the analysis in (i), what we have designated as the predicate phrase is labeled by its head, an auxiliary verb indicating past tense. On the assumption that *tense* is the salient property of these auxiliaries, we can replace **?** with **T** for 'tense' – a standard designation in linguistics. Structurally, a predicate would be defined as a tense phrase resulting from the merger of the tensed element with another syntactic unit (usually some kind of verb phrase but possibly an adjective phrase as underlined in *it is unlikely that he will arrive on time* or a prepositional phrase as underlined in *they are in the house*).

With the analysis of the predicate in (i) it is one simple step to the analysis of full clause consisting of a subject plus a predicate. In the case of the simple sentence *these books were written by philosophers*, the noun phrase *these books* is merged with the predicate (i) to form a complete clause. What the syntactic label of the resulting syntactic unit is remains the only outstanding question for the syntactic analysis of the clause.

If we limit the labels of syntactic units to the syntactic categories of items in the lexicon, then labels like *sentence* and *clause* are impossible in principle. That leaves two possibilities: N that labels the subject noun phrase and T that labels the predicate. Defining a clause as a noun phrase has never been seriously considered in linguistics. One point against this is that under this analysis the predicate of the clause would be a structural subpart of the subject noun phrase – which rejects the traditional understanding of a clause as two distinct units, a subject plus a predicate. Instead, T is taken to be the structural head of a clause, where the subject noun phrase and the predicate T phrase (for example, T plus a verb phrase in (i)) are constituents.

Taking T as the head of a clause yields (k) as the analysis of the simple sentence *these books were written by philosophers*.

(k)

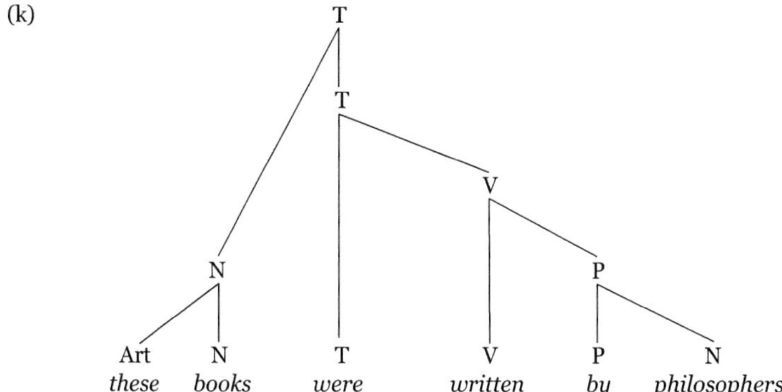

While it might seem at this point that the structure of the relative clause *which were written by philosophers* is simply a matter of replacing *these books* in (k) with the relative pronoun *which*, the syntax of (English) relative clauses turns out to be a bit more complicated.

This complication unfolds from a consideration of the syntactic variation that is possible with finite relative clauses. The relative clause examples discussed so far have all contained the relative pronoun *which* where the pronoun stands in for the noun *books* that the relative clause modifies and where the relative pronoun is interpreted as the subject of the relative clause. This constitutes an ANAPHORIC RELATION (therefore a word/word relation – in contrast to reference, which is a word/world relation) between *books* and *which*. As illustrated in (l) there is an alternative and synonymous version that omits the relative pronoun and contains instead a *that*.

(l)   1. *books which have been written by philosophers*
         2. *books that have been written by philosophers*

The word *that* in (l.2) cannot be interpreted as either a pronoun (as in *that is a mistake*) or a modifier of a noun (as in *that book*), both of which are inherently singular (compare **that are mistakes* and **that books*). Therefore, *that* does not stand in for the relative pronoun *which* and is not interpreted as the subject of the relative clause.

Exactly what function *that* in (l.2) has and where it sits in the hierarchical structure of a relative clause is easier to understand from a comparison with a further pair of synonymous expressions given in (m).

(m)   1. *books which philosophers have written*
         2. *books that philosophers have written*

In (m.2) *that* occurs in front of the noun *philosophers*, which is the subject of the verb *written* in the relative clause. Thus the relative clause in (m.2) results from the merger of a tense phrase with *that*. This lexical item *that* announces that the following clause is a subordinate clause, this one embedded in the noun phrase headed by *books*. It also indicates that the subordinate clause must have a finite T as its head. Interpreting this dependency between T and *that* as an instance of selection (where finite T selects *that*) yields a hierarchical structure in which the label of *that* is the label of the phrase created by merging a tense phrase with the subordinating particle *that*, as shown in (n).

(n)

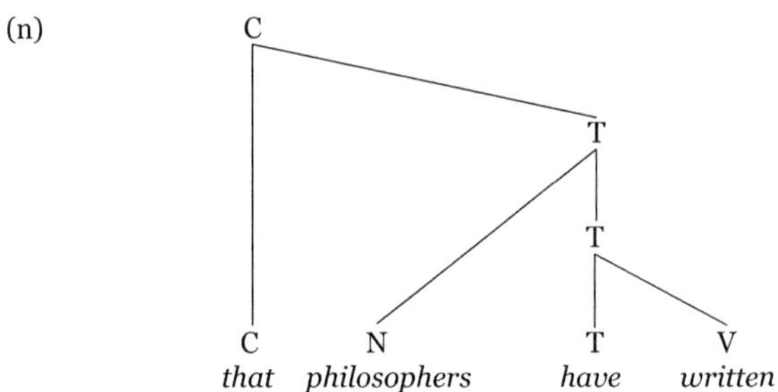

The label C for a subordinating particle like *that* is standard in linguistics.[5] (n) gives the syntactic structure for the phonetic form of the relative clause in (m.2), but is not the complete structure for its cognitive form, where there must be some unpronounced element that connects the relative clause to the noun it modifies.

As for the phonetic form of (m.1), the relative pronoun is pronounced at the beginning of the relative clause in front of the clause subject *philosophers*. Given that *which* is a pronoun, a type of noun, it is distinct from the subordinating particle *that* and therefore does not occupy the syntactic C position when *that* is

---

[5] C is an abbreviation for the technical term 'complementizer' – basically an element that turns a clause into a 'complement' (another technical term from linguistics that has been in use since 1970). Functionally, a relative clause is a modifier of a noun, whereas the clausal complement underlined in *they reported that John left on time* does not modify the verb *reported* and instead functions like an object of the verb (compare *they reported the theft*). The parallelism between the two constructions is dramatically illustrated in examples that are ambiguous between a relative clause interpretation and a clausal complement interpretation, as in *we have a report that John left on time*. On the relative clause reading, the example is synonymous with *we have a report which John left on time*. On the complement interpretation, the verb *left* is interpreted instead as intransitive (that is, without an object – as in the simple sentence *John left on time*). To modify *we have a report that John left on time* so that its interpretation is unambiguously that of the clausal complement would require separating the noun *report* and the clause with a verbal element – for example, *we have a report **saying** that John left on time*. Replacing the subordinating particle *that* with the relative pronoun *which* – yielding *we have a report which John left on time* disambiguates in the other direction because of the presence of the relative pronoun *which* (itself interpreted as the object of the verb *left* and taking the noun *report* as its antecedent).

not part of the phonetic form. The syntactic structure of (m.1) would then be (o), where the C phrase in (n) is extended to include *which* as a constituent part.

(o)

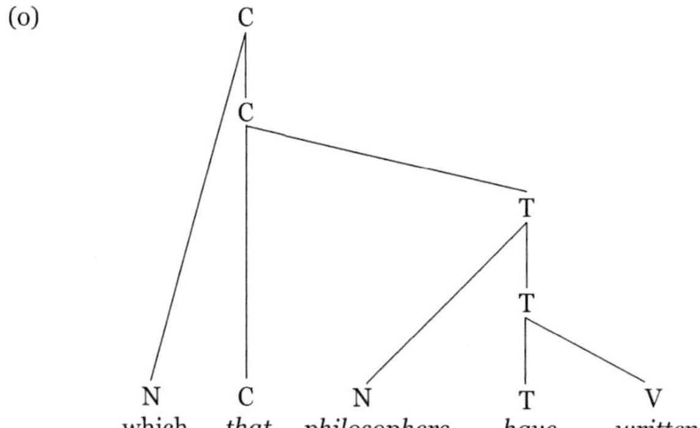

The strikethrough of the subordinating *that* simply indicates that it is not pronounced, hence absent from phonetic form.

Although *which* occurs in front of the subject *philosophers*, it is nonetheless interpreted as the object of *written* in the exactly same way that *these books* in the sentence *philosophers have written these books* is interpreted. This relative clause can be represented in cognitive form with a simple modification of (o) as (p).

(p)

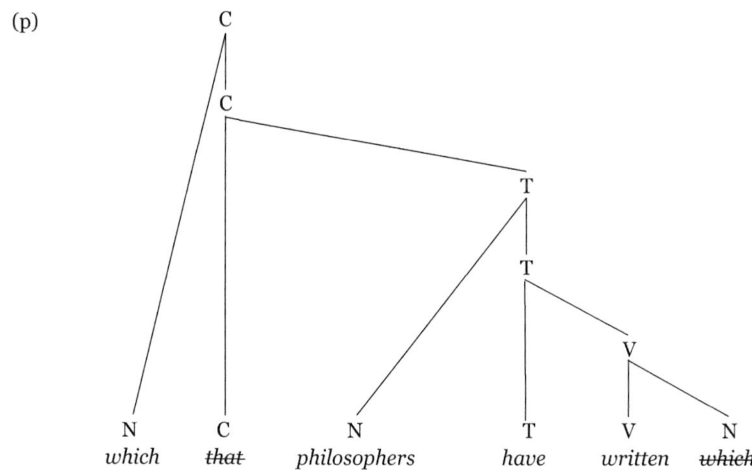

The syntactic representation in (p) shows how *which* is interpreted as the object of *written*, but is pronounced at the front of the clause. This phenomenon, where a syntactic unit is pronounced in one position, but interpreted as if it occupies another, is called in linguistics DISPLACEMENT. As will be discussed in Chapters 5 and 7, displacement occurs elsewhere in English syntax.

Given (p) as the syntactic structure of the relative clause in *books which philosophers have written*, there remains a question about the structure of the relative clause in *books that philosophers have written* (m.2), where the subordinating particle is pronounced, but the relative pronoun is not. To account for the interpretation of the relative clause, where the noun *books* is understood as the object of *written*, an unpronounced relative pronoun *which* would occur in the verb phrase, as in (p). The question is whether or not an unpronounced *which* also occurs at the beginning of the relative clause.

One answer would be to take (p) as the underlying structure of both (m.1) and (m.2), thus two variants (of phonetic form) for the same relative clause. This would mean that both relative clauses, although different in phonetic form, have the same cognitive form (they are understood in exactly the same way) – which would account for their synonymy.[6] Under this analysis, the definition of displacement as the phenomenon where a syntactic unit is pronounced in one syntactic position but interpreted as if it occupied a different position would have to be modified to include relative clauses like (m.2), where displacement has no phonetic effects. In effect, displacement is simply a phenomenon in which a syntactic unit occurs in more than one context in the cognitive form of a linguistic expression (e.g. a sentence).

One piece of evidence that supports this analysis of relative clauses is the impossibility of visible displacement in examples like **books which I met the philosopher who wrote*, where *which* is interpreted as the object of *wrote*. Such examples demonstrate that there are constraints on the syntactic distance across which displacement can occur.[7] The same constraints could apply when there is no visible displacement, thus **books that I met the philosopher who wrote*. Under the analysis that the syntactic variants of relative clauses all have the same underlying structure, the constraint on visible displacement generalizes to invisible displacement. Otherwise, we would need a different explanation for the impossibility of the second case.

There is a third possible variation for the relative clauses in (n) where neither the relative pronoun *which* nor the subordinating particle *that* is pronounced, as illustrated in (q) – what is called a 'reduced' relative clause.

(q)   *books philosophers have written*

---

[6] For readers who have been taught that there is an interpretive difference between relative clauses with *that* and *which*, see Section 4.4.3. Note that the same point about synonymy can be established with the relative clauses in *philosophers who I have met* and *philosophers that I have met*.

[7] Research on these constraints for language in general has been a lively and fruitful area of research in linguistics since the early 1960s, continuing today.

And for reduced relative clauses, the same constraint on displacement also applies. Thus, *books I met the philosopher who wrote* is equally impossible, that is equally deviant.

The reduced relative clause option is prohibited in certain configurations. Consider, for example, the following paradigm, where the underlined parts constitute a relative clause that modifies *philosophers*:

(r)   1. *philosophers who have written books*
         2. *philosophers that have written books*
         3. **philosophers have written books*

While the first two examples in (r) can occur as the object of a verb like *meet* (as in *I have met philosophers who have written books* and *I have met philosophers that have written books*), the third example cannot (as in *I have met philosophers have written books*). In contrast, the two examples in (m) and the reduced relative clause *books philosophers have* written can all occur as the object of a verb like *buy* (as in *I have bought books which philosophers have written, I have bought books that philosophers have written*, and *I have bought books philosophers have written*).

To summarize, a relative clause is structurally a clause consisting of a subject (usually a noun phrase, but see Chapter 5 for another possibility) and a predicate (a T phrase consisting of a T element merged with (again usually) a verb phrase). As a subordinate clause, a relative clause also contains a subordinating particle C (*that* for finite relative clauses), which can in some circumstances be invisible in phonetic form but nonetheless exists in cognitive form. Taking C as the head of syntactic unit created from the merger of C with a T phrase, a relative clause is structurally a C phrase. This C phrase is extended by the displacement of the relative pronoun to the left edge of the C phrase. Like the subordinating particle, the displaced relative pronoun can be silent in phonetic form. When the relative pronoun is interpreted as part of the predicate, neither it nor the subordinating particle need be pronounced in phonetic form; however both cannot be pronounced together. A reduced relative clause results when neither is pronounced in phonetic form. When the relative pronoun is interpreted as the subject of the relative clause, then the reduced relative clause (containing neither an overt relative pronoun or an overt subordinating particle *that*) is not a viable option – either the subordinating particle or the relative pronoun must be pronounced.

4.2.1   *Syntactic variation in relative clauses*

Although the reduced relative option is not available in these constructions in so-called 'standard' English (SE), it is possible in a variety of English dialects including those spoken Belfast, Northern Ireland; Newfoundland; and in the United States, in the Ozark and Appalachian Mountains. In addition, this variety of English is spoken in African American communities in the United

States (henceforth AAE),[8] as illustrated in the following quotation of reported speech in a novel by Walter Mosley (*And Sometimes I Wonder About You* (Doubleday 2015), p. 211).[9]

(s)   *But I'm telling you the truth. The men shot at you killed Hector*
         Laritas and the man you call Hiram Stent.

In AAE the verb phrase *shot at you* is interpreted as a reduced relative clause that modifies *men* (compared to the full relative clause (either *who shot at you* or *that shot at you*)). The verb *killed* would then be interpreted as the main verb of the sentence. In SE, which doesn't allow these reduced relative constructions, *shot* could only be parsed as the main verb of the sentence (as in the simple sentence *the men shot at you*), leaving the verb phrase *killed Hector Laritas and the man you call Hiram Stent* syntactically untethered. This demonstrates a difference between the grammars of these two varieties of English.

One consequence of this difference between SE and AAE involves the perception of sentences like the following:

(t)   *The horse raced past the barn fell.*

Typically on the initial reading, SE speakers will misinterpret *raced* as the past tense of the intransitive verb *race* and consequently the main verb of the sentence, leaving the verb *fell* syntactically untethered – in which case (t) is not recognizable as a legitimate sentence of English. Nonetheless, (t) can be assigned a legitimate syntactic structure if *raced* is interpreted instead as the passive participle of *race* and *raced past the barn* is interpreted as an extremely reduced relative clause (with neither the relative pronoun *which* nor the subordinating particle *that* in addition to the elimination of the passive auxiliary *was*) modifying the noun *horse*. A comparison of the two parsing choices (the incorrect active past tense of the intransitive verb *race* versus the correct passive participle of the transitive verb *race*) suggests that in parsing – that is, assigning a hierarchical structure to a linear string of lexical items – there is a general preference for the simpler choice (here active and intransitive) over the more complicated choice (here passive and transitive). Examples like (t) (see also *the ship sailed out to sea sank*) are called 'garden path sentences' because they typically mislead readers (or hearers) to parse them incorrectly by opting for the illegitimate simpler structure even though they

---

[8] For more information, see the Yale Grammatical Diversity Project in North America (online) under the heading "subject contact relatives". For a more detailed and technical discussion of AAE, see Walter Sistrunk's PhD dissertation "The Syntax of Zero in African American Relative Clauses" (Michigan State University, 2012).

[9] I'm indebted to Professor Lisa Green, Department of Linguistics, University of Massachusetts at Amherst for discussion of the material which follows.

have a perfectly legitimate but more complicated syntactic analysis. For writers (and readers) the point of this analysis is to beware of reduced relative clauses that trigger a garden path reading. Just because a sentence can be written with fewer words doesn't mean it always should be.

Perhaps surprisingly (but not if you consider the syntactic facts), AAE speakers do not parse examples like (t) incorrectly where *raced* is an interpreted as the verb of the main clause predicate, the garden path interpretation. Instead, AAE speakers can interpret *raced past the barn* as the predicate of a reduced relative clause modifying *horse*, where the verb is interpreted as past tense rather than the passive participle (as in *the horse which raced past the barn*). As a result, constructions like (t) do not create a garden path effect for speakers of AAE. AAE speakers can also interpret (t) as ambiguous between *the horse which raced past the barn* and *the horse which was raced past the barn*, though the latter is less likely because passives are not always natural in AAE (Lisa Green, p.c.). If there is a general parsing strategy to opt for the simplest structural analysis, then the interpretation in AAE of *raced* in (s) as a passive participle might appear to be more difficult even though the computational system allows it, as illustrated by the acceptability of *the man was questioned by the police owns that brown car* under the interpretation that is synonymous with *the man questioned by the police owns that brown car* (Lisa Green, p.c.).

4.3   Infinitival clauses

Although reduced relative clauses with covert subjects are not possible in SE where the clause is finite, these constructions are possible when the clause is infinitival (where T is realized as the infinitival *to* as in *a topic to research*). Thus in (u) the noun phrase object of *suggested* (underlined) contains an infinitival relative clause modifying the noun *topic*.

(u)   *They suggested <u>a topic to research.</u>*

The reduced relative clause *to research* contains two visible elements: the infinitival *to* – label it T – and the verb *research* (the bare form of the verb and therefore uninflected for present or past tense). In addition to the two overt elements, the cognitive form of this relative clause contains a covert relative pronoun, which establishes an anaphoric relation with *topic* serving as the basis for the modification relation between *topic* and the relative clause. The covert relative pronoun is interpreted as the object of *research*. Thus the representation of the infinitival T phrase in cognitive form would be rendered as (v), where the covert subject of the verb *research* is represented as Ø.

(v)

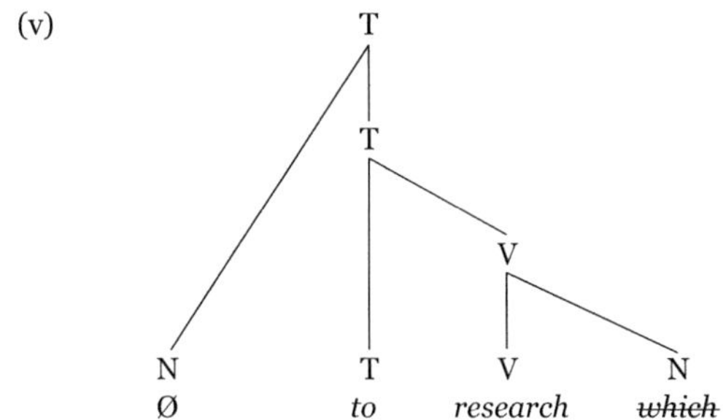

Ø in (v) is open to three possible interpretations, where (u) is synonymous with (1) *they suggested a topic for them to research* (*they = them*), (2) *they suggested a topic for someone else to research* (not including *they*), or (3) *they suggested a topic for everyone to research* (including *they* and others).

The structure of the infinitival clause in (v) is essentially the same as the finite clauses in (l) and (o): compare (v) with the finite clause *they will research that topic*. In (v) the bare form of the verb *research* selects *to*, the same V-selects-T relation that holds in finite clauses. All clauses are therefore T phrases.

As mentioned above, the bare form of a verb can also select a modal auxiliary (*will*, *can*, etc.), suggesting that modal auxiliaries are also labeled T in the lexicon. Furthermore, while it is possible for infinitival *to* to occur with either a perfective or progressive auxiliary (or both) as illustrated in (w), it impossible for *to* to occur with a modal auxiliary.

(w)   1. *For them to have arrived on time is unlikely.*
          2. *For them to be arriving on time is unlikely.*
          3. *For them to have been arriving on time was unlikely.*
          4. **For them to will arrive on time is unlikely.*
          5. **For them will to arrive on time is unlikely.*

(w) illustrates how infinitival *to* never occurs with modal auxiliaries, establishing that these two lexical elements are in COMPLEMENTARY DISTRIBUTION, and thereby providing strong evidence that they are lexical items belonging to the same lexical category T. In (w.4) the bare form verb *arrive* selects the auxiliary *will*, but *will* itself is not a bare form – there is no **to will* – and therefore cannot itself select the infinitival *to*. Similarly, in (w.5), while *arrive* selects *to*, *to* is not a bare verb form that can select *will*. In this way, the complementary distribution of infinitival *to* and modal auxiliaries motivates the analysis of the latter as lexical instances of T.

In writing, infinitival clauses are always subordinate – thus embedded in larger syntactic constructions. And like finite subordinate clauses, they can occur with both an overt subject (sometimes) and an overt subordinating particle, as in (x) where the infinitival clause is underlined.

(x)   *For Fred to arrive on time* is highly unlikely.

The infinitival tense phrase *Fred to arrive on time* is merged with the subordin-ating particle *for* – not to be confused with the preposition *for* that takes a noun phrase object as in *a present for Mary* – in the same way the finite tense phrase *they will arrive on time* is merged with the subordinating particle *that* in a corresponding sentence *that Fred will arrive on time is highly unlikely*. Thus the full structure of the subordinate clause in (x) would be (y).

(y)

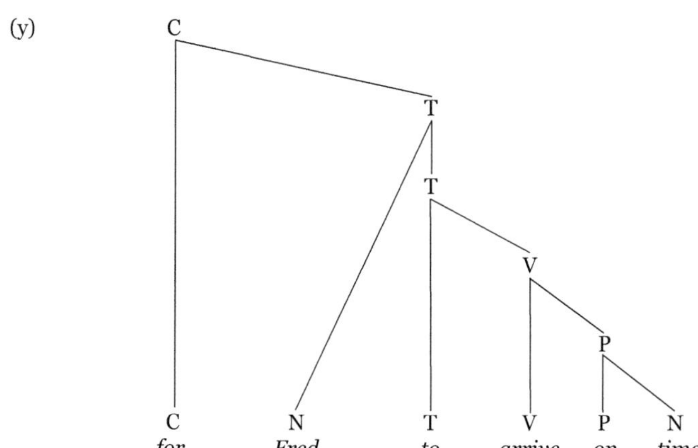

As in finite subordinate clauses, the T-selects-C dependency also holds – where infinitival T *to* selects the infinitival C *for* as opposed to the finite C *that*. In this way the syntactic structure of subordinate clauses in general is determined largely in terms of selection relations (V selects T, which selects C).

In addition to reduced infinitival relative clauses as illustrated in (u), there are also full infinitival relative clauses, as in *a topic for Fred to research,* where the relative clause is also a C-phrase. This C-phrase contains the verb phrase *research* ~~which~~ (as in (v) above). The full infinitival relative clause corresponds structurally to the full finite relative clause, as in *a topic that Fred should research* and *a topic which Fred should research* (with the same selectional relations: V selects T, and T selects C). But unlike the finite form, this full infinitival relative cannot occur with an overt relative pronoun, hence the deviance of **a topic which Fred to research* (compare with *a topic which Fred should research*) and **a topic which for Fred to research*. Also, the infinitival relative cannot occur with a visible subordinating C (*for*) and a phonetically empty subject, as in **a topic for to research* – although there are varieties of English in which such relative clauses are possible.

Given that infinitival relative clauses are C phrases, whether they manifest covert displacement of the invisible relative pronoun as proposed for the analysis of finite relative clauses in Section 4.2 remains to be answered. There are two factors that suggest a positive answer: (1) maintaining the symmetry between finite and infinitival relative clauses, and (2) there is one case where visible displacement of a relative pronoun occurs in an infinitival relative (see (ee.2) in Section 4.3.1).

Reduced infinitival relative clauses are just one form of infinitival clauses without overt subjects, what is called a BARE INFINITIVAL CLAUSE to indicate that it occurs without a visible subject in phonetic form. A bare infinitival clause can also express the purpose of an action, as in *we arrived early to make sure of getting a seat* or alternatively, *to make sure of getting a seat, we arrived early*.

The following example (from a British newspaper article about *an ugly spat* between a Nobel Prize-winning economist and the head of research at the International Monetary Fund) contains both kinds of bare infinitival and illustrates the kind of problems that can arise with their use.[10]

(z)   *He used a lunchtime debate last week to launch his rival's book to unleash a fierce attack.*

One problem with (z) is that the modifier *last week* could apply to either the verb *used* or the noun *debate*, as illustrated in (aa) where the first infinitival modifier has been eliminated.

(aa)   *He used a lunchtime debate last week to unleash a fierce attack.*

There are three possible syntactic analyses for the modification relations in (aa), which can be represented by color-coding the modifiers to match the lexical items they modify.

(bb)   1. *He used* A LUNCHTIME DEBATE *last week to unleash a fierce attack*.
            2. *He used* A LUNCHTIME DEBATE LAST WEEK *to unleash a fierce attack*.
            3. *He used* A LUNCHTIME DEBATE LAST WEEK TO UNLEASH A FIERCE ATTACK.

---

[10] *The Independent*, Saturday July 6, 2002, www.independent.co.uk/news/business/news/econo mists-at-war-how-a-difference-of-opinion-over-globalisation-turned-personal-183076.html.

Thus in (bb.1) *last week* modifies *used*, while in the other two examples it modifies *debate*. In terms of hierarchical structure, the noun phrase *last week* would be merged with the verb phrase *used a lunchtime debate*, whereas in (bb.2–3) *last week* would be merged as part of the larger noun phrase *a lunchtime debate last week*, which functions as the object of the verb *used*.

The assignment of one structure instead of the other has consequences for the interpretation of the infinitival clause *to unleash a fierce attack* in (aa). Hierarchical structure does not support the nonexistent interpretation color-coded in (cc), where *last week* modifies *used*, but *to unleash a fierce attack* would modify *debate*.

(cc)   *He used A LUNCHTIME DEBATE last week TO UNLEASH A FIERCE ATTACK.

Note that in (bb), the infinitival clause has two distinct functions: *to unleash a fierce attack*, which modifies the verb *used*, functions as a purpose clause with the interpretation of 'in order to V-phrase', while TO UNLEASH A FIERCE ATTACK, which modifies the noun *debate*, functions as a relative clause (compare *a debate which unleashed a fierce attack*).

One problem for (z) is that the sentence contains two consecutive infinitival clauses, inviting multiple interpretations for modification relations. The only viable interpretation of (z) given the context of the newspaper article is (dd).

(dd)   He used A LUNCHTIME DEBATE LAST WEEK TO LAUNCH HIS RIVAL'S BOOK *to unleash a fierce attack*.

However, if there is a preference for attaching time expression modifiers to verbs rather than nouns, then the resulting hierarchical structure, where *last week* is merged with *used a lunchtime debate*, prohibits both infinitival clauses from being analyzed as modifying the noun *debate*. In this analysis *to launch his rival's book* must be read as a purpose clause where the covert subject of *launch* is interpreted as identical to the subject of the verb *used*, so that $\emptyset = he$ = the head of research at the IMF (which of course makes no sense given that *he* is attacking his rival's book, not trying to promote it). This reading also leaves the second infinitival clause *to unleash a fierce attack* untethered in much the same way as the garden path examples discussed in Section 4.2.1.[11]

One way to eliminate the problem of the time expression is to transform it into a possessive, *last week's lunchtime debate*. That will not completely eliminate the potential garden path problem with the resulting sentence: *he used last week's lunchtime debate to launch his rival's book to unleash a fierce attack*. At this point, it is an empirical question whether readers will misinterpret the first infinitival clause as a purpose clause rather than an infinitival

---

[11] The reason why I noticed this sentence when I first read it.

relative. One way to eliminate this potential problem is to turn the infinitival relative clause into a finite relative clause, as in *he used last week's lunchtime debate that launched his rival's book to unleash a fierce attack.*

It is worth noting that there is no way to punctuate (z) that will eliminate the structural ambiguity with *last week* or force the infinitival relative clause reading for *to launch his rival's book.* While the proposed revision at the end of the last paragraph eliminates both problems, there remains a further potential ambiguity with the interpretation of the purpose clause infinitival *to unleash a fierce attack.* Although the context in which the sentence occurs motivates the interpretation of the infinitival as modifying *used*, it is also syntactically possible that the same infinitival could modify the verb *launched* in the relative clause (making it part of the relative clause). If we substitute *read about* for *used*, yielding *he read about last week's lunchtime debate that launched his rival's book to unleash a fierce attack*, the most plausible interpretation is the one in which *to unleash a fierce attack* modifies *launched* and where the covert subject of the infinitival clause would be interpreted as *debate.*

A further modification of the revised sentence will eliminate the potential ambiguity of the purpose clause – one that involves punctuation: *he used last week's lunchtime debate, which launched his rival's book, to unleash a fierce attack.* It is a convention of English punctuation that a nonrestrictive relative clause can be identified in writing by placing a comma at the beginning and at the end. The second comma indicates that the infinitival clause that follows is not part of the relative clause and therefore cannot be interpreted as modifying the verb of the relative clause. Note further that this comma eliminates the possibility of interpreting the infinitival clause as a relative clause modifying *book*, implausible as this may be.

4.3.1   *Ending a relative clause with a preposition*

When a relative pronoun is interpreted as the object of a preposition (as in (ee.1) and (ee.2)), there are four synonymous syntactic variants of the relative clause that presumably share the same cognitive form, as illustrated in (ee).

(ee)   1. *Mary finally found a topic <u>which she can write about</u>.*
     2. *Mary finally found a topic <u>about which she can write</u>.*
     3. *Mary finally found a topic <u>that she can write about</u>.*
     4. *Mary finally found a topic <u>she can write about</u>.*

In (ee.1) the overt relative pronoun *which* is pronounced at the front of the relative clause, but not following the preposition. In contrast, the relative pronoun forms a syntactic unit with the preposition in (ee.2), where the whole prepositional phrase is pronounced at the front of the relative clause. Where the preposition occurs without a following object noun phrase, the preposition is designated as 'stranded' in the verb phrase, a phenomenon that linguists refer to as PREPOSITION STRANDING. When the relative pronoun that functions as the object of a preposition is covert (not pronounced) in a relative clause (as in (ee.3) and (ee.4), the preposition is unavoidably stranded. Of the four variants, (ee.2) is distinctly more formal than the others and also less natural (see Section 4.4.1 for further discussion).

Infinitival relatives allow fewer variants – in fact just two, one with an overt relative pronoun and another with a covert relative pronoun, as in (ff).

(ff)   1. *Mary finally found a topic about which to write.*   (compare (ee.3))
        2. *Mary finally found a topic to write about.*   (compare (ee.2))
        3. **Mary finally found a topic which to write about.*   (compare (ee.1))

Here too, the variant (ff.2) with the stranded preposition sounds more natural than the variant (ff.1), in which the prepositional phrase *about which* occurs at the front of the relative clause. But unlike finite relative clauses, which allow a preposition and its overt relative pronoun object to be separated (as in (ee.1)), the corresponding variant for infinitival relative clauses is deviant, as demonstrated by (ff.3).

In contrast to a relative pronoun that is interpreted as the object of a preposition, when the relative pronoun is the possessive *whose*, as in *a philosopher whose classes they have attended*, the only option for the phonetic form of such relative clauses is where the possessive and the noun it modifies occur at the beginning of the relative clause. However, when the relative pronoun *whose* occurs in the object of a prepositional phrase, the informal/ formal (or natural/less natural) options are again available, as in *a philosopher whose books they have blogged about* versus *a philosopher about whose books they have blogged*. Given the synonymy of these two examples, they presumably share the same cognitive form; however, precisely what that form is is not obvious.

4.4   Mental grammar vs. prescriptive rules

In the history of commentary on the English language, various constructions have been singled out for criticism – the stranded preposition, the 'split' infinitive, the passive voice. Use of these constructions has been branded as bad writing and improper usage by the self-appointed guardians of the language, and their prohibition in writing has been endorsed by generations of English teachers (see the quotation from *Grammar Alive!* on page viii of the Preface). However, a basic understanding of the English syntax easily dispels the illusion that there is something wrong with these constructions, revealing them to be useful parts of the natural syntax of English. The mistake is not using these constructions in writing, but rather in branding them as illegitimate. In general, when you find yourself violating some prescriptive rule of grammar, one that has to be taught and then reinforced, the chances are that the construction is part of your mental grammar of English, which explains why you keep making these 'mistakes' even though you certainly understand the prohibition the rule is intended to impose.

Given that the stranded preposition is a natural part of English syntax, as established in Section 4.3.1, Section 4.4.1 examines some of the commentary on this construction, showing that it fails to support a general prohibition. Section 4.4.2 discusses the syntax of adverbs in infinitival clauses, showing how the so-called split infinitive is both a natural part of English syntax and, furthermore, stylistically preferable in some contexts. Section 4.4.3 considers a prohibition against using *which* in certain relative clauses. The syntax of the passive construction is explicated in the next chapter, along with a review of the history of criticism of the construction, a twentieth-century phenomenon that unfortunately continues into the twenty-first.

4.4.1   *The stranded preposition mistake*

Beginning with John Dryden's short essay "Defence of the Epilogue" (1672) and continuing to the present (for example, Steven Pinker's *The Sense of Style: The Thinking Person's Guide to Writing in the 21st Century* (2014)), preposition stranding has been a subject of commentary and criticism.

Dryden (Poet Laureate of England 1668–70) in his essay is writing about *impropriety in language*, where he cites as an example the following sentence from the poet and playwright Ben Jonson's *Catiline His Conspiracy*, a play about the first-century BC Roman senator who was involved in a conspiracy to overthrow the Roman Republic, where the sentence contains two lines of verse about the result of a massacre:[12]

> *The [maws] and dens of beasts could not receive*
> *The bodies that those souls were frighted from.*

He calls this an example of a *synchysis, or ill-placing of words* and writes of this example: *The preposition in the end of the sentence; a common fault with him, and which I have but lately observed in my own writings.* There are two problems with Dryden's criticism. First, the stranded preposition is not an example of *synchysis*, which according to the *Oxford English Dictionary* is *a confused arrangement of words in a sentence, obscuring the meaning*. Neither

---

[12] The version published in the Oxford University Press edition of Dryden's selected essays, edited by W.P. Ker, misquotes *maws* as *waves*.

is the arrangement of words in this example confused or confusing, nor is the meaning obscure. Second, there is no way to simply reposition the preposition at the end of the relative clause that ends the sentence because the relative clause contains no overt relative pronoun. The alternative is to replace *that* with *which*, which destroys the alliteration between *that* and *those* – an important poetic effect for Jonson's verse. And if the second line is rewritten as *the bodies from which those souls were frighted*, then the alliteration between *frighted* and *from* is lost, as well as destroying the meter of the second line (which would also happen if the line were recast as *the bodies those souls were frighted from*). As a result, Dryden's foray into language criticism simply misfires – although unfortunately the stricture against ending a sentence with a preposition caught on and is still with us, as the continued commentary on this construction demonstrates.

Just over a century later the issue of preposition stranding shows up in Robert Lowth's *A Short Introduction to English Grammar* (1775). Lowth, the Oxford Professor of Poetry, writes on pp. 95–6:

The preposition is often separated from the relative which it governs, and joined to the verb at the end of the sentence, or of some member of it: as, "Horace is an author, whom I am much delighted with." "The world is too well-bred, to shock authors with a truth, which generally their booksellers are the first that inform them of." This is an idiom, which our language is strongly inclined to: it prevails in common conversation, and suits very well with the familiar style in writing: but the placing of the preposition before the relative, is more graceful, as well as more perspicuous; and agrees much better with the solemn and elevated style.

This rather mild proposal was by the early twentieth century (if not before) transformed into an apparently widely held prohibition against ending a sentence or clause with a preposition. The 1931 3rd edition of *The King's English* (first published in 1906 by Oxford University Press) by the British grammarians H.W. and F.G. Fowler refers to this prohibition as a *modern superstition* – and in the revised 3rd edition of *The New Fowler's Modern English Usage* by R.W. Burchfield (2000), it is characterized as *one of the most persistent myths about prepositions in English*. The fact that recent books about English written for the general public, like Pinker's, still bother to discuss the myth attests to its vitality in spite of numerous refutations, starting with Lowth's initial proposal on which it is based.[13]

What appears to be true of modern English for the past several centuries is that preposition stranding in relative clauses (and questions) has been a

---

[13] In addition to quoting two sentences that end in a preposition, Lowth himself strands a preposition in *This is an idiom, which our language is strongly inclined to* where he could have just as well written *This is an idiom, to which our language is strongly inclined* – so perhaps with intended irony as one might expect from an Oxford Professor.

legitimate alternative to constructions in which the preposition and a following relative (or interrogative) pronoun form an overt phrasal unit, as illustrated by the previous *in which* in this sentence.[14] Lowth tries to distinguish the non-stranding construction as *more graceful* and more clearly understood (*perspicuous*) than the construction in which the preposition is stranded. *Graceful* is a value judgment whose value depends on a preference for *the solemn and elevated style* (or from another perspective, *stuffy and uptight*) – one that is not exactly what we find in today's prose.

Given that both constructions share the same cognitive form, the criterion of perspicuousness (how easily a construction is understood) depends on how readers parse these constructions. Is it significantly easier for a reader to connect a prepositional phrase containing a relative pronoun at the beginning of a relative clause to a verb in the relative clause than to connect a bare relative pronoun at the beginning of the clause to a preposition contained in verb phrase of the clause? This is in essence an empirical question, an answer to which must account for speakers' judgments about the contrast between the four variants for relative clause constructions discussed in Section 4.3.1, as illustrated in a slightly different example in (gg).

(gg)   1. *topics about which philosophers write*
          2. *topics which philosophers write about*
          3. *topics that philosophers write about*
          4. *topics philosophers write about*

If my own judgments are not out of the ordinary, then (gg.4) is completely natural as are (gg.2–3), and (gg.1) is, if anything, less natural – all of which suggests that preposition stranding is not the problem in English syntax it has been purported to be.

Although Pinker endorses the view that a prohibition against preposition stranding is a superstition, he nonetheless attempts to distinguish the two options (stranding vs. nonstranding), noting that the nonstranding version *sounds better in a formal style* (which reiterates one of Lowth's points). He also suggests that the nonstranding version would be preferable when *a stranded preposition would get lost in the hubbub of little grammatical words*, citing as an example: *One of the beliefs which we can be highly confident in is that other people are conscious.* The trouble with this characterization is that

---

[14] Notice that the alternative to this sentence, in which the preposition *in* is stranded sounds rather awful: *What appears to be true of modern English for the past several centuries is that preposition stranding in relative clauses (and questions) has been a legitimate alternative to constructions **which** the preposition followed by a relative (or interrogative) pronoun form an overt phrasal unit **in**, as illustrated by the previous* in which *in this sentence.* The same holds for the stranded version of the previous sentence before the colon: notice that the alternative to this sentence, **which** the preposition *in* is stranded **in** sounds rather awful.

the words in this sentence have a precise and unique hierarchical syntactic structure that we unconsciously assign to them, so how this *hubbub of little grammatical words* creates confusion is unclear. One potential problem with the example is that the preposition in *confident in* may seem odd to some speakers (myself included), where *confident about* is preferable (but compare *confidence in*, which is fine). The adjacency between the preposition *in*, the copular verb *is*, and the subordinating particle *that* remains in the version of the relative clause where the noun *confidence* substitutes for the adjective *confident*, as in *one of the beliefs which we can have a lot of confidence in is that other people are conscious*, a sentence which seems completely natural, even though it contains the same hubbub of little grammatical words that Pinker is criticizing.[15] Substituting *confident about* for *confident in*, as in *One of the beliefs which we be highly confident about is that other people are conscious*, yields another equally natural variant of the relative clause (plus two other equally natural variants, one where *that* substitutes for *which* and the other which has neither *that* nor *which*). If *about* is equivalent to *in* in the status of *little grammatical word*, then these too should be unacceptable, contrary to fact so it seems.

Pinker refers to Theodore Bernstein, who claims *that a sentence ending with a preposition is sometimes clumsy, often weak* (*The Careful Writer: A Modern Guide to English Usage* (1965), pp. 342–3), and cites Bernstein's example sentence, *He felt it offered the best opportunity to do fundamental research in chemistry, which was what he had taken his Doctor of Philosophy in*, which Bernstein says *is like the last sputter of an engine going dead*, a description that Pinker quotes, saying that this is the result of ending a sentence *with a word that is too lightweight to serve as its focal point* (p. 221). Whether this is true remains to be argued because the sentence cited in support of this criticism of preposition stranding doesn't actually make the case. First consider how the sentence could be revised to eliminate the offending stranded preposition. *He felt it offered the best opportunity to do fundamental research in chemistry, which was in what he had taken his Doctor of Philosophy* is questionable and certainly not significantly stronger or less clumsy than the original, and **He felt it offered the best opportunity to do fundamental research in chemistry, in which was what he had taken his Doctor of Philosophy* is simply deviant. The clumsiness of the sentence involves the *which was what* construction; try instead *He felt it offered the best opportunity to do fundamental research in chemistry, which he had taken his Doctor of Philosophy in* (or if you prefer, *He felt it offered the best opportunity to do fundamental research in chemistry, in which he had taken his Doctor of Philosophy*). Note further that there is a

---

[15] The other two variants of the relative clause, with *that* instead of *which* or with neither are equally natural.

certain awkwardness in the connection between the relative pronoun, which here refers to a field of academic study, and the noun *chemistry*, which here refers to a body of knowledge and topic of research. This can be eliminated by recasting the sentence as *He felt it offered the best opportunity to do fundamental research in chemistry, the field in which he had taken his Doctor of Philosophy* (or as the stranded preposition version). But at this point the relative clause is a wordy and superfluous modifier of the noun *field*, so that the sentence could be simply recast as *He felt it offered the best opportunity to do fundamental research in chemistry, the field of his PhD.*

In his brief discussion of preposition stranding, Pinker also cites examples where a stranded preposition is required, claiming that this is motivated by a principle of composition that prefers light-before-heavy material in a sentence. His first two examples, *music to read by* and *something to guard against*, involve bare infinitival relative clauses where the absence of a relative pronoun forces the stranding of the preposition. However, with an overt relative pronoun, the infinitival relative clause cannot support the stranded preposition, thus compare *music by which to read* vs. **music which to read by*, and *something against which to guard* vs. **something which to guard against*. On Pinker's analysis, the preposition in these examples *contributes a crucial bit of information* and therefore should be stranded in adherence to the principle. Nonetheless, the alternatives without a stranded preposition are equally grammatical even if they are in comparison more formal, wordy, clumsy, and fussy as well as less colloquial and less natural.

Unlike the examples with infinitival relative clauses, the next sentence that Pinker cites (hh.1) as an example of a stranded preposition at the end of a sentence where the preposition *contributes a crucial bit of information* has no natural alternative version where the preposition is not stranded (hh.2).

(hh)   1. *That's what this tool is for.*
        2. **That's for what this tool is.*

The syntactic analysis of (hh.1) is complicated by a couple of factors. The word *what* is interpreted as the object of *for* but occurs at the front of the clause, which parallels the syntactic behavior of overt relative pronouns like *which*. Also, if *what* is a relative pronoun then there is no overt noun to which it is anaphorically linked – and in fact there cannot be one (try **the purpose what this tool is for*). Furthermore, the phrase *what this tool is for* can occur as the subject of a clause as in *what this tool is for eludes us* in contrast to a relative clause with an overt relative pronoun *which*. Nor is it possible to substitute *which* for *what* in this construction. One plausible syntactic analysis of (hh.1) is that *what* is a noun that heads a noun phrase where the clause *this tool is for* constitutes a relative clause in which the relative pronoun and subordinating particle are both unpronounced. On this analysis the subordinate clause in (hh.1) parallels the infinitival relative clause examples that Pinker cites, where the absence of an overt relative pronoun forces the stranded preposition.

The last three examples that Pinker cites are identified as containing idioms (underlined in (ii)), where the stranded preposition is justified *when it pins down the meaning of an idiom.*

(ii)   1. *It is nothing to sneeze at.*
           2. *He doesn't know what he's talking about.*
           3. *She a woman who can be counted on.*

(ii.1) involves an infinitival relative clause without an overt relative pronoun, so the stranded preposition follows from basic syntactic properties regardless of the idiomatic character of the noun phrase *nothing to sneeze at.* The stranded preposition in (ii.2) again seems to follow from general constraints on syntactic structure because it is the only option in non-idiom constructions like *he couldn't say what she had talked about* (compare **he couldn't say about what she had talked*). For some thus far undetermined reason, English appears to block prepositional phrases where *what* alone is the object of the preposition. The stranded preposition in (ii.3) follows from the fact that *be counted on* involves a passive participle, so the relative pronoun *who* is interpreted as the syntactic subject of the relative clause as well as the object of the complex verb *counted on.* The passive construction forces the stranding of the preposition, where in active constructions the idiomatic interpretation allows two possibilities with the preposition stranded or not: *she is a woman who(m) they can count on* as well as *she is a woman on who(m) they can count* (again discounting the clumsiness of the nonstranded version).

In general, syntactic structure determines where stranded prepositions can and/or must occur, without recourse to informal principles of composition. As H.W. Fowler notes, *the fact is that the remarkable freedom enjoyed by English in putting its prepositions late & omitting its relatives is an important element in the flexibility of the language* (A Dictionary of Modern English Usage (Oxford 1926), p. 458). And he goes on to comment that *even now immense pains are daily expended in changing spontaneous into artificial English.* Concluding the entry on "Preposition At End", Fowler offers the following reasonable advice:

Follow no arbitrary rule, but remember that there are often two or more possible arrangements between which a choice should be consciously made; if the abnormal, or at least unorthodox, final preposition that has naturally presented itself sounds comfortable, keep it; if it does not sound comfortable, still keep it if it has compensating vigour, or when among awkward possibilities, it is the least awkward.

Notice how the advice favors the stranded preposition alternative, and nonetheless, Fowler avoids stranding *between*, where there are two potential alternatives (where *between* is in boldface): *two or more possible arrangements which a choice should be consciously made **between*** (which sounds significantly worse than Fowler's version and may be just deviant) and **two or more possible arrangements which a choice **between** should be consciously made* (which may be worse than the previous alternative and is actually deviant). In fact, there is a third alternative, *two or more possible arrangements a choice between which should be consciously made*, where the preposition is not stranded, but even so, sounds less natural than Fowler's version. In the unquestionably deviant example the prepositional phrase is interpreted as modifying the noun *choice*, and therefore syntactically part of the noun phrase headed by *choice*. The deviance demonstrates that a relative pronoun that is interpreted as subpart of a subject noun phrase cannot be syntactically separated from that noun phrase. Extending this constraint to the prepositional phrase whose object is a relative pronoun yields the conclusion that in Fowler's example, *between which* modifies the verb *made* and not the noun *choice* – and therefore does not violate the syntactic constraint against separating a relative pronoun that occurs as a subpart of a subject noun phrase. Unlike the prohibition against preposition stranding, this constraint is not taught in school nor is it discussed in the general literature on English grammar, usage or style, but is however in linguistics a lively topic of research on syntactic structure.

Fowler considers the ability of English to omit relative pronouns as a *remarkable freedom* that constitutes *an important element in the flexibility of the language* – to which we should add the freedom to omit the subordinating particles *that* in finite relative clauses and *for* in infinitival relative clauses, as well as the reduced relative clauses discussed in this chapter. It is worth considering how this freedom and flexibility connects with the question of concision in writing, formulated as an *elementary principle of composition* in what NPR commentator on language Geoffrey Nunberg calls *the gospel according to Strunk and White* (their *The Elements of Style*), specifically the famous dictum *omit needless words* (see also Chapter 3, Section 3.5). According to Strunk and White, *vigorous writing is concise* and therefore *a sentence should contain no unnecessary words*. Among the few examples that they cite are two examples of relative clauses where a reduced relative clause is preferred to its non-reduced counterpart: not *his brother, who is a member of the same firm* but rather *his brother, a member of the same firm*; and not *Trafalgar, which was Nelson's last battle* but rather *Trafalgar, Nelson's last battle*. However, they don't insist on eliminating the subordinating particle *that* when it is possible. In a group of examples designed to show that the words *the fact that* are perhaps always needless, Strunk and White cite *I was unaware of the fact that* and reduce this to *I was unaware that* (*did not know*), where the *that* is also strictly speaking not necessary. Given the discussion of relative clauses in this chapter, we might wonder whether such clauses without either a relative pronoun or a subordinating particle are by this principle preferable to their fuller counterparts. Given Strunk and White's examples, their purported principle would prefer *books written by philosophers* to *books which were written by philosophers*; but would this principle also argue for *books by philosophers* over *books written by philosophers*? An answer depends on whether all words that can be omitted are 'needless' and ultimately whether this kind of concision necessarily produces more vigorous writing.

4.4.2   *The split infinitive mistake*

Another prescriptive rule of grammar that contradicts the natural syntax of English is the prohibition against 'splitting an infinitive', which Pinker (2014) dubs as the *quintessential bogus rule*. In practice, the rule prohibits the placement of an adverb or a negative (for example, *not*) between the infinitival particle *to* and the uninflected verb to which it is syntactically linked in a selection relation (see above).

Exactly where this prohibition was first articulated seems to be unknown. Lowth's eighteenth-century grammar, the first prescriptive English grammar, does not mention it; neither does Lindley Murray's popular nineteenth-century prescriptive grammar[16] – though both grammars discuss infinitival constructions and adverbs. Strunk and White comment that precedents for the construction occur from the fourteenth century to the present, but advise nonetheless that *this construction should be avoided unless the writer wishes to place unusual stress on the adverb*, citing *to diligently inquire* vs. *to inquire diligently* as an example.[17] In *The King's English* (1906), H.G. and F.W. Fowler begin the entry for 'Split' Infinitive with the following statement:

The 'split' infinitive has taken such hold upon the consciences of journalists that, instead of warning the novice against splitting his infinitives, we must warn him against the curious superstition that the splitting or not splitting makes the difference between a good and a bad writer. (p. 319)

---

[16] *English Grammar* (New York: Collins & Perkins, 1809).

[17] Without more context, the claim that the preverbal adverb receives *unusual stress* compared to the postverbal adverb is not obvious.

Nonetheless they go on to claim that the construction is *an ugly thing* but caution that *it is one among several hundred ugly things, and the novice should not allow it to occupy his mind exclusively.*[18] Twenty years later in *A Dictionary of Modern English Usage*, Henry Fowler drops the claim that split infinitives are ugly, offering instead a more nuanced view in terms of types of writers, including those who can recognize a split infinitive but nonetheless prefer the construction to either *real ambiguity* or *patent artificiality*.

To understand how ambiguities can arise in the interaction between adverbs and infinitival constructions, and also why exactly this prohibition against these constructions is bogus – that is, how it contradicts natural English syntax – we need to take a look at the syntax of adverbs in English.

In the simplest case, an adverb can occur after a verb or in front of it, as in *he lied strategically* or *he strategically lied*. This shows that an adverb that forms a syntactic unit with a verb can be linearized in either direction. Changing from past tense to future tense requires the addition of the modal auxiliary *will*, an overt instance of T (as discussed earlier), yielding both *he will lie strategically* and *he will strategically lie*. These sentences have the same hierarchical syntactic structure, but different linear orders as demonstrated in (jj).

[18] Among the "ugly" examples they cite are the following four, all from *The Times* newspaper (rendered here with the "split" T and V in boldface and the intervening adverbial in small caps).

1. *The time has come to* ONCE AGAIN **voice** *the general discontent.*
2. *It should be authorized to* IMMEDIATELY **put** *in hand such work.*
3. *Important negotiations are even now proceeding to* FURTHER **cement** *trade relations.*
4. *We were not as yet strong enough in numbers to* SERIOUSLY **influence** *the poll.*

The motivation for designating these examples as "ugly" – aside from claiming that they constitute deviant sentence structure – is unclear. Moreover, it's questionable that repositioning the modifiers (in small caps) anywhere else in these sentences yields a better result. Placing the modifier in front of *to* creates a potential ambiguity, where the modifier could be interpreted as modifying the main clause predicate rather than the subordinate clause infinitival verb. For example, in this variant of (3) (*important negotiations are even now proceeding* FURTHER *to cement trade relations*) are negotiations proceeding futher or are they further cementing trade relations? Placing the modifier after the infinitival verb (for example as in *we were not as yet strong enough in numbers to influence* SERIOUSLY *the poll*) creates an awkward break between the verb and its object, and in the case of FURTHER in (3) creates an ambiguity between *further influence* and *further trade relations*, where the adverb could also be interpreted as an adjective. The other possible placement of the modifier at the end of the sentence opens the possibility to interpret the modifier as modifying the main clause predicate, thereby introducing unwanted ambiguity (*proceeding further* vs. *cementing futher*). Thus by seriously considering the possible alternatives to the sentences the Fowlers cite, it becomes clear that the examples they cite are the only clear alternatives. That they are "ugly" for some reason remains to be established.

(jj)

1.

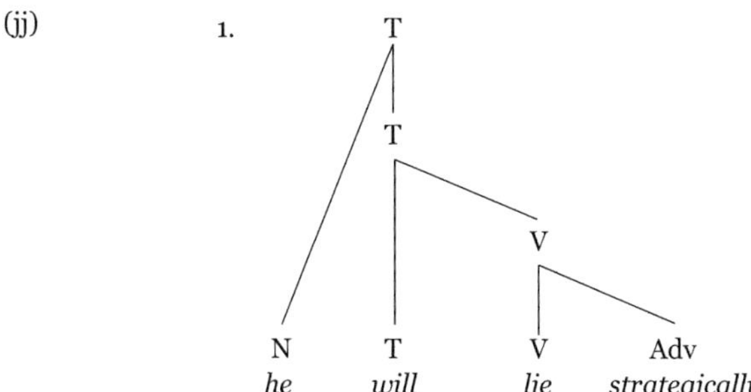

2.

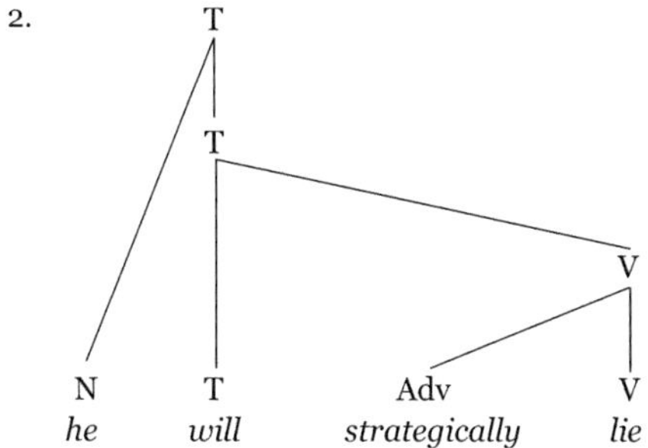

Substituting T *to* for T *will* yields both infinitival structures, as in *he is planning to lie strategically* and the so-called split infinitive version *he is planning to strategically lie*. To account for the fact that the subject of *planning* is also interpreted as the subject of *lie*, we can postulate a covert subject Ø that replaces *he* in (jj.1–2) and that stands in an anaphoric relation with the subject of *planning* in the same way a relative pronoun relates to the noun the relative clause modifies. Thus *he* is the antecedent of Ø.

The linear order where the adverb *strategically* separates the tense particle *to* and the verb *lie* has a distinct hierarchical structure, which is represented in (kk).

(kk)

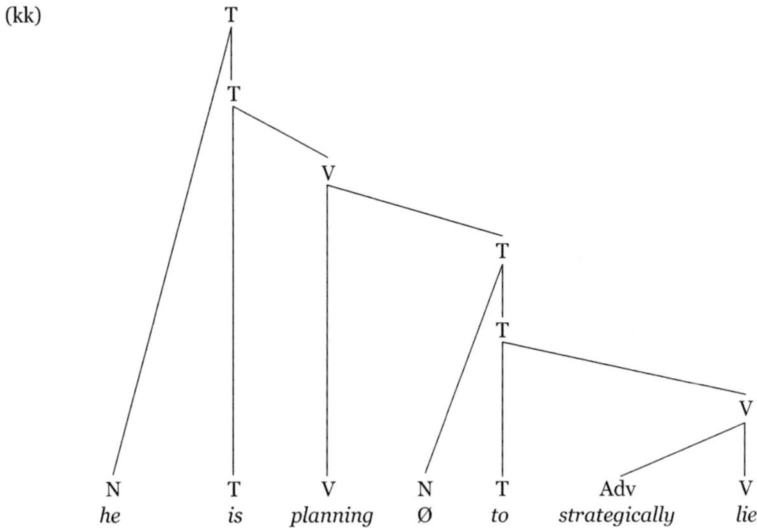

The adverb *strategically*, which here forms a syntactic unit with the verb *lie*, is linearized at the left edge of the verb phrase. The hierarchical structure in (kk) supports an alternate linear order where the adverb is linearized instead at the right edge of the verb phrase. This is shown in (ll).

(ll)

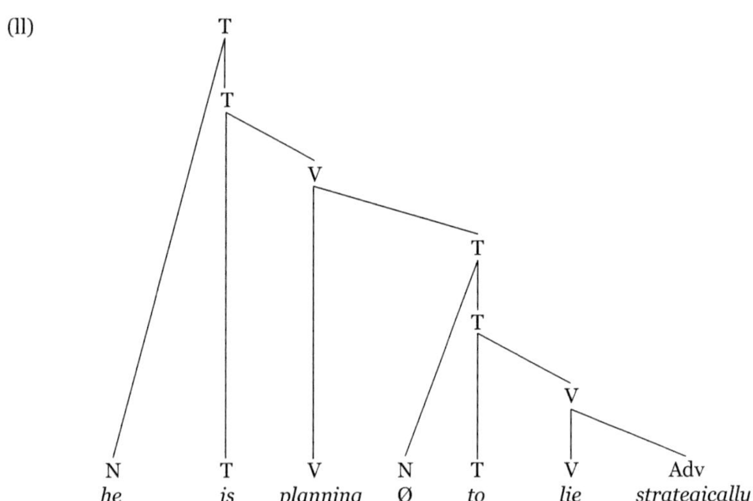

However this same linear order also corresponds to a very different hierarchical structure where the adverb *strategically* does not form a syntactic unit with the verb *lie*, but rather forms a syntactic unit with the verb phrase *planning to lie*. This is shown in (mm).

(mm)

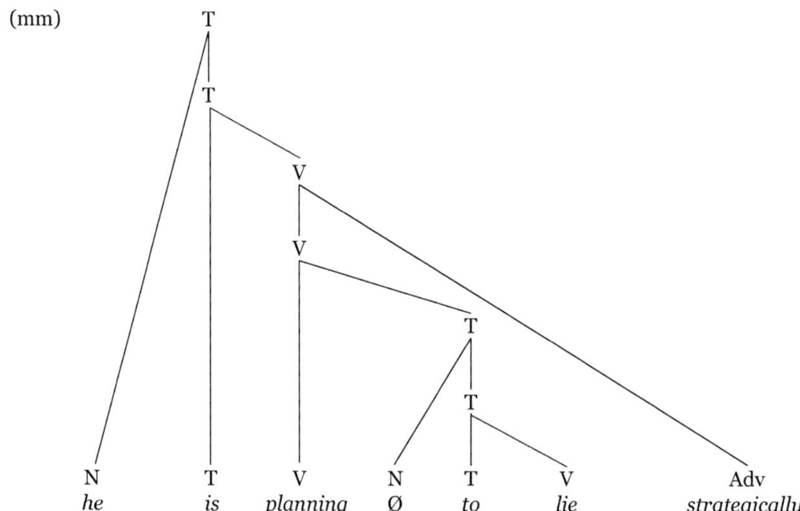

Thus in (mm) the adverb *strategically* modifies the verb *planning* and not the verb *lie*, whereas in both (ll) and (kk) the converse is true. In (mm), the adverb is linearized at the right edge of the verb phrase, but with that hierarchical structure it could have equally well been linearized at the left edge of the verb phrase, yielding the unambiguous *he is strategically planning to lie*.

What this analysis demonstrates is that of the two possibilities for linearizing adverbs modifying verbs, linearizing the adverb at the left edge of the verb phrase, which renders the adverb adjacent to the verb it modifies, does not create structural ambiguity – whereas, linearizing the adverb on the right edge of the verb phrase is compatible with multiple hierarchical structures, thus creating structural ambiguities. All other things being equal, linearization of the adverb at the left edge of the verb phrase is in fact stylistically preferable given that one of the mostly unmentioned properties of good style is the absence of unintended ambiguity. This is mostly common sense, but you won't find it stated in Strunk and White's *The Elements of Style* or in Pinker's more recent *The Sense of Style*, which does discuss both lexical and structural ambiguities.

An explicit analysis of clause structure of the sort presented in this chapter demonstrates that finite and infinitival clauses share the same basic structure.

Once we realize that the so-called infinitive form of a verb (for example, *to lie*) contains two separate lexical elements, then the claim that the so-called split infinitive construction improperly places an adverb inside a presumably single lexical unit (the infinitive) simply evaporates – leaving us with no grammatical reason not to linearize an adverb at the left edge of a verb phrase in an infinitival clause.

Prescriptive rules like the prohibitions against preposition stranding and split infinitives have to be both taught and then enforced, because they do not conform naturally to the computational system in the mind of the speaker. Knowing the prescriptive rule does not guarantee adherence in practice. In contrast, there are constraints on structure-building operations of the computational system that are understood without instruction and enforcement. English speakers do not have to be taught that *a philosopher whose we have studied books* is not a possible alternative to *a philosopher whose books we have studied*. As mentioned before, the precise formulation of these constraints is a lively and fruitful area of research in linguistics – and has been for over half a century.

4.4.3   that *vs.* which*: restrictive vs. nonrestrictive relative clauses*

Relative clauses that are set off with commas have a particular interpretation that distinguishes them from relative clauses not bounded by commas. Consider the examples in (nn).

(nn)   1. Martians, who live in glass houses, get sunburned.
         2. Martians who live in glass houses get sunburned.
         3. Martians that live in glass houses get sunburned.
         4. #Martians, that live in glass houses, get sunburned.

There are two ways to interpret the relative clause *who live in glass houses*. Under the interpretation of the relative clause represented in (nn.1), it applies to all Martians. Such relative clauses are designated as NONRESTRICTIVE. Without the commas, the relative clauses in (nn.2–3) are interpreted as RESTRICTIVE in that they identify only a subgroup of Martians that live in glass houses and therefore there must be other Martians who do not.

As (nn.3–4) indicates, a relative clause with an overt subordinating particle (and consequently with a covert relative pronoun) is not interpreted as a nonrestrictive relative clause. As a result, such relative clauses are not usually punctuated as nonrestrictive relative clauses in standard English orthography. This appears to be something that speakers of English know without instruction. Furthermore, speakers of English also know that a relative clause with an overt relative pronoun can have two distinct interpretations – as a restrictive or a nonrestrictive modifier. This distinction applies as well to other modifiers, for example prenominal adjectives as in *brilliant Caltech biologists are leading the field*. Under the nonrestrictive interpretation, all Caltech biologists are brilliant; whereas under the restrictive interpretation only those Caltech biologists that are brilliant (and not all of them are) are leading the field. With prenominal adjectives punctuation cannot be used to disambiguate between the two readings. However, paraphrasing the two interpretations using relative clauses instead of prenominal adjectives can be distinguished orthographically as *Caltech biologists, who are brilliant, are leading the field* (nonrestrictive: all Caltech biologists are brilliant) versus *Caltech biologists who are brilliant are leading the field* (restrictive: some Caltech biologists are brilliant, but not all).

The restrictive/nonrestrictive ambiguity is not always relevant for the interpretation of relative clauses. Consider another modification of *he used a lunchtime debate last week to launch his rival's book to unleash a fierce attack* ((z) above) that converts the infinitival relative clause into a finite clause, but eliminates the purpose clause.

(oo)   1. *He participated in last week's debate that launched his rival's book.*
        2. *He participated in last week's debate, which launched his rival's book.*
        3. *He participated in last week's debate which launched his rival's book.*

The restrictive relative clause in (oo.1) presumably distinguishes a particular debate that occurred *last week* from all the other debates that were taking place then. However, it seems implausible that (oo.1) would be read in this particular way. In contrast, the nonrestrictive relative clause in (oo.2) raises no issue of other debates. The nonrestrictive reading fits the context, but does not seem especially relevant because both readings are essentially the same.

The third variant in (oo) includes an overt relative pronoun *which* (= *debate*) where the relative clause is punctuated as a restrictive relative clause –that is, without commas that bracket it. (oo.3) violates a spurious prescriptive rule of syntax that the *The King's English* proposed to readers concerned with the finer points of English grammar. The rule, stated simply, is that a relative clause beginning with an overt relative pronoun *which* or *who* should always be interpreted as a nonrestrictive relative clause and therefore must be punctuated as one, with a comma separating the noun modified by the relative clause and the relative clause itself. However, in fairness to the Fowlers, their discussion is more nuanced: even they recognized exceptions to their proposal, which still occur in contemporary English prose in spite of the continued efforts of prescriptive grammarians to enforce it (including the annoying grammar checker of Microsoft's widely used word processing program *Word*). For commentary on the spurious nature of this rule, see Geoffrey Pullum's article in *The Chronicle of Higher Education* "A Rule Which Will Live in

Infamy" and Mark Liberman's blog post in *Language Log* "A decline in *which*-hunting?".[19]

If a relative clause with an overt relative pronoun can be interpreted as either restrictive or nonrestrictive, then the use of punctuation to distinguish the two interpretations can be useful. Furthermore, the use of commas to bracket the nonrestrictive interpretation matches a difference in the way this relative clause is pronounced (its prosody), where a slight pause occurs before and after the nonrestrictive clause but not with the restrictive clause. Whether this corresponds to a difference in syntactic structure is an interesting question, an answer to which depends on the analysis of the syntactic structure of relative clauses.

The syntactic analysis of relative clauses developed in Section 4.2 distinguishes *that* as a subordinating particle C from the relative pronouns *who* and *which*, which are nouns. With this in mind, consider the pair of examples introduced in (n) above (repeated here with the relative clauses underlined):

(n) 1. *books <u>which philosophers have written</u>*
  2. *books <u>that philosophers have written</u>*

Recall that syntactically the relative clause in (n.2) is a C-phrase where the subordinating particle *that* forms a syntactic unit with the T-phrase *philosophers have written* ~~*which*~~, the strikethrough indicating an element that is interpreted but not pronounced. In contrast, the pronoun *which* in (n.1) is pronounced in front of *philosophers*, the subject of relative clause, but is nonetheless interpreted as the object of the verb *written* ($\neq$ the displacement phenomenon). To account for this interpretation we can assume that in the cognitive representation of (n.1) *which* forms a syntactic unit with *written*, as in *philosophers have written books* and also as in the cognitive representation of (n.2). To account for the pronunciation of (n.1), *which* must also occur in front of *philosophers*, the subject of the relative clause.

Recall that in Section 4.2 the relative clauses in (n.1 and n.2) are analyzed as having the same underlying cognitive form given the synonymy of the sentences in which one can be substituted for the other without any change in interpretation (for example: *he never reads books which philosophers have written* versus *he never reads books that philosophers have written*). Taking (pp) to be the cognitive form of (n.1), where the relative pronoun is pronounced at the front of the relative clause and the subordinating particle is unpronounced, (n.2) is derived by pronouncing the subordinating particle, but not the relative pronoun.

---

[19] Pullum: http://chronicle.com/blogs/linguafranca/2012/12/07/a-rule-which-will-live-in-infamy/; Liberman: http://languagelog.ldc.upenn.edu/nll/?p=5479.

(pp)

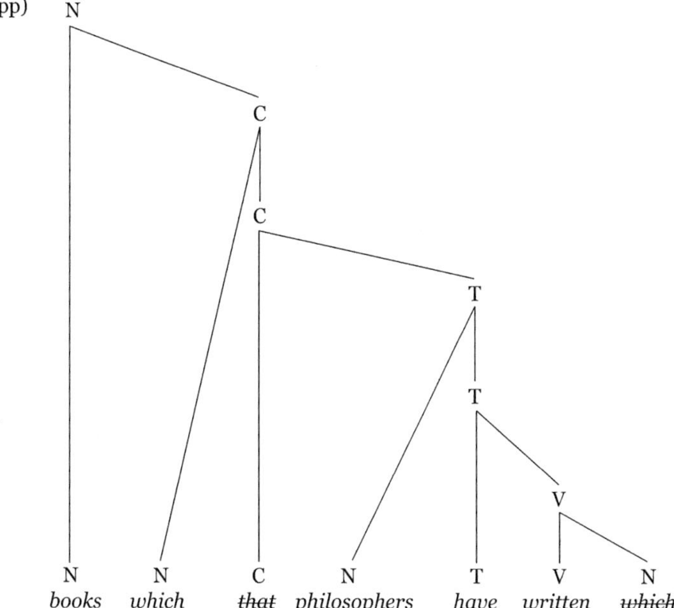

And the third variant in phonetic form is derived by not pronouncing either the relative pronoun or the subordinating particle.

In the sentence *he never reads books which philosophers have written*, only the restrictive interpretation of the relative clause seems plausible. The nonrestrictive interpretation would entail that being written by philosophers is a defining property of books. And even if the relative clause were punctuated as nonrestrictive (as in *#he never reads books, which philosophers have written*), it is not obvious that the punctuation alone would force this bizarre interpretation. This suggests that the restrictive/nonrestrictive ambiguity of some relative clauses may depend on interpretive possibilities that engage a speaker's knowledge of the world and beliefs about it.

Given the syntactic structure of relative clauses, there appears to be a strict correlation between phonetic form and the restrictive interpretation of relative clauses. When the clause contains a visible finite subordinating particle *that*, the restrictive interpretation is the only one possible. This also applies to relative clauses which contain neither the finite subordinating particle nor a relative pronoun in phonetic form. However, when the relative clause contains an overt relative pronoun (*who* or *which*), it can be interpreted as either restrictive or nonrestrictive – and in the latter case, is set off by commas in written text.

This contradicts the prescriptive analysis where the subordinating particle *that* is considered to be a relative pronoun corresponding to the restrictive interpretation and where the relative pronoun *which* is taken to be the relative pronoun introducing the nonrestrictive relative clause. But the prescriptive analysis is based on the misanalysis of the subordinating particle *that* as a pronoun. Moreover, it is contradicted by common usage, where writers frequently use *which* in restrictive relative clauses in the same way that they use *who*.

Coda

This chapter explores another ambiguity in English, one involving noun phrases containing more than one prepositional phrase, where the second of two consecutive prepositional phrases can be interpreted as modifying either the adjacent noun or the one that occurs in front of first prepositional phrase. The difference in interpretation corresponds to a difference in hierarchical structure, demonstrating once again that hierarchical structure not linear order determines the interpretations of modifiers.

The prepositional phrase modifier *by philosophers* in the ambiguous title of this chapter can be replaced with the verb phrase *written by philosophers*, given that, for example, *books by philosophers* is essentially synonymous with *books written by philosophers*. And this verb phrase can be further expanded as a full finite relative clause *which were written by philosophers*. Spelling out the syntactic structure of this relative clause reveals the syntactic structure of clauses generally as T phrases, both subordinate and non-subordinate. The analysis also provides a general analysis of subordinate clauses as C phrases. Extending the analysis of finite relative clauses to what is possible in English reveals how these constructions have a range of variation in phonetic form involving the presence or absence at the front of the clause of the finite subordinating particle *that* and the relative pronoun.

The verb phrase modifier *written by philosophers* can also be analyzed as a form of relative clause (as in *books* ~~which were~~ *written by philosophers*). This form of reduced relative clause can create a problem in written texts when the passive participle form of the verb can be misread as the past tense of the same verb (as in *the horse raced past the barn fell* or *the ship sailed out to sea sank*), creating a 'garden path' reading where the actual main verb of the sentence doesn't fit. However, there are dialects of English in which, for example, *raced past the barn* in *the horse raced past the barn fell* is interpretable as a reduced relative clause (~~which~~ *raced past the barn*) modifying *horse* in the same way the unreduced relative clause (underlined) in *the horse <u>that raced past the barn fell</u>* does – escaping the garden path reading.

The T phrase/C phrase analysis for finite relative clauses generalizes to infinitival relative clauses, although the latter allow much less variation in phonetic form. One natural variant of infinitival relative clauses involves the stranding of a preposition at the end of the clause (for example, *Mary finally found a topic to write about* (with the relative clause underlined), in contrast to the more formal and perhaps less natural version where the relative pronoun occurs in phonetic form in a prepositional phrase at the front of the relative clause (the corresponding *Mary finally found a topic about which to write*).

Bare infinitival clauses can also be utilized to indicate purpose associated with an action (expressed by a verb), for example *they wrote to their senators (in order) to register their opposition to the President's judicial nomination.* This creates the potential for ambiguity between the two interpretations in some constructions, an extreme case of which is examined in the chapter.

The final section of this chapter employs the understanding gained from the analysis of clause structure developed in this chapter to evaluate three prescriptive prohibitions against the use of specific syntactic structures in English: stranded prepositions, split infinitives (which involves the syntax of adverbs), and the relative pronoun *which* in restrictive relative clauses. The discussion of each case reviews the formulations of these prohibitions in various commentaries on English usage, including the specific sentences they cite as examples of 'bad' or 'improper' English, demonstrating how these prohibitions contradict normal English syntax and are therefore essentially unfounded.

5   *Bob is certain to succeed.*

Although the title of this chapter, unlike the previous four, is unambiguous, it too exemplifies a nontrivial linguistic property concerning the correspondence between the interpretation of this sentence and its covert syntactic representation. The title, given as example (a), contains 5 words: a noun *Bob*, 2 T elements (*is* and *to*), an adjective *certain* and a verb *succeed*.

(a)   *Bob is certain to succeed.*

Structurally, the infinitival clause *to succeed* combines with *certain* to form a predicate adjective phrase. As is usually the case, a predicate adjective that combines with an infinitival clause can also combine with a finite clause. With *certain* there are two options, illustrated in (b).

(b)   1. *It is certain that Bob will succeed.*
           2. *Bob is certain that he will succeed.*

In (b.1) *it* functions as a placeholder for the subject without any interpretive connection with the predicate *is certain*. In (b.2) the subject *Bob*, in contrast to *it* in (b.1), has an interpretive connection with the predicate *is certain*. As is apparent immediately, the sentence (a), which is essentially synonymous with sentence (b.1), is interpreted differently from sentence (b.2) even though in both (a) and (b.2) *Bob* is the subject of the main clause.

5.1   The structure and interpretation of infinitival clauses: displacement

The synonymy of sentences (a) and (b.1) is easily demonstrated by showing that asserting the truth of one while at the same time denying the truth of the other leads to a logical contradiction. Thus *%Bob is certain to succeed, but it is not certain that Bob will succeed* is a contradiction (indicated by the %). Or conversely: *%It is certain that Bob will succeed, but Bob is not certain to succeed.* These are not grammatically deviant examples, which would be designated with a *, but they are deviant in terms of the basic logic that underlies our interpretation of language.

The nonsynonymy of sentences (a) and (b.2) is likewise easily demonstrated with the same test. Asserting the truth of one sentence while at the same time denying the truth of the other does not lead to a logical contradiction, but instead a perfectly sensible interpretation. Neither *Bob is certain to succeed, but Bob is not certain that he (=Bob) will succeed* nor (conversely) *although Bob is certain that he (=Bob) will succeed, Bob is not certain to succeed* constitutes a contradiction.

The essential synonymy of sentences (a) and (b.1) suggests that their cognitive representations would share similar properties. Consider first the syntactic analysis of (b.1), given in (c).

(c)

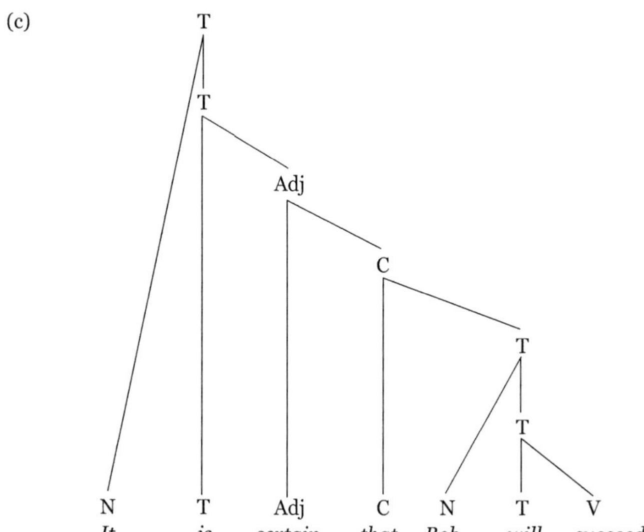

The subordinate clause *that Bob will succeed* is merged with the adjective *certain* to form an adjective phrase. Given this structure, *certain* applies to the proposition 'Bob will succeed'; interpretatively speaking, 'certainty' is being predicated on a state of affairs ('Bob's success') or an event ('Bob succeeds'). So *Bob* is interpreted only as the subject of *succeed* in the subordinate clause. While the subject of the main clause *it* has the same phonetic form as the third person neuter singular pronoun *it*, this *it* has no interpretation beyond being grammatically singular and third person – in agreement with the finite copula *is*, which is also grammatically singular and third person. The *it* in (b.1) is simply a placeholder, a pleonastic element that is required because without it the resulting linguistic expression is deviant – in this case, *is certain that Bob will succeed*, which is not a sentence of English.

In sentence (a) *Bob* is also interpreted as the subject of *succeed*. The simplest way to account for this is to postulate that *Bob* occupies the subject position in the infinitival clause covertly. Thus the infinitival clause in cognitive representation would be as given in (d).

(d)

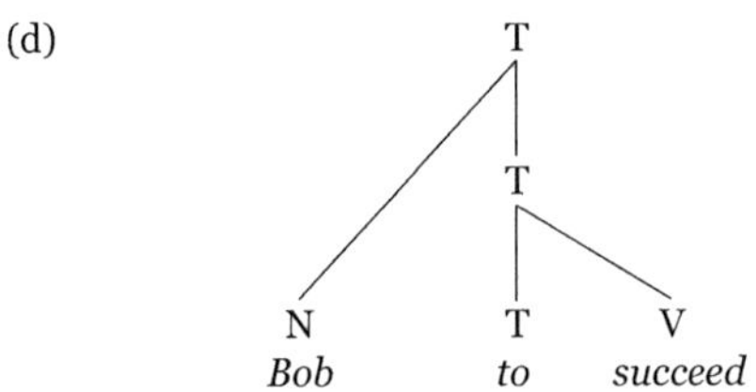

While *Bob* is interpreted in this position, this syntactic unit is not pronounced in this position, but instead is pronounced as the subject of the main clause. Furthermore, although *Bob* in (a) occurs overtly as the subject of the main clause, it is not interpreted as the subject of *certain* as it is in (b.2), where *certain* describes 'Bob's state of mind', and thus (a) and (b.2) are not synonymous as demonstrated above. In this way, (a) demonstrates an asymmetry between interpretation and pronunciation where a syntactic unit is interpreted in a position in which it is not pronounced and also pronounced in a position in which it is not interpreted – another instance of displacement in English syntax in addition to the displacement of relative pronouns in relative clauses discussed in the previous chapter. (See Section 5.5 for discussion of the utility of this property.)

But while sentences (a) and (b.1) are essentially synonymous in that both ascribe certainty to an event (roughly, Bob's succeeding), there is nonetheless an important cognitive difference between them: (a) is a sentence about *Bob* in a way that (b.1) is not. Therefore, the cognitive representation of (a) must also include the overt *Bob* as the subject of the main clause.

In effect, the syntactic unit *Bob* must occur in two distinct contexts in the cognitive representation of (a): the subject position of the infinitival clause, where it is assigned a semantic function by a predicate (the verb *succeed*), and also the subject position of the main clause, where it is not assigned a semantic function by the predicate of that clause (the adjective *certain*). To see how this is handled by the computational system, consider the syntactic representation *is certain to succeed* in the title, which extends (d) to (e).

(e)

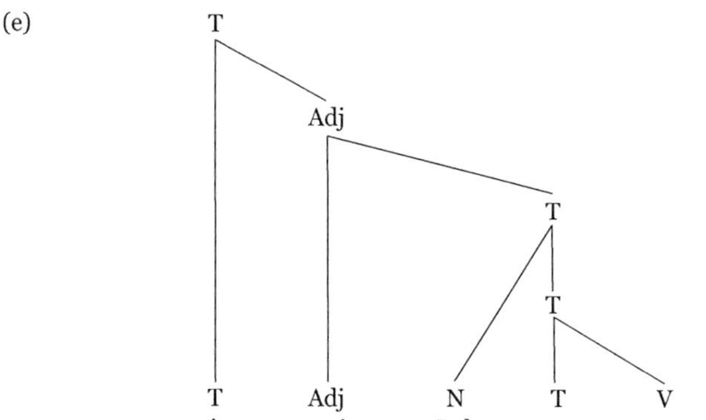

The hierarchical structure of (e) is constructed by the operation Merge stepwise, starting with the merger of T *to* and V *succeed* and proceeding with the merger of a lexical item to a syntactic structure created by a previous operation of Merge. In each case, Merge operates on unconnected syntactic units. Another option for Merge is to operate on two syntactic units where one is contained in the other, which is exactly what happens in the construction of the cognitive representation of (a) given in (f).

(f)

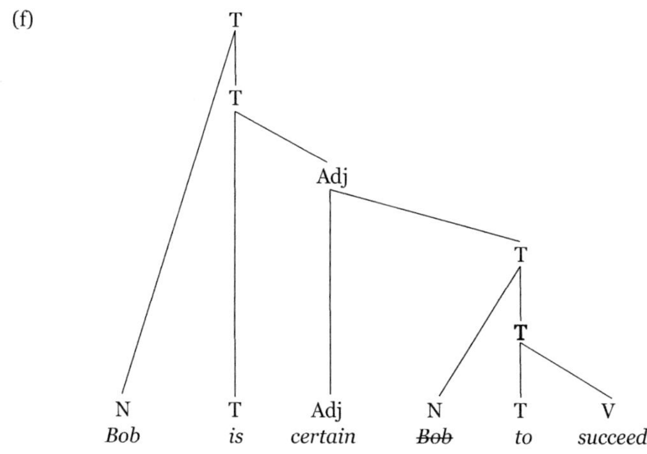

That is, Merge combines the syntactic unit (e) with the syntactic unit *Bob* that is contained in (e). In this way Merge accounts for the phenomenon of displacement by creating a syntactic representation in which a single syntactic unit (in this case *Bob*) acquires two distinct syntactic contexts, where context can be explicitly defined in terms of the sister relation (see Chapter 3). One context is the subordinate T phrase *to succeed*; the other, the main clause predicate *is certain ~~Bob~~ to succeed*. When this hierarchical structure is linearized as a phonetic form, *Bob* occurs in one context only – the position in which it is pronounced. ~~Bob~~ in (f) indicates the position where *Bob* is interpreted as the subject of *succeed*, but not pronounced.

Given that (a) cannot also be interpreted as synonymous with (b.2), where *Bob* is assigned a semantic function as the subject of *certain*, it appears that displacement involving a (single) syntactic unit that is assigned multiple semantic functions by multiple predicates is not possible. (b.2) avoids the problem by having a pronoun *he*, an independent syntactic unit, which on the relevant interpretation takes *Bob* as its antecedent. This strategy can be extended to examples like *Bob is eager to succeed*, where *Bob* is interpreted as a semantic subject of both *eager* and *succeed*, by postulating a covert subject Ø in the cognitive representation of the infinitival clause (as was done for the analysis of infinitival relative clauses in the Chapter 4). In *Bob is eager to succeed* this covert pronominal subject of the infinitival clause (Ø) must take *Bob* as its antecedent.

Thus there are two strategies for interpreting the subject of bare infinitival clauses (that is without overt subjects): displacement vs. a covert pronoun Ø or covert relative pronoun. This can be seen again in the contrast between *Bob is eager to please* versus *Bob is easy to please*, which in terms of phonetic form constitute a syntactic minimal pair. With *eager* the subject of the infinitival clause is a covert pronoun Ø as just discussed, whereas with *easy* there is a covert pronominal subject Ø which cannot be interpreted as having *Bob* as its antecedent. Instead, *Bob* in this example is interpreted as the object of *please*. Furthermore, *Bob is easy to please* can be paraphrased with the synonymous *it is easy to please Bob*, where *it* is non-referring. Thus *Bob is easy to please* apparently involves displacement, where *Bob* is interpreted as the semantic object of *please* and is assigned no semantic function by the main clause predicate *easy*.

5.2   The displacement of clauses

The displacement analysis that we have been illustrating with subordinate infinitival clauses can be extended to subordinate finite clauses in a slightly different way, as illustrated by the syntactic analysis of the synonymous pair of sentences in (g).

(g)   1. *It is certain that Bob will succeed.* (= (b.1))
         2. *That Bob will succeed is certain.*

The syntactic analysis of (g.1) given in (c) shows that the finite clause *that Bob will succeed* is merged with *certain* to form an adjective phrase. In this configuration the finite clause is assigned a semantic function by the predicate adjective *certain*. The subject position of the main clause in (c) is filled by non-referring *it*, demonstrating that this syntactic position is not assigned any semantic function by *certain*. As noted in the previous section, it is not an option in English to have a phonetically null and therefore unpronounced main clause subject – that is, **is certain that Bob will succeed* is simply deviant. Under the displacement analysis of (g.2), the subordinate clause *that Bob will succeed* is interpreted as a syntactic unit that merges with the predicate adjective *certain* but is pronounced as a syntactic unit that merges with the main clause predicate *is certain*. Therefore the cognitive representation of (g.2) would contain the finite subordinate clause *that Bob will succeed* in two contexts as shown in (h).

(h)

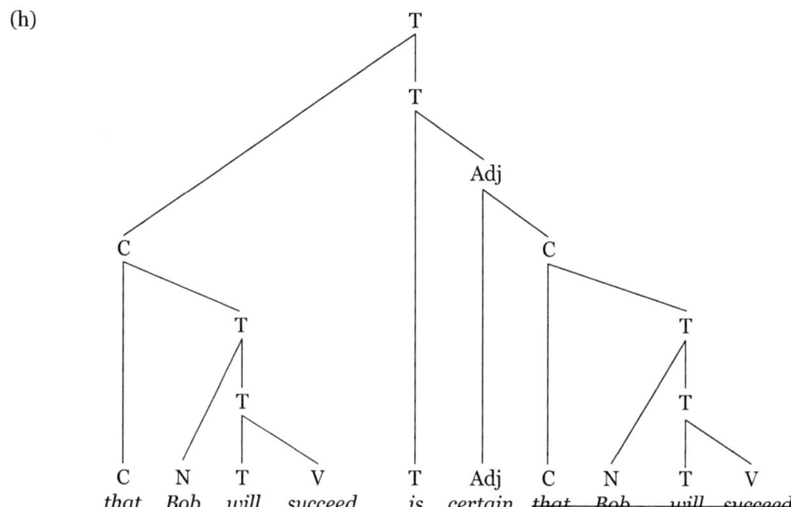

There is, however, another possibility to consider where certainty is predicated of the subordinate finite clause as the subject of the main clause – in which case, the *that Bob will succeed* will occur in only one context in the cognitive representation of (g.2).

To see why this second possibility doesn't work, we need to consider a somewhat more complicated example. Changing *certain* in (g) to *inevitable* yields the same two alternatives for the position of the finite subordinate clause (underlined): *it is inevitable that Bob will succeed* and *that Bob will succeed is inevitable*. Combining the two adjectives in a single sentence yields the two options shown in (i)

(i)   1. *It is certain that it will be inevitable that Bob will succeed.*
          2. *That it will be inevitable that Bob will succeed is certain.*

With both examples in (i), what is inevitable is that Bob will succeed and what is certain is that it is inevitable that Bob will succeed.[1] Changing *will be inevitable* to *to be inevitable* yields *it is certain to be inevitable that Bob will succeed* – with essentially the same interpretation as the sentences in (i). In addition, there is another alternative, given in (j), where the finite subordinate clause *that Bob will succeed* replaces non-referring *it*.

(j)   *That Bob will succeed is certain to be inevitable.*

The cognitive representation of (j) must show that the underlined finite subordinate clause in the main clause subject position is in fact assigned a semantic function by the adjective *inevitable* – that is, as a syntactic unit that combines with *inevitable* to form an adjective phrase – as illustrated in (k).

(k)

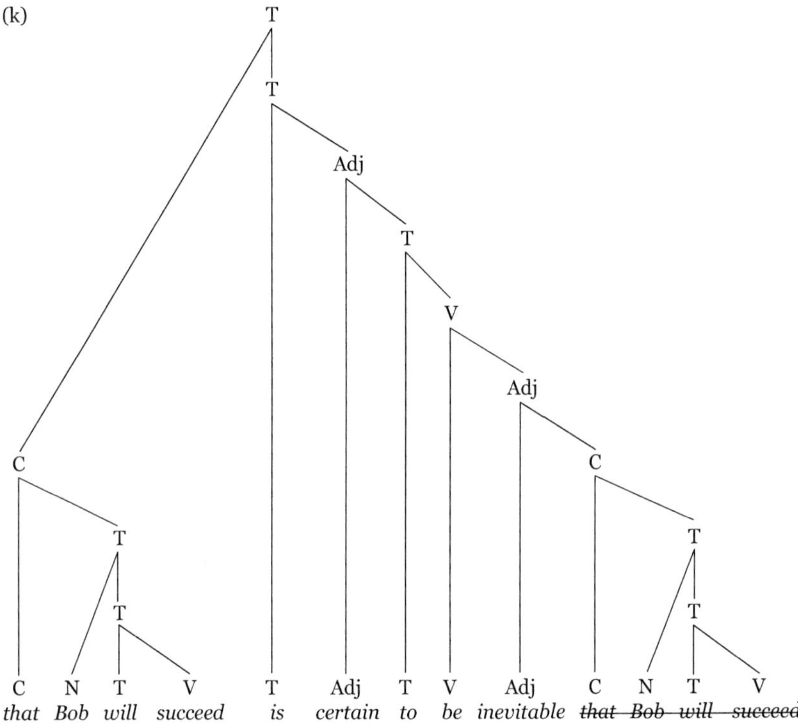

---

[1] Replacing the remaining *it* in (i.2) with *that Bob will succeed* yields the highly unnatural *that that Bob will succeed will be inevitable is certain.*

Thus (j) is unequivocally a case of displacement where the predicate *is certain* does not assign a semantic function to its subject. What is *certain* is the inevitability that Bob will succeed, not merely that Bob will succeed. Given this, it seems certain that (g.2) can only be interpreted as the displacement represented in (h).

It is worth noting that given (i.1), it is not possible to displace just the subordinate finite clause *that Bob will succeed* because this yields a deviant utterance, **that Bob will succeed is certain that it will be inevitable*. Our understanding that this utterance is not part of the language is something we know without instruction or other external evidence. What it is about the computational system of speakers of English that accounts for this is a lively area of research in linguistics, but need not concern us further.

The displacement of finite subordinate clauses also occurs with verbs, as can be seen by replacing *is certain* in (j) with *might seem* yielding *that Bob will succeed might seem to be inevitable*. The cognitive representation of this new sentence will be almost identical to (k) except with T *might* substituted for T *is* and V *seem* substituted for Adj *certain*. And without displacement, the alternative with non-referring *it* as the subject of the main clause will be *it might seem to be inevitable that Bob will succeed*.

There is however a difference between constructions with predicate adjectives like *certain* (*inevitable, likely, probable,* and *possible*) and verbs like *seem* and *appear*. Where both the displacement and non-displacement structures are possible with the adjectives (as in (g)), only the non-displacement structure is possible with the verbs when they form a syntactic unit with a finite subordinate clause: *it seems that June has won a lottery* vs. **that June has won a lottery seems*. And like certain predicate adjectives (*certain* and *likely*), but not others (*inevitable, probable,* and *possible*), these verbs support displacement of an infinitival subject to their subject position, as in *June seems to have won a lottery* (contrast **June is possible to have won a lottery* vs. *June is likely to have won a lottery*).

With infinitival clauses where both the subordinating particle and the subject are overt, as in *for June to have won a lottery*, the possibilities are significantly restricted compared to the corresponding finite clause (compare *that June has won a lottery*). If a predicate adjective can form an adjective phrase with a full infinitival clause, then the displacement construction is also possible, as illustrated in (l).

(l)   1. *It is possible for June to have won a lottery.*
          2. *For June to have won a lottery is possible.*

In contrast, if *probable* replaces *possible* in (l), the result seems distinctly less acceptable. Furthermore, whether the replacement of *possible* in (l) with either *likely* or *inevitable* yields sentences that speakers of English judge acceptable may vary from speaker to speaker.

The two possibilities for displacement, with either the subject phrase of an infinitival clause or a finite subordinate clause, also exist with another subclass of English verbs, as illustrated in (m).

(m)   1. *We reported that June had won a lottery.*
          2. *It was reported (by us) that June had won a lottery.*
          3. *That June had won a lottery was reported (by us).*
          4. *June was reported (by us) to have won a lottery.*

The main clause verb *reported* in (m.1) is the past tense form in the ACTIVE VOICE, whereas *reported* in (m.2–4) does not express past tense – the auxiliary verb *was* does that – and is instead a participial form that along with the auxiliary *was* indicates the PASSIVE VOICE. In active voice form *reported* cannot occur with a non-referring *it* subject, in contrast to the passive voice form *reported* in (m.2) where it can. As with the other English constructions discussed in this chapter, where a non-referring *it* subject is possible, a displaced clause or noun phrase can also occur. This turns out to be a useful structural property of English syntax, as will be discussed in Section 5.5.

5.3   Displacement and passive voice

The alternation between active and passive voice of course also occurs in SIMPLE finite clauses, which do not contain any subordinate clause, as illustrated in (n).

(n)   1. *A grand jury indicted those bankers for fraud.*
          2. *Those bankers were indicted for fraud (by a grand jury).*

In (n.1) the syntactic subject *a grand jury* is interpreted as the agent of the action *indicted* (in the past tense) and the syntactic object *those bankers* is interpreted as the target of this action. In (n.2) *those bankers*, which is now the syntactic subject, is still interpreted as the target of the action *indicted* (in the passive participle form). So the cognitive representation of (n.2) contains a verb phrase *indicted those bankers*, as does the cognitive representation of (n.1) – and therefore simple passive clauses also involve displacement, where the semantic object occurs as the syntactic subject in phonetic form. Displacement in simple passives is obligatory because the alternative where non-referring *it* occurs as the structural subject is not possible – thus **it was indicted those bankers (by a grand jury)* is deviant, which demonstrates that the noun phrase that is interpreted as the object of the passive verb cannot ever be pronounced in this position.

In simple passives, the agentive *by* in conjunction with the passive participle *indicted* (n.2) assigns the same semantic role to *a grand jury* as the active form *indicted* assigns to its structural subject in (n.1). Therefore, the noun phrase that is interpreted as the subject of the active clause apparently occurs in a different syntactic configuration for the passive. Furthermore, in the active voice the agent of the action must be expressed in phonetic form whereas in the passive the agentive *by*-phrase is optional. Thus *those bankers were indicted* is a perfectly grammatical sentence of English (see Section 5.5 for further discussion).

The designations 'active' versus 'passive' voice are categories that have been part of grammatical description since the late Middle Ages (see P.H. Matthews, *The Concise Oxford Dictionary of Linguistics*, 2nd edition (2007)). They are purely technical terms for distinguishing two verb forms that occur in different syntactic configurations. The passive form usually occurs with some form of an auxiliary verb *be*, as in *the review was written by two philosophers*. This passive auxiliary *be* should be distinguished from the auxiliary *be* that occurs with progressive form of the verb (which is inflected with a suffix *–ing* and designates ongoing action – referred to in traditional grammar as PRO-GRESSIVE ASPECT), as in *two philosophers are writing the review*. Both passive voice and progressive aspect can occur together, as in *the review was being written by two philosophers*, where the passive auxiliary is inflected with the progressive suffix and the progressive auxiliary (*was*) is inflected for past tense.

The passive participle of the main verb which occurs with the passive auxiliary is always identical in phonetic form to the corresponding perfective participle, which occurs with the auxiliary *have*[2] – for example, *was written* (passive) vs. *has written* (active perfective). In this case, both the passive and

---

[2] English also has a main verb *have* and thus there are sentences in English that can have both, as in *many students had had trouble with writing assignments during their college careers*. So it is grammatically possible to have two consecutive instances of *had* in a grammatical sentence. In November 1955, *Eureka* (the journal of the Archimedians, the Cambridge University Mathematical Society; Junior Branch of the Mathematical Association) published a mathematical problem titled "By Induction or Ever Been Had?" which concerns the following sentence:

(1)   *John where Willie had had had had had had had had had had had full marks.*

The first part of the problem is to punctuate (1) to show that it is actually a well-formed sentence of English. The second part is demonstrating that there are "intelligible sentences containing (14*3n–3) successive *had*'s, where *n* is any non-negative integer."

The problem includes the solution to both parts, but we will only consider the first, which involves a trick. The journal's solution is given in (2).

(2)   *John, where Willie had had 'had,' had had 'had had'; 'had had' had had full marks.*

The instances of *had* inside single quotes do not function in the syntax of the sentence as auxiliaries or main verbs in the way that the non-quoted instances of *had* do. Furthermore, the sentence as analyzed consists of two finite clauses that are spliced together with a semicolon. The distinction between the two uses of *had* is somewhat easier to see if we distinguish them

perfective participles are inflected with the *–en* suffix (*write* + *en*).[3] This syncretism between corresponding passive and perfective participles (where morphosyntactically distinct suffixes share the same phonetic form) sometimes extends to the past tense of the verb, as in *the bankers were indicted* (passive) vs. *the grand jury has indicted the bankers* (active perfective) vs. *the grand jury indicted the bankers* (active past tense), where all three forms are inflected with the suffix *–ed*.

5.4   Displacement inside noun phrases

Some properties of the active/passive alternation in clauses also occur in the syntax of noun phrases where the head of the phrase constitutes a nominalization of the verb, for example the relation between the verb *indict* and the noun *indictment*. Thus the sentences in (n) correspond to the noun phrases in (o), where (o.1) corresponds to the active clause (n.1) and (o.2) corresponds to the passive clause (n.2).

(o)   1. *the grand jury's indictment of those bankers for fraud*
         2. *those bankers' indictment for fraud by the grand jury*

As illustrated in (o.1), the noun phrase *the grand jury* at the beginning of the whole noun phrase is interpreted as the agent and source of the indictment, corresponding to the subject of the active clause. In (o.2) the noun phrase *those bankers* occurs in the same position but is nonetheless interpreted as the object of the indictment, corresponding to the object of the active clause. This suggests that the cognitive representation of (o.2) might, like the passive clause (n.2), involve displacement. However, unlike passive clauses, displacement in these noun phrase constructions is optional because it is also possible to express this noun phrase as *the indictment of those bankers for fraud by the grand jury*.

---

graphically by translating the quoted forms into boldface, yielding *John, where Willie had had **had**, had had **had had**; **had had** had had full marks*. Notice that (1) is in fact ambiguous between the interpretation represented in (2) and *John, where Willie had had **had had**, had had had; **had had** had had full marks* – which the solution to the second part mentions in the solution to $n = 1$, in citing another example of the finite clause following the semicolon as: **had had had had had had had had had had** *had had two possible interpretations*. Notice that the 11 instances of *had* in boldface in this phrase can only be interpreted as a string of 11 words with the same phonetic form where no syntactic or semantic interpretation is assigned to any of the individual words in the string.

[3] Another case where the *–en* suffix appears in corresponding passive and perfective participles involves verbs whose past tense form changes the vowel in the root instead of adding the past tense suffix *–ed*. Thus the past tense of *steal* is *stole* and the corresponding passive (and perfective) participle is *stolen*.

Given that displacement phenomena can occur with nominalizations, these structures can be ambiguous, where distinct cognitive representations have the same phonetic form. Consider the case of *the banker's indictment* (switching to the singular because it's simpler – one banker to one indictment). On one interpretation, someone or some group is indicting the banker – that is, accusing that banker of a crime. But it is also possible to interpret this noun phrase as the banker who is making the indictment (for example, against her CEO or the financial industry). However it is not possible to interpret this noun phrase as 'the banker is accusing herself of a crime' – a fact which supports the idea that displacement cannot involve two syntactic positions that are both assigned a distinct semantic role.

Nouns like *indictment* have an internal structure consisting of distinct parts, their MORPHOLOGY. Consider the plural noun *indictments*, which has three distinct overt parts: a verbal ROOT *indict*, a suffix *–ment*, and a plural suffix *–s*. How these parts are put together constitutes the morphological structure of *indictments*, represented in (p).

(p)

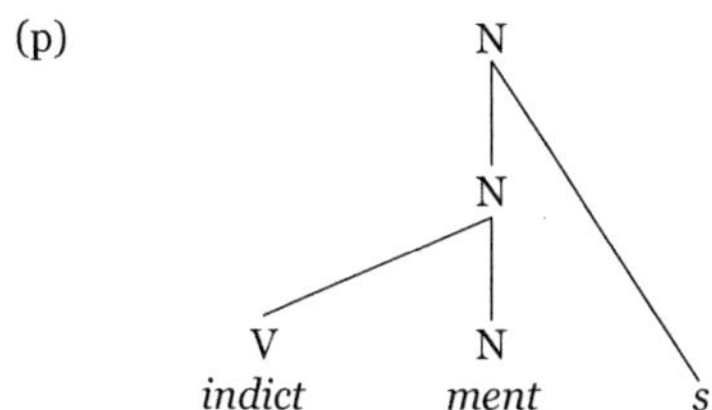

(p) shows that the syntactic category of the suffix *–ment* determines the syntactic category of the word as a noun. In contrast, because the plural suffix *–s* has no inherent syntactic category, it can only inflect the noun for number, adding the small bit of information 'more than one' to the morphological unit it combines with. In terms of interpretation, the combination of *indictment* and the plural suffix is compositional, where each part has a distinct recognizable interpretation. The suffix *–ment*, on the other hand, radically affects the interpretation of the verbal root *indict* with which it combines to form a morphological unit. Moreover, the suffix *–ment* cannot be assigned a distinct meaning such that the interpretation of the morphological unit *indict + ment* is compositional in that way that inflectional suffixes (for number, person, tense, aspect, and voice in English) clearly are. Identifying a single clear interpretation for the suffix *–ment* is actually impossible given the variety of nominalizations it occurs in – consider for example the relation between the interpretations of the following list of verbs and their corresponding nouns.

(q)   *argue*   *argument*
        pay   *payment*
        state   *statement*
        govern   *government*
        move   *movement*
        manage   *management*
        entertain   *entertainment*
        bewilder   *bewilderment*

For instance, if *payment* is interpreted as 'what is paid', a corresponding interpretation fails for the rest of the list with perhaps the exception of *statement* interpreted as 'what is stated'. The noun *bewilderment* is interpreted as 'a state of being bewildered', an interpretation ('a state of being Ved') that corresponds to none of the other nouns listed in (q).

One further difference between the inflectional suffix for plural and the nominalizing suffix *–ment* that turns a verbal root into a noun concerns their productivity in the lexicon. With few exceptions, the plural suffix combines with countable nouns generally; whereas the nominalizing suffix *–ment* does not combine generally with most verbs.[4]

English has another nominalizing suffix that is illustrated in (r).

(r)   1. *The grand jury's indicting of those bankers for fraud* will shock Wall Street.
        2. *The grand jury's indicting those bankers for fraud* will shock Wall Street.
        3. *The grand jury indicting those bankers for fraud* will shock Wall Street.

The suffix *–ing* attaches to the verbal root *indict* producing the form *indicting*, called in traditional grammar a GERUND. In terms of phonetic form the gerund is identical to the progressive participle (as in *they are **indicting** those bankers*), but it is interpreted as noun whereas the participle is interpreted as a verb that normally occurs with some form of the progressive auxiliary *be*. (r) gives three alternative syntactic configurations for subject noun phrases (underlined) that have a gerund as the head of the phrase.

The variation in (r) involves the syntactic rendering of both *the grand jury*, which functions as the subject of the gerund, and *those bankers*, which functions as its object. In (r.1) and (r.2), *the grand jury* is inflected as a possessive (with a possessive suffix *–'s*[5]), while in (r.1) *those bankers* is

---

[4] This is easily verified by trying to apply the suffix *–ment* to a set of verbs from any text.

[5] Although the phonetic form shows the possessive affix *–'s* attaching to a noun (in this case the compound noun *grand jury*), larger noun phrases suggest that syntactically the affix attaches to the whole phrase rather than a single noun. Consider, for example, *that mathematician from Princeton's accent* where the *accent* is possessed by *that mathematician*, not by *Princeton* (town or university). Thus *–'s* modifies the head of this noun phrase, not the adjacent noun to which it is attached in phonetic form.

separated from the gerund by a semantically empty preposition *of*. These are distinctly nominal properties as shown by substituting the corresponding derived nominal *indictment* for the gerund in (r). Only the revised (r.1), yielding (o.1) *the grand jury's indictment of those bankers for fraud shocked Wall Street*, with the syntactic structure (s), is possible in English.

(s)

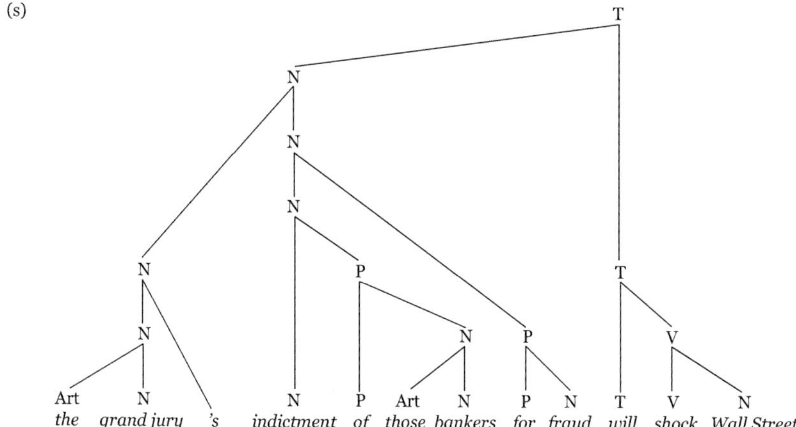

The syntactic structure of (r.1) is identical to (s), with the gerund *indicting* replacing the derived nominal *indictment*.

Lacking both nominal properties, the gerund in (r.3) appears to behave syntactically like a verb rather than a noun. But labeling this gerund a verb – and thus labeling the subject of *shock* (*the grand jury indicting those bankers for fraud*) a verb phrase – leaves open the question of the gerund in (r.2) that manifests one nominal property (the possessive affix) and one verbal property (the noun phrase object immediately following the gerund). Furthermore, verb phrases do not generally serve as subjects of verbs.

Another reason for distinguishing the gerund from the verbal form *indicting* is that (r.3) is actually ambiguous between two distinct interpretations, one in which the act of indicting those bankers for fraud is what will shock Wall Street, and the other where it is the grand jury that is interpreted as the subject of *shock*. The latter interpretation is synonymous with *the grand jury which is indicting those bankers for fraud will shock Wall Street* – which reveals *indicting those bankers for fraud* to be a reduced relative clause – overtly a verb phrase – modifying *grand jury*, where the relative pronoun, the subordinating particle, and the verbal auxiliary of the progressive participle (*indicting*) are all silent in phonetic form.[6] Under this interpretation, *indicting* is unquestionably a verb. In contrast, the interpretation where the act of indicting the bankers for fraud is what will shock Wall Street, then the nominal interpretation of *indicting* automatically distinguishes the gerund as a form of noun and therefore as distinct from the progressive participle, which is unquestionably a form of verb.

There is one combination of nominal and verbal properties that is not possible for gerunds in English, illustrated in (t).

(t)   *The grand jury indicting of the bankers for fraud shocked Wall Street.*

Why the presence of the semantically empty *of* requires that the subject of the gerund be inflected as possessive remains to be determined. Nonetheless, the pronounced contrast between (t) and the three variants in (r) show that all three are viable configurations of the English gerund.

Another impossible gerundive construction relates to the parallelism between nominalization *indictment* and the gerund *indicting*. Given *the indictment of those bankers for fraud by the grand jury*, it is possible to substitute the gerund to derive *the indicting of those bankers for fraud by the grand jury*. Modification by the definite article *the* is a nominal property that marks *indictment/indicting* as nouns. This property cannot co-occur with the verbal property where the gerund forms a syntactic unit with its object noun phrase without an intervening semantically empty preposition *of*. Thus **the indicting the bankers for fraud* is deviant. Again, why modification of a gerund by an article requires the use of the semantically empty preposition *of* awaits an explanation. But the comparison provides strong evidence that the semantic subject of the gerund can occur in a prepositional phrase (an agentive *by*-phrase) following the gerund.[7]

In English, a gerund can also be formed by adding the nominalizing *–ing* suffix to auxiliary verbs, as (u) demonstrates.

(u)   1. *Wall Street objects to the grand jury having indicted those bankers for fraud.*
        2. *Wall Street objects to those bankers being indicted for fraud by the grand jury.*

It is also possible to add the possessive inflection to *the grand jury* in (u.1) and to *those bankers* in (u.2). In (u.1) the gerundive suffix *–ing* turns the perfective auxiliary *have* into some form of noun, where the remaining part of the

---

[6] The full relative clause can further be interpreted as either restrictive or non-restrictive. However, the reduced relative clause only has the restrictive interpretation.

[7] There is, however, a striking difference between the gerundive and non-gerundive nominalizations. Gerunds require the presence of the semantic object – compare *the indictment by the grand jury* vs. **the indicting by the grand jury*.

gerundive clause *indicted those bankers for fraud* is a straightforward verb phrase headed by the perfective participle *indicted*. (u.1) shows that the requirement that the perfective participle must occur with some form of the perfective auxiliary can be satisfied by the gerundive nominalization of the verbal auxiliary.

In (u.2) the gerundive suffix turns the uninflected passive auxiliary *be* (as opposed to *is/am/are* and *was/were*, which are inflected for tense, number, and person) into a nominal form. The following verb phrase is a passive construction in which *indicted* is interpreted as the passive participle, and the syntactic unit *those bankers* is interpreted as the object of *indicted* even though it is not pronounced in this position. Thus the syntactic structure of (u.2) involves two contexts for *those bankers*, a covert position where it is assigned a semantic role by the verb *indicted* and an overt position in which it is pronounced. Suppressing the optional *by*–phrase in (u.2) yields a syntactic structure (v) that is virtually identical in hierarchical structure to that of (u.1).

(v)

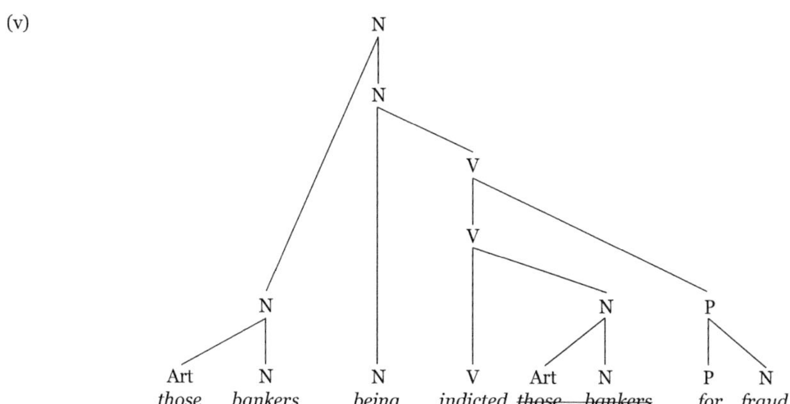

(v) differs from (u.1) in that the verb form *indicted* is interpreted as a passive participle in (v) as opposed to a perfective participle in (u.1). In (u.1) the two noun phrase positions are occupied by different noun phrases, whereas in (v) they are occupied by the same noun phrase. As in clauses, the passive participle in this gerundive noun phrase requires some form of the passive auxiliary *be* – in this case, gerundive nominal *being*, just as the perfective participle requires some form of the perfect auxiliary *have*. And just like regular clausal passives, the gerundive with a passive participle requires displacement with a noun phrase that is pronounced in subject position interpreted as the object of the passive verb. Thus *those bankers*, while interpreted as the object of the passive participle *indicted*, shows up in phonetic form in the subject position of the gerundive construction. This analysis extends to the slightly more complicated gerundive construction with both the perfect and passive auxiliaries, as in *Wall Street objects to those bankers having been indicted by the grand jury*.

It is worth noting that (u.2), like (r.3), is actually ambiguous between a relative clause interpretation and a gerundive clause interpretation. On the relative clause interpretation, *being indicted for fraud by the grand jury* is a reduction of *who are being indicted for fraud by the grand jury*, modifying *bankers* – thus the reduced relative clause is a verb phrase in which *being* is the progressive form of the passive auxiliary. On this analysis, Wall Street is objecting to the bankers. Like the gerundive construction in (v), this relative clause would also involve displacement, where the relative pronoun *who* is interpreted as the object of *indicted*. In contrast, on the gerundive interpretation Wall Street is objecting to a state of affairs (*being indicted for fraud by the grand jury*) that the bankers find themselves in.

This chapter has focused on displacement phenomena in English syntax, where a syntactic unit pronounced in one syntactic position is interpreted as if it occupies a different syntactic position. The units involved can be either noun phrases or clauses (both finite and infinitival). The syntactic constructions that manifest displacement can include both complex and simple sentences, and can be as small as a single noun phrase. The phenomenon of displacement in the various constructions considered in this chapter is simply part of the repertoire of the computational system for English, and thus part of the natural English syntax.

5.5   On the utility of displacement

The utility of displacement in clauses is easily stated in terms of the traditional analysis of a clause as consisting of a subject plus a predicate. The subject announces the topic that the clause is about, while the predicate comments on the topic. Displacement allows a writer to shift the focus of a clause – most importantly a main clause and therefore the entire sentence – by turning a phrase that is nonetheless interpreted as part of the predicate into a topic of the clause. Consider for example the title of this chapter compared with two variants where the infinitival clause is replaced by a finite clause (*it is certain that Bob will succeed* and *that Bob will succeed is certain*). In terms of truth conditions, if one is a true statement then the other two must also be true statements, as discussed at the beginning of Section 5.1. With respect to the two finite clause variants this is easily verified by constructing a compound sentence that affirms one and negates the other, which yields an obvious contradiction, a sentence that can never be true under any interpretation. Thus *%It is certain that Bob will win but that Bob will win is not certain*, which is a syntactically legitimate sentence in English, constitutes a contradiction. Although the three sentences are synonymous in terms of truth conditions, they are different in terms of focus. The sentence that is title of this chapter is about *Bob*, whereas *that Bob will succeed is certain* is a sentence about the proposition *that Bob will succeed*. The version that has non-referring *it* as the subject of the main clause cannot be about *it*, which is essentially a placeholder, and therefore functions as a comment without a stated topic, strange as that may seem.

5.5.1   *Criticism of the passive voice: a brief history*

Although the passive voice is simply one syntactic device that produces displacement in English, it has been a special subject of criticism in the literature on English usage for over a century, starting at the beginning of the twentieth century. What follows is a review of these criticisms that will attempt to demonstrate how the various justifications offered against the use of passive voice collapse under careful consideration of the syntactic structure of the examples cited, which generally involve other problems. Once we see that there is actually nothing wrong with passive voice per se, we can return to the utility of displacement, which involves evaluating the use of sentence forms in the context of other sentences (in discourse), which in writing leads us to a consideration of the structure of paragraphs.

The discussion of English usage originates in Oxford Professor of Poetry Robert Lowth's *A Short Introduction to English Grammar* (1775), which is, according to his preface, the first published grammar of English that attempts to distinguish correct from incorrect usage. He writes:

The principal design of a Grammar of any Language is to teach us to express ourselves with propriety in that Language, and to enable us to judge of every phrase and form of construction, whether it be right or not. —The plain way of doing this, is to lay down rules, and then illustrate them by examples. But, besides shewing what is right, the matter may be further explained by pointing out what is wrong. I will not take upon me to say, whether we have any Grammar, that sufficiently instructs us by rule and example; but I am sure we have none, that, in the manner here attempted, teaches us what is right by shewing what is wrong; though this perhaps may prove the more useful and effectual method of instruction. (pp. viii–ix)

However, when discussing the passive voice, he gives only a straightforward description of the passive construction.

When the Verb is a Passive, the Agent and the Object change places in the Sentence; and the thing acted upon is in the Nominative case, and the Agent is accompanied with a Preposition: as, "The Persians were conquered by Alexander." (p. 74)[8]

Lowth's grammar contains no comment on the purported misuse of the passive voice.

Criticism of the use of passives appears to have started in the early twentieth century, with H.W. Fowler and F.G. Fowler's *The King's English* (1906), where §26 of Part II under the subheading "Grammar" criticizes a construction called a *compound passive*. According to the book, the active construction *...have attempted to justify this step* has two alternatives in the passive: (1) *this step has been attempted to be justified* and (2) *it has been attempted to justify this step*. Only the first alternative constitutes a compound passive, which the book characterizes as *an incorrect and slovenly makeshift, although licensed by usage*. The judgment *licensed by usage* is supported by ten citations of the double passive (including one each from the writers Hazlitt, Balfour, Burney, Dickens, and Carlyle – the others from the British newspaper *The Times*). Of both passive alternatives, the book comments: *in point of clumsiness, there is perhaps not much to choose between the two passive constructions, neither of which should be used when it can be avoided*. Thus the first criticism of the passive was that it can produce clumsy prose in specific instances.

According to *The King's English*, what is wrong with the example of the compound passive cited above is that *the true object of 'have attempted' is the whole phrase 'to justify this step'* and therefore *this step*, not being the object of *attempted*, cannot be the subject of the passive that corresponds to the active *...have attempted to justify this step*. This analysis suggests that the deviant sentence **to justify this step was attempted* should be possible in English. Furthermore, this analysis does not extend to perfectly acceptable *compound passive* constructions like *this step was reported to have been justified*.[9] The *true object* of *reported* would also be the infinitival clause *to have been justified*, in which *this step* is interpreted as the object of *justified*.

---

[8] Unlike Latin, German, and Russian, English does not distinguish common nouns with a case inflection that affects the phonetic and morphological shape of the noun. However, third person pronouns in English do manifest case distinctions. Thus if we replace *Alexander* and *Persians* in Lowth's example *The Persians were conquered by Alexander* with the personal pronouns *they* and *him*, then Lowth's passive example becomes *they were conquered by him*, with the corresponding active *he conquered them*. *He* and *him* have the same interpretation 'third person, masculine, singular'. The only difference is that *he* is in the Nominative case, while *him* is not. If we talk about 'Alexander's conquest of the Persians' as *his conquest*, then *his* is the Genitive case form for the third person masculine singular pronoun. *Him* is the "Objective" case form – the form that occurs when the pronoun is either the object of a verb or preposition. The same distinctions apply to the third person plural forms. Similarly, English also distinguishes first person pronouns in terms of case (*I – me – my* and *we – us –our*).

[9] Twenty years later, Henry Fowler discusses these acceptable double passives in *The Dictionary of Modern English Usage*. See below for commentary.

But this *true object* cannot occur as either the subject of a passive clause or the object of an active clause, as the deviance of both **to have justified this step was reported* and **they reported to have justified this step* shows.[10]

The difference between the deviant passive constructions cited in *The King's English* and the legitimate construction cited above can be explained in terms of the properties of the verbs involved. Given that both examples contain *justified* as the main verb of the subordinate clause, the difference between the two compound passive constructions rests on the difference between the lexical properties of *report* and *attempt*. When *attempt* combines with an infinitival clause, the infinitival clause can only have a covert subject Ø whose antecedent is the syntactic subject of *attempt*. Thus the infinitival clause cannot contain an overt subject, as illustrated by the deviance of **they attempted their scientific team to justify this step* and which generalizes to the deviance of **they attempted this step to be justified by their scientific team*, where the subordinate clause is both infinitival and passive. In contrast, *report* does not permit an infinitival subordinate clause lacking an overt subject since **they reported to justify this step* is deviant as noted above; whereas this verb does allow an overt subject in the infinitival clause (in contrast to *attempt*), as in *they reported their scientific team to have justified this step*, a property that generalizes to the passive version of the infinitival subordinate clause, as in *they reported this step to have been justified by their scientific team*. The problem with the book's double passive example is that *attempt* does not have the prerequisite property (occurring with an infinitival subordinate clause that has an overt subject) for a main clause verb in a compound passive construction.

The other passive construction cited in the book (*it was attempted to justify this step*) raises other problems. The book refers to *it* as *an introductory 'it'*, presumably the non-referring pleonastic *it* discussed in Section 5.1. However, neither the active or passive form of *attempt* (in contrast to active *seem* and passive *reported*) can occur with this *it* as its subject in any grammatical sentence. But if *it* is interpreted as the third person referential pronoun, then there is an interpretation of the sentence under which it is grammatical – namely, where the infinitival clause is interpreted as a purpose clause along the lines of 'something (= it) was attempted in order to justify this step').

A year after the publication of *The King's English*, Edwin C. Woolley, an assistant professor of English at the University of Wisconsin, Madison,

---

[10] Given the analysis of the infinitival clause as the object of *attempt*, another option suggests itself – namely, *to justify this step was attempted several times without success* (which sounds a bit more natural than ending the sentence with the passive verb). I suspect that this variant sounds a great deal less "clumsy" than the two alternatives cited in *The King's English*, but nonetheless a bit odd compared to *justifying this step was attempted several times without success*, where the gerundive subject is syntactically a noun phrase (compare *the climb was attempted several times without success*).

published his *Handbook of Composition: A Compendium of Rules regarding Good English, Grammar, Sentence Structure, Paragraphing, Manuscript Arrangement, Punctuation, Spelling, Essay Writing, and Letter Writing*, which comments on the *misuse of passive voice* in a section titled "structure of sentences". This section (on p. 20) states two rules for the use of passive voice and gives a pair of sentences for each, one labeled *Bad* and the other, *Right*, a practice that Professor Lowth would have appreciated. The first rule states: *Do not use the passive voice when such use makes a statement clumsy or wordy*. It is illustrated by a comparison between the passive sentence *your letter was received and carefully read by me* (Bad) and its active counterpart *I received and carefully read your letter* (Right). As noted previously, a full passive sentence – one that expresses the agent in a prepositional phrase – will always contain two single-syllable function words (some form of the passive auxiliary *be* and the preposition *by*) that do not occur in the corresponding active sentence. But it is just silly to think that therefore all passive sentences are 'wordy' compared to their active counterparts because they contain two additional function words.[11] So these examples simply do not illustrate the wordiness of the passive construction.

In the margin, the misuse of the passive in this example is characterized as *resulting in awkwardness*. Exactly how this example is clumsy and/or awkward is not explicitly stated. There is, however, an obvious source in the coordination of the verbs *receive* and *read*. If I read your letter, that entails that I received it – which then doesn't need to be stated. So the active counterpart of the disparaged passive sentence is both unnecessarily wordy and because of the implied redundancy of *received* in the context of *read*, clumsy/awkward. And this carries over the passive counterpart. So far, there seems to be nothing wrong with the passive version specifically.

Pullum (2014), discussing a similar pair of sentences in Strunk and White's *The Elements of Style* (see below), identifies the problem as ending a sentence with *by me*, proposing that the passive version violates a more general discourse constraint where the noun phrase object of passive *by must denote something at least as new in the discourse as the subject* (p. 64). The constraint would appear to rule out any passive construction containing *by* me. Consider, however, *your letter has been carefully read by me in particular* or *your letter has been carefully read in particular by me* (where this version ends the sentence with *by me*), which both seem less awkward than the active counterpart *I in particular have carefully read your letter*. Nonetheless, the first prescriptive grammar of English (Lowth's 1775 edition of *A Short*

---

[11] See Geoffrey Pullum's "On the myth that passives are wordy" (www.sense-online.nl/files/ jubilee-conference/jubilee-public/674-esensemagazine-issue-37-april-2015-gk-pullum-on-myths-about-passives/file) for a more detailed refutation of this criticism.

Introduction to English Grammar) cites the pair *I love Thomas* and *Thomas is loved by me* to illustrate the active/passive alternation (on p. 26); apparently the use of *by me* in a passive construction was not a problem in the eighteenth century.

The second rule in Woolley's book states *Do not, by using the passive voice, leave the agent of the verb vaguely indicated, when the agent should be clearly indicated*, and is illustrated with the comparison between the passive sentence *that was a crisis in my life, which will never be forgotten* (Bad) and its active counterpart *that was a crisis in my life, which I shall never forget* (Right). This putative misuse of the passive voice is identified as *resulting in vagueness*. But is this passive actually vague? If we can assume that people generally do not forget crises in their lives, then leaving out the agentive *by*-phrase – which would be another *by me* construction – does not make this passive sentence vague.[12] Moreover, given this assumption, the sentence with a by-phrase would be an unnecessary statement of the obvious, which contributes to its weakness. This passive example contains an unnecessary relative clause, which makes the sentence wordy compared to *that crisis in my life will never be forgotten*. And if wordiness is a consideration, then *that unforgettable crisis in my life* is of course less wordy than *that crisis in my life will never be forgotten*. But this adjective now implicates the passive voice via the interpretation of the suffix *–able* as 'able to be Ved' – in this case, 'able to be forgotten' – an infinitival passive that is negated by the prefix *un* (thus interpreted 'not able to be forgotten').

Woolley's criticism of the passive as leading to clumsy sentences reiterates the point made in *The King's English* but with a less complex example. The criticism of the truncated passive as a source of vagueness is new to the discussion. The second rule is surely correct: when the agent in a passive construction *should be clearly indicated*, then leaving it out is surely wrong. But whether the agent needs to be clearly indicated in a passive construction depends on the larger discourse in which the passive occurs.

The critique of the passive voice as an occasional source of *bad grammar, false idiom, or clumsiness* is expanded in Henry Fowler's *A Dictionary of Modern English Usage* (Oxford University Press, 1926) under an entry titled *Passive Disturbances*. The entry identifies four problematic passive constructions, beginning with the so-called 'double passive' that was identified twenty years earlier in *The King's English* as the *compound passive* as discussed above. But unlike the discussion in the earlier book, this entry contrasts a deviant example of a double passive (**the order was attempted to be carried out* as derived from *they attempted to carry out the order*) with a legitimate

---

[12] Unless the agent includes other people in addition to *me*; for example, what is meant is that this crisis will not be forgotten by anyone involved.

example of the construction that results when *people believed him to have been murdered* is changed to the double passive *he was believed to have been murdered*. The entry characterizes the deviant example as *clumsiness or worse* and refers the reader to another entry under the heading of "Double Passives", which denounces the deviant constructions – **the point is sought to be evaded*, the example cited – as *monstrosities (which are as repulsive to the grammarian as to the stylist)* and suggests that their source might be a false analogy with *the superficially similar* legitimate double passive, citing *the man was ordered to be shot*.

The second problematic passive construction discussed in Fowler's *Dictionary* concerns the impossibility of a passive variant of *avail oneself of*, for which Fowler cites the deviant **We understand that the credit will be availed of by three months' bills, renewable three times, drawn by the Belgian group on the British syndicate*. However, the example, which contains no corresponding reflexive pronoun, does not justify Fowler's conclusion that it constitutes a problematic use of the passive, but rather shows that there is no English expression *avail of* (as opposed to *avail ourselves of*). Presumably, the active counterpart of this example would be *we understand that we will (can?) avail ourselves of credit for three months' bills* (where *for* replaces the confusing *by*, and the prepositional phrase which modifies *credit* is not separated from the noun it modifies), another factor that contributes to the awkwardness of the example.[13] The alternative is to interpret *three months' bills* as the semantic subject of the verb *availed* and *the credit* thus the object of that verb, which makes no sense at all.

The third problematic passive construction is designated as *active do after passive verb*, a simple formulation which masks the complexity of the example cited, *Inferior defences could then, as now, be tackled, as Vernon did at Porto Bello, Exmouth at Algiers, & Seymour at Alexandria*. The end of the sentence coordinates three reduced clauses, the last two more reduced than the first. This can be demonstrated by rebuilding these coordinated clauses in steps to their corresponding full clauses. Step one reintroduces the verbal element *did* in the last two: *as Vernon did at Porto Bello, Exmouth did at Algiers, & Seymour did at Alexandria*. Step two replaces the verbal element *did* with a complete verb phrase: *as Vernon tackled inferior defenses at Porto Bello, (as) Exmouth tackled inferior defenses at Algiers, & (as) Seymour tackled inferior defenses at Alexandria*. These reduced clauses exemplify ellipsis phenomena, which involve the deletion of phonetic material, to be discussed in detail in Chapter 8.

---

[13] This assumes that *we* in Fowler's example refers to the debtors rather than the creditors. It is also possible to interpret *we* as the creditors. On either interpretation Fowler's example verges on gibberish.

They also involve a more detailed treatment of English auxiliary verbs, including *did* in this example, as will be discussed in Chapter 7.

The fourth problematic construction, which is titled simply as "As.", is illustrated with the passive sentence *the great successes of the Co-operators hitherto have been won as middlemen*, comparing it to the active sentence *the Co-operators have won their successes as middlemen*. Fowler comments: *Conversion to the passive has had the effect of so tying up the co-operators with of that it is not available, as in the active form, for as middlemen to be attached to*. Once again, the active and passive versions are not an exact match. In the active sentence, *the Co-operators* is the subject of the clause and *their successes* is the object of *won* (assuming that *the Co-operators have as middlemen won their successes* is an equivalent paraphrase). But in Fowler's passive version, *the Co-operators* occurs in a prepositional phrase *of the Co-operators* that modifies *successes*, the object of *won* but now shorn of the possessive pronoun *their* and sporting instead the adjective *great* along with the definite article *the*.

Fixing the mismatch requires a decision about what the phrase *as middlemen* modifies in the active sentence. There are two possibilities: either *as middlemen* modifies *successes*, in which case it forms a noun phrase *successes as middlemen*, or it modifies the *won* and merges with the verb phrase *won their successes*. The first results in a passive sentence *their successes as middlemen were won* (*by the Co-operators*), which is syntactically well formed but semantically odd, in part because 'win successes' is essentially redundant given that *success* is a nominalization of *succeed*, which is very close in meaning to *win*. Furthermore, the use of the pronoun *their* at the beginning of the sentence suggests that its antecedent *the Co-operators* is already known – in which case *by the Co-operators* adds no new information. But then *their successes as middlemen were won* is distinctly odd.

In contrast, if *won as middlemen* qualifies how the Co-operators' successes have been achieved, the redundancy of 'win successes' does not arise. In *the Co-operators' successes hitherto have been won as middlemen*, which is the passive sentence that most closely corresponds to the active example cited (*the Co-operators have won their successes as middlemen*), the interpretation of *Co-operators* as *middlemen* does not seem to be blocked – certainly, not in the way claimed for the passive example. And finally, it is worth noting that the subordinate finite clause used in the explanation cited above (*it is not available, as in the active form, for <u>as middlemen</u> to be attached to*) contains an infinitival passive that is demonstrably deviant, worse than the example that discussed in Fowler's *Dictionary*. Under any interpretation where *as middlemen* modifies *won* there will be no direct syntactic attachment (via Merge) with the phrase *the Co-operators*, and thus the connection must be made via some interpretive process that establishes the connection between *Co-operators* and *middlemen.*

What this entry on *passive disturbances* demonstrates is that writers can get into trouble when they use complex syntax.[14] Blaming this on the use of passive voice is no more justified than blaming these examples on use of infinitival subordinate clauses or ellipsis.

None of the books discussed above suggest that the active voice is in general preferable to the passive, a proposal that first appears in the privately published 1918 first version of *The Elements of Style* by William Strunk Jr., who was teaching English composition at Cornell University. Thirteen years after Strunk's death in 1946, a revised version of *The Elements of Style* co-authored by his former student, the writer E.B. White, was published by Macmillan, followed by a paperback edition in 1962. The book has been enormously successful, with a fourth edition in 1999, an edition illustrated by the artist Maira Kalman in 2005, and a 50th anniversary edition in 2009 – according to Roger Angell, E.B. White's stepson, in his 1999 foreword to the 4th edition, this book *has been in print for forty years, and has offered more than 10 million writers a helping hand.*[15] In part II, titled "Elementary Principles of Composition", the third principle reads *Use the active voice.*

The formulation of this principle in *The Elements of Style* is actually vague simply because it does not state when a writer should use the active voice. It seems to be more a way of saying 'avoid the passive voice'. And if not, then when is the active voice to be preferred to the passive? The discussion of the principle cites the following active sentence *I shall always remember my first visit to Boston,* which is claimed to be *much better than* its passive counterpart, *my first visit to Boston will always be remembered by me.* These examples appear to be a conflation of Woolley's pair of examples discussed above, where *my first visit to Boston* replaces *a crisis in my life* and *remember* replaces *forget.* However, unlike Woolley's handbook, *The Elements of Style* does not criticize the example passive sentence as 'awkward' or 'clumsy'. Instead, the

---

[14] For a more contemporary example, consider the following sentence by Arundhati Roy, winner of the 1997 Man Booker Prize for Fiction:

> *Our tragedy today is not just that . . . – it is also that the language of the Left, the discourse of the Left, has been marginalized and is sought to be eradicated.*

> *Things that Can and Cannot Be Said: essays and conversations* by John Cusack and Arundhati Roy (Haymarket Books, 2016), p. 37.

While it is possible to *seek to eradicate* something, that something cannot be said to be *sought to be eradicated.* The double passive here is simply deviant.

[15] Foreword to the 4th edition of *Elements of Style* (Pearson/Longman), in *This Old Man: Roger Angell all in pieces* (Doubleday, 2015), pp. 18–19.

commentary on *Use the active voice* begins with an almost categorical statement, *the active voice is usually more direct and vigorous than the passive*, which the two examples are supposed to illustrate. The adverb *usually* raises the unanswered question of when the passive could be *more direct and vigorous* than the active. This criticism rests on an interpretation of the adjectives *direct* and *vigorous* that is not obvious. If by *direct* the authors mean 'straightforward', then how is a normal passive sentence – perhaps not one that ends awkwardly with *by me* (for example, *the Persians were conquered by Alexander*) – less straightforward than its active counterpart? *The Elements of Style* does not say. The adjective *vigorous* is if anything more problematic. If it is interpreted as a synonym for *active* (as applied to a person), then this criticism is based on a confusion of the technical grammatical terms *active* and *passive* applied to the category of voice with their interpretations as nontechnical common adjectives.

Of the passive sentence *my first visit to Boston will always be remembered by me* (and by extension the passive voice), *The Elements of Style* claims that it is *less direct, less bold, and less concise*. *Less concise* reiterates Woolley's unfounded charge (see above) that passive sentences are wordy. *Less direct* restates the claim that the active voice is *more direct*, but is equally unhelpful. That leaves *less bold*, which leaves us with the problem of explaining how one syntactic construction is 'bolder' than another systematically related syntactic construction. A statement can be judged to be 'bold' in terms of what it says in a particular context, but a bold statement will be 'bold' regardless of whether it is formulated as an active or a passive sentence.

The Elements of Style offers as a further criticism of the passive voice that by allowing the elimination of the *by*-phrase, it leads to *indefinite* sentences. While *my first visit to Boston will always be remembered by me* can be made *more concise by omitting "by me"*, the resulting sentence is "indefinite" because it does not say whether this visit will be remembered by *the writer, or some person undisclosed, or the world at large*. In essence, the criticism reiterates the analysis (and in essence the example) given in Woolley's 1907 handbook.

The following paragraph of *The Elements of Style* begins with a statement that virtually undermines the principle the book is attempting to justify: *This rule does not, of course, mean that the writer should entirely discard the passive voice, which is frequently convenient and sometimes necessary*. As an example, the book compares the passive sentence *the dramatists of the Restoration are little esteemed today* with the active sentence *modern readers have little esteem for the dramatists of the Restoration*, pointing out that in a paragraph about the dramatists of the Restoration, the passive sentence would be preferred to the active sentence, but in a paragraph about the tastes of modern readers, the active sentence is preferable. So the choice between active and passive voice is really a question about focus and context (see below for further discussion). In this particular case, though, the active *have little esteem for* is not actually the grammatical counterpart of the passive *were little esteemed*. The active counterpart would be the somewhat stilted *modern readers little esteem the dramatists of the Restoration*, which compared to its actual passive counterpart *the dramatists of the Restoration are little esteemed by modern readers* (or the synonymous *modern readers have little esteem for the dramatists of the Restoration*, which converts the verb *esteem* into a noun) may actually seem quite stilted.

While *The Elements of Style* appears to be the first book to offer a general criticism of the passive voice, the idea that there is something generally wrong with the passive voice shows up five years later in the revised and enlarged edition of *Sentences and Thinking* by Norman Foerster and J.M. Steadman Jr., originally subtitled *A Practice Book in Sentence Making* in 1919, which changes to *A Handbook of Composition and Revision*. Part of the expansion includes a comment on *weak passive voice*, the title of section 82 in Chapter VII (Emphasis) of Book II (Principles of Revision), which claims: *The passive voice is properly used only when the agent is unknown or unimportant, or when the receiver of the action is more important than the agent.* The example cited, *four hundred men were wounded in the battle*, lacks a *by*-phrase that would identify the agent of the action. Who wounded 400 men in a battle is presumably neither unknown nor unimportant; however, *four hundred men were wounded in the battle by the opposing forces* states the obvious and moreover emphasizes this with the *by*-phrase placed at the end of the sentence – the real reason for preferring the passive if the focus of the paragraph is the victims of the battle and not the armies that fought it. Immediately after the example, this handbook advises *in all other cases avoid the passive voice, for it detracts from the smoothness, interest, and emphasis of the sentence.* The text does not justify the claims about *smoothness* or *interest* with any examples or further discussion. It offers two pairs of sentences, each labeled *unemphatic* versus *better* to illustrate the claim about emphasis. The first, *a delightful time was had by all* versus *all had a delightful time*, is problematic because *have* is not a normal transitive verb, given that the truncated passive *a delightful time was had* is peculiar at best (compare also: *Joan had the book* and **The book was had by Joan*). The second pair, *I was thanked by both of them with a smile* versus *both thanked me with a smile*, is also a poor comparison – first because the active version shortens *both of them* to *both* making the active clearly more concise than the passive, and second because the passive version *by both of them* separates the verb *thanked* from the modifying PP *with a smile*, which is more awkward than *I was thanked with a smile by both of them*. Here again the general denunciation of the passive voice is revealed as unjustified.

Fowler's *Dictionary* does not recommend the use of the active voice over the passive as Strunk's *Elements* and Foerster & Steadman's *Sentences and*

Thinking do, focusing instead on particular syntactic configurations where problematic sentences involve the passive voice. At the other extreme, the conclusion of George Orwell's famous essay "Politics and the English Language" (1946) proposes as a rule for the improvement of written English: *Never use the passive where you can use the active.* The motivation for such rules is expressed in the second paragraph of the essay:

Modern English, especially written English, is full of bad habits which spread by imitation and which can be avoided if one is willing to take the necessary trouble. If one gets rid of these habits one can think more clearly, and to think clearly is a necessary first step toward political regeneration: so that the fight against bad English is not frivolous and is not the exclusive concern of professional writers.

However, the essay never explains how the passive voice, in contrast to the active, leads to unclear thinking.

The only other mention of passive voice occurs in a section titled "Operators or Verbal False Limbs" which complains about the use of phrases instead of 'simple' *verbs*: *The keynote is the elimination of simple verbs.* Of the simple verbs mentioned (*break, stop, spoil, mend, kill*), not one clearly corresponds to the phrases complained about (*render inoperative, militate against, make contact with, be subjected to, give rise to, give grounds for, have the effect of, play a leading part (role) in, make itself felt, take effect, exhibit a tendency to, serve the purpose of*). The closest pairing (*render inoperative* and *break*) are not synonymous; one can render something (a machine for example) inoperative without breaking it temporarily or permanently. In this context, the essay's complaint against the passive voice seems to be that it requires an auxiliary verb *be* in addition to the main verb, thereby presumably replacing a simple verb with a phrase. But this just ignores the displacement property of passives, which is a useful tool in writing.

What the essay actually says in this section is: *In addition, the passive voice is wherever possible used in preference to the active, and noun constructions are used instead of gerunds (<u>by examination</u> of instead of <u>by examining</u>).* That the complaint against the passive voice is itself formulated in the passive voice (*is wherever possible used*) is ironic, most likely unintentional. The passive voice occurs elsewhere in the essay as well, notably in discussing motivation for writing the essay (cited above) where it refers to the bad habits of writers of English *which can be avoided if one is willing to take the necessary trouble.* It also occurs stunningly in the following succession of three sentences (cited below), which Orwell uses to illustrate how *political speech and writing* employ *euphemism, question-begging and sheer cloudy vagueness* because they *are largely the defence of the indefensible* (his examples of the indefensible being *the continuance of British rule in India, the Russian purges and deportations, the dropping of the atom bombs on Japan*):

Defenceless villages are bombarded from the air, the inhabitants driven out into the countryside, the cattle machine-gunned, the huts set on fire with incendiary bullets: this is called <u>pacification</u>. Millions of peasants are robbed of their farms and sent trudging along the roads with no more than they can carry: this is called <u>transfer of population</u> or <u>rectification of frontiers</u>. People are imprisoned for years without trial, or shot in the back of the neck or sent to die of scurvy in Arctic lumber camps: this is called <u>elimination of unreliable elements</u>.

According to linguist Geoffrey Nunberg in a 2009 radio commentary, the passive voice in this passage is *the syntax Orwell turned to when he talked about the victims of history.* And of the passage Nunberg comments: *Nothing limp about <u>that</u>.*[16]

Regrettably, in spite of an arguably total lack of justification (see also Geoffrey Pullum's article "Fear and Loathing of the English Passive"[17]), the passive voice in English continues to be denigrated in commentary on English usage, which offers advice on what constitutes 'good writing'. In the latter half of the twentieth century, a successful handbook for college writers by Frederick Crews, Professor of English at the University of California at Berkeley, *The Random House Handbook* (2nd edition 1977), advises *Rely on the active voice*, echoing *The Elements of Style*. Although this book notes that *a passive construction is sometimes called for*, as it is in this formulation (compared to Strunk & White's *sometimes necessary*), it goes on to claim that *the habitual use of the passive* results in *a colorless, evasive, and sometimes ambiguous impression, and it disguises the relation between the doer and the thing done*. Here again, as usual, the claim is without merit. As for *habitual use of the passive*, this is refuted by the Orwell passage cited above. As a justification of this criticism of the passive voice, the book cites three active/passive sentence pairs:

(w)   1. *It is believed by the candidate that a ceiling must be placed on the budget by Congress.*
       2. *The candidate believes that Congress must place a ceiling on the budget.*

(x)   1. *The consequences of thermonuclear war could not be escaped by any country in the world.*
       2. *No country in the world could escape the consequences of thermonuclear war.*

(y)   1. *Their motives were applauded by us, but their wisdom was doubted.*
       2. *We applauded their motives but doubted their wisdom.*

It offers no discussion of how these passive sentences compared to their active counterparts create *a colorless, evasive, and sometimes ambiguous impression* or how the passive version *disguises the relation between the doer and the thing done*, which may be a new addition to the list of the purported failings of

---

[16] "Our Friend the Passive Voice" (http://people.ischool.berkeley.edu/~nunberg/passive.html)
[17] *Language & Communication*, 37 (2014), 60–74.

the passive voice. Instead it claims that *in each instance the active construction is more vivid and succinct* (again echoing *The Elements of Style*), and further that the *by*-phrases in the passive constructions in (x) and (y) *occupy more or less clumsy positions*, generalizing to all *by*-phrases the criticism that originates in Woolley's 1907 handbook, but without justifying this.

However, it is far from clear that these pairs actually demonstrate what *The Random House Handbook* is claiming. Given that *budget* in the sentences in (w) refers to the federal budget, which Congress sets, then *by Congress* is simply redundant and therefore the passive version ought to be revised as *it is believed by the candidate that a ceiling must be placed on the federal budget*. Furthermore, the subordinate clause in (w.1) could occur as the subject of the main clause (*that a ceiling must be placed on the federal budget is believed by the candidate*). Which version is preferable ultimately depends on the discourse context in which these examples occur. The wordiness of *no country in the world* aside (*no country* suffices), the problem with the passive variant (x.1) is that *escape the consequences of X* is more a fixed phrase than a regular transitive verb that takes a noun phrase object. There seems to be no context in which the passive participle *escaped* is even marginal. Consider for example the putative passive **the consequences of its massive deficit cannot be escaped by America*, compared to *America cannot escape the consequences of its massive deficit*.[18] So (x) is just another example that does not demonstrate an inherent weakness of the passive voice. And so too with (y). The passive sentence (y.1) coordinates two clauses, which are punctuated with a comma after the first conjunct. In contrast, the active sentence (y.2) coordinates two verb phrases, where *we* is the subject of both *applauded* and *doubted*. Because there is no way to convert the single clause (y.2) into a passive sentence that is also a single clause, the two sentences in (y) do not constitute a legitimate active/passive pair. On top of this, the passive sentence (y.1) illustrates both of Woolley's criticisms of the misuse of the passive voice: the first conjunct contains a *by*-phrase with a first person pronoun (*us*) and the second conjunct contains no *by*-phrase – and therefore is a weak example if the identity of the agent is crucial information that should have been stated. A better comparison for (y) would be (z).

(z)   1. *Their motives were applauded, but their wisdom was doubted.*
         2. *We applauded their motives but doubted their wisdom.*

Adding *by us* to one or both clauses in (z.1) detracts from the concision of the statement and would probably be unnecessary given the context in which it is written. Whether (z.1) or (z.2) is preferable depends ultimately on the

---

[18] The title of a 2012 article in *Business Insider* (www.businessinsider.com/america-can-not-escape-the-consequences-of-its-massive-deficit-2012-9).

paragraph in which the sentence occurs. If the paragraph is about us, what we did and what we think about their motives and wisdom, then (z.2) is preferable, but if the paragraph is about their motives and wisdom, then (z.1) is.

In the final decade of the twentieth century, Strunk & White's general criticism of the passive voice shows up again in Joseph M. Williams's excellent *Style: Towards Clarity and Grace* (1991). He writes in chapter 2, titled "Clarity": *We can usually make our style more vigorous and direct if we avoid both nominalizations and unnecessary passive verbs* (p. 36), echoing also Orwell's essay in linking passives with nominalizations.

To illustrate, Williams offers the following comparison, where the passive voice is highlighted in boldface:

*A new approach to toxic waste management **detailed** in a chemical industry plan **will be submitted**. A method of decomposing toxic by-products of refinery processes **has been discovered** by Genco Chemical.*

versus a revision which replaces the three instances of passive voice with the active voice:

*The chemical industry **will submit** a plan that **details** a new way to manage toxic waste. Genco Chemical **has discovered** a way to decompose toxic products of refinery processes.*

However, the problem with the first passive sentence of the first version is that it says literally that *a new approach* will be submitted, where clearly it is *a chemical industry plan* that is being submitted as the revision states. Although *a chemical industry plan* precedes the predicate phrase *will be submitted*, it cannot be interpreted as the syntactic subject of this predicate phrase because it functions syntactically as the object of the preposition *in* inside a reduced relative clause (~~which is~~ *detailed in a chemical industry plan*) that modifies *approach*. Passive voice is not the problem with this sentence, which could be revised maintaining the passive voice: *A new approach to toxic waste management **is detailed** in a chemical industry plan **to be submitted***. This revision raises the question of what the writer intends to focus on as the main action, detailing the new approach as expressed in this revision or submitting a plan based on it as expressed in the revision by Williams.

The other problem with both of Williams's versions is that the second sentence shifts the focus from the submission of a chemical industry plan to Genco Chemical's discovery. In addition, there are the repetitions of *way* and *toxic* in the second sentence, which are unnecessary if the two sentences are combined into a single sentence, as shown in (aa).

(aa)   The chemical industry **will submit** a detailed plan for **managing** toxic waste **based** on Genco Chemical's new method of **decomposing** the by-products of refinery processes.

The revision in (aa) replaces the noun *way* with the more precise noun *method*. The adjective *detailed* replaces the verb *details*, eliminating the relative clause. The gerunds *managing* and *decomposing* replace their infinitival forms *to manage* and *to decompose*. This revision reformulates the second independent sentence in Williams's two formulations as a reduced relative clause (~~which is~~ based on *Genco Chemical's new method of decomposing the by-products of refinery processes*) modifying *plan* in the first sentence. Note that the main verb of that relative clause *based* is the passive participle and that it would be awkward at best to change it into an active main verb.

The general criticism of the passive voice, which begins with *The Elements of Style* at the beginning of the twentieth century, has survived into the twenty-first. Most recently, Steven Pinker's *The Sense of Style* (2014) lists *unnecessary passives* (a term that originates in Williams's book on style discussed above) as one of ten bad habits (including clichés and mixed metaphors) that result in *soggy prose*. It identifies the *overuse* of passives as a feature of *excessive abstraction*, and refers to the *enervating use of passives*. Such criticisms buy into the view that there is something wrong with the passive voice. Yet this view conflicts with some of the book's other comments about the passive voice, which it calls *unfairly maligned* (chapter 4). In chapter 1 it states that *telling writers to avoid the passive voice is bad advice* and claims that *linguistic research has shown that the passive construction has a number of indispensable functions because of the way it engages a reader's attention and memory*, functions that are discussed in chapter 4. This conflict shows clearly how ingrained the antipathy toward the passive voice remains.

5.5.2 *The role of displacement in discourse*

In spite of the persistent criticism of the passive voice, its utility has long been understood, even by the critics. Strunk & White make this clear when they say in commenting on their sentences about Restoration dramatists (see **p. xx** above) *the need of making a particular word the subject of the sentence will often, as in these examples, determine which voice is to be used*. Cleanth Brooks and Robert Penn Warren (*Modern Rhetoric*, 2nd edition 1958) say that the choice between active and passive voice *usually turns upon the matter of what constitutes proper emphasis* because as they note *we can state the basic facts by means of either construction* (p. 756). For Joseph Williams, this choice depends on the answers to three questions, the first being *must our audience know who is performing the action?*. If not, then the passive voice removes the necessity of identifying the agent of the action. The second concerns whether the writer is *maintaining a logically consistent string of subjects* – which ensures the cohesion of a group of connected sentences in a text. A consistent topic (subject) string *focuses attention on a circumscribed set of* [related – RF] *concepts.* The third question for Williams is whether the consistent topic string is the right one – which goes beyond questions of sentence structure.

How these concepts apply can be seen more clearly if we examine a concrete example like Chomsky's paragraph about linguistics as the scientific study of language cited in Chapter 3 and repeated below (with passive predicates in boldface[19]).

*For about 30 years, the study of language – or more accurately, one substantial component of it – **has been conducted** within a framework that understands linguistics to be a part of psychology, ultimately human biology. This approach attempts to reintroduce into the study of language several concerns that have been central to Western thought for thousands of years, and that have deep roots in other traditions as well: questions about the nature and origin of knowledge in particular. This approach has also been concerned to assimilate the study of language into the main body of the natural sciences. This meant, in the first place, abandoning dogmas that are entirely foreign to the natural sciences and that have no place in rational inquiry, the dogmas of the several varieties of behaviorism, for example, which seek to impose a priori limits on possible theory construction, a conception that would properly **be dismissed** as entirely irrational in the natural sciences. It means a frank adherence to mentalism, where we can understand talk about the mind to be talk about the brain at an abstract level at which, so we try to demonstrate, principles **can be formulated** that enter into successful and insightful explanation of linguistic (and other) phenomena that **are provided by observation and experiment**. Mentalism, in this sense, has no taint of mysticism and carries no dubious ontological burden. Rather, mentalism falls strictly within the standard practice of the natural sciences and in fact, is nothing other than the approach of the natural sciences applied to this particular domain. This conclusion, which is the opposite of what **is often assumed**, becomes understandable and clear if we consider specific topics in the natural sciences: for example, 19th century chemistry, which sought to explain phenomena in terms of such abstract notions as elements, the periodic table, valence, benzene rings, and so on – that is, in terms of abstract properties of then unknown, perhaps still unknown physical mechanisms. This abstract inquiry served as an essential preliminary and guide for the subsequent inquiry into physical mechanisms. Mentalistic inquiry in the brain sciences is quite similar in approach and character to the abstract inquiry into properties of the chemical elements, and we may expect that this abstract inquiry too will serve as an essential preliminary and guide for the emerging brain sciences today; the logic is quite similar.*

This paragraph, which consists of 10 sentences, has the following topic string: {*the study of language, this approach* (to the study of language), *this approach, this, it, mentalism, mentalism, this conclusion* (that mentalism falls strictly within the standard practice of the natural sciences etc.), *this abstract inquiry, mentalistic inquiry*}. The interpretation of both *this* and *it* as referring

---

[19] Although the third sentence contains what looks like a passive (*has also been concerned*), there is no clear active counterpart.

to the assimilation of *the study of language into the main body of the natural sciences* reveals the coherence of the topic string, which connects the study of language to abstract inquiry in the natural sciences via mentalism.

The main clause of the first sentence of the paragraph is in the passive voice and further does not identify an agent in a *by*-phrase. Therefore, the first sentence could have identified who has conducted the study of language within this framework either with a *by*-phrase (*by researchers* or some more specific noun like *linguists* or *linguists and psychologists*, or *linguists, psychologists, and philosophers*, etc.) or by converting the passive voice into the active – yielding: *For about 30 years, researchers have conducted the study of language – or more accurately, one substantial component of it – within a framework that understands linguistics to be a part of psychology, ultimately human biology*. The revised active sentence makes *researchers* the subject/topic of the sentence, which undermines the coherence of the topic string of the paragraph. Adding a *by-phrase* raises the question of where it should be placed because there are two options. For one, the *by*-phrase can be inserted between *conducted* and the prepositional phrase headed by *within*. Thus *conducted by researchers* would be a verb phrase which merges with the *within* phrase to yield the sentence: *For about 30 years, the study of language – or more accurately, one substantial component of it – has been conducted **by researchers** within a framework that understands linguistics to be a part of psychology, ultimately human biology*. The alternative is to merge the *by*-phrase with the verb phrase *has been conducted within a framework that understands linguistics to be a part of psychology, ultimately human biology*, yielding the sentence: *For about 30 years, the study of language – or more accurately, one substantial component of it – has been conducted within a framework that understands linguistics to be a part of psychology, ultimately human biology, **by researchers***.

Of the three alternatives, the third is distinctly worse than the other two because the end of a sentence is, in terms of discourse, a position of special emphasis. In general, the subject of a sentence announces the topic that the sentence is about and the predicate provides new information about the that topic. Once the topic has been established in a paragraph, it becomes old information and thus each sentence in a paragraph can be divided into two parts, old information + new information, whose greater importance is being stressed at the end of the sentence. Placing *by researchers* at the end of the sentence stresses the phrase as containing the most important new information in the sentence, which of course it doesn't. The same unwanted emphasis results when the prepositional phrase *for about 30 years*, which begins Chomsky's sentence, is located at the end, yielding: *The study of language – or more accurately, one substantial component of it – has been conducted within a framework that understands linguistics to be a part of psychology, ultimately human biology, for about 30 years*. Like the *by*-phrase, the prepositional phrase *for about 30 years* could also be located inside the verb phrase headed by *conducted*. Thus the verb phrase could contain three prepositional phrases, PP_{within}, PP_{for}, and PP_{by}. And depending on which phrase is merged first and which last, there will be six different hierarchical structures, which will correspond to six different linear orders for the three prepositional phrases and thus six distinct sentences. The issue of stress on the information that comes as the end of a sentence aside, none of the alternatives with *by researchers* preferable to Chomsky's original simply because this *by*-phrase adds almost nothing to our understanding of the sentence without it. Note also that it is possible to switch the positions of PP_{within} and PP_{for}, yielding a rather dreadful sentence in terms of discourse properties: *Within a framework that understands linguistics to be a part of psychology, ultimately human biology, the study of language – or more accurately, one substantial component of it, has been conducted for about 30 years*. And while the sentence improves if PP_{within} is placed as a modifier of *the study of language*, as in *the study of language within a framework that understands linguistics to be a part of psychology, ultimately human biology – or more accurately, one substantial component of it – has been conducted for about 30 years*, the result is still a poor sentence in terms of discourse properties – because the revised sentence emphasizes *has been conducted for 30 years*, which is subsidiary to the main point of the sentence. Nonetheless, all of these alternatives to Chomsky's sentence are equally legitimate and viable sentences of English, but distinctly less preferable in terms of discourse and, more specifically, the context of Chomsky's paragraph.

A similar demonstration is possible for each of the other sentences in Chomsky's paragraph, which is left for the reader to experiment with. Examples of how the paragraph could be revised in ways that makes it worse writing are discussed in Section 5.6.1.

At this point, it should be clear that the utility of displacement – to a large extent – concerns discourse properties of sentences involving the organization of information (old vs. new, relative importance and stress) within a single sentence and especially in the context of other sentences, including the structure of the paragraph, which is discussed in the next section.

5.6   The structure of paragraphs

In addition to the way sentences in a paragraph cohere in terms of conceptually related topics, there is also the question of how the paragraph itself is structured. Consider the following wonderfully concise and perfectly structured paragraph from John Mortimer's *Rumpole Rests His Case* (Viking, 2002):

In the varied ups and downs, the thrills and spills in the life of an Old Bailey hack, one thing stands as stone. Your ex-customers will never want to see you again. Even if you've seen them through the rocks of the prosecution case and brought them out to the calm waters of a not-guilty verdict, they won't plan further meetings, host reunion dinners or even send you a card on your birthday. If they catch a glimpse of you on the Underground, or across a crowded wine bar, they will bury their faces in their newspapers or look studiously in the opposite direction.

In this four-sentence paragraph, one sentence stands out: *your ex-customers will never want to see you again.* This sentence is the main point that the paragraph is making, the other sentences are distinctly subsidiary. The last two sentences constitute a discussion of this point, illustrating it with concrete examples. The first sentence introduces what the paragraph is about.

This structural analysis, which is discussed in more detail in Joseph Williams's *Style: Towards Clarity and Grace*, divides a paragraph into two major parts, the sentences which introduce the topic the paragraph is about, followed by those sentences which expand on the topic identified – what Williams calls *the issue* and *the discussion*. The one sentence that is the main point of the paragraph, which Williams unsurprisingly calls *the point*, is usually (but not necessarily always) located at the end of the issue (as in the Mortimer paragraph) or at the end of the discussion.

We can represent this analysis of paragraphs more graphically with colors in the following manner, where the point is also rendered in boldface small caps:

*In the varied ups and downs, the thrills and spills in the life of an Old Bailey hack, one thing stands as stone. **YOUR EX-CUSTOMERS WILL NEVER WANT TO SEE YOU AGAIN.** Even if you've seen them through the rocks of the prosecution case and brought them out to the calm waters of a not-guilty verdict, they won't plan further meetings, host reunion dinners or even send you a card on your birthday. If they catch a glimpse of you on the Underground, or across a crowded wine bar, they will bury their faces in their newspapers or look studiously in the opposite direction.*

The issue is marked in blue, the discussion in green. The Chomsky paragraph, which is significantly more complex, has exactly the same structure:

*For about 30 years, the study of language – or more accurately, one substantial component of it – has been conducted within a framework that understands linguistics to be a part of psychology, ultimately human biology. This approach attempts to reintroduce into the study of language several concerns that have been central to Western thought for thousands of years, and that have deep roots in other traditions as well: questions about the nature and origin of knowledge in particular. **THIS APPROACH HAS ALSO BEEN CONCERNED TO ASSIMILATE THE STUDY OF LANGUAGE INTO THE MAIN BODY OF THE NATURAL SCIENCES.** This meant, in the first place, abandoning dogmas that are entirely foreign to the natural sciences and that have no place in rational inquiry, the dogmas of the several varieties of behaviorism, for example, which seek to impose a priori limits on possible theory construction, a conception that would properly be dismissed as entirely irrational in the natural sciences. It means a frank adherence to mentalism, where we can understand* *talk about the mind to be talk about the brain at an abstract level at which, so we try to demonstrate, principles can be formulated that enter into successful and insightful explanation of linguistic (and other) phenomena that are provided by observation and experiment. Mentalism, in this sense, has no taint of mysticism and carries no dubious ontological burden. Rather, mentalism falls strictly within the standard practice of the natural sciences and in fact, is nothing other than the approach of the natural sciences applied to this particular domain. This conclusion, which is the opposite of what is often assumed, becomes understandable and clear if we consider specific topics in the natural sciences: for example, 19th century chemistry, which sought to explain phenomena in terms of such abstract notions as elements, the periodic table, valence, benzene rings, and so on – that is, in terms of abstract properties of then unknown, perhaps still unknown physical mechanisms. This abstract inquiry served as an essential preliminary and guide for the subsequent inquiry into physical mechanisms. Mentalistic inquiry in the brain sciences is quite similar in approach and character to the abstract inquiry into properties of the chemical elements, and we may expect that this abstract inquiry too will serve as an essential preliminary and guide for the emerging brain sciences today; the logic is quite similar.*

The first three sentences are about the study of language, with the third introducing the point of the paragraph, the assimilation of the study of language *into the main body of the natural sciences*. Although the *also* in this sentence implicates the previous sentence, the sentences that follow are a discussion of what the point means and how it works.

As an example of a paragraph where the point occurs at the end of the discussion, consider the following from Oliver Sachs's chapter on "Brainworms, Sticky Music, and Catchy Tunes" in *Musicophilia* (Alfred A. Knopf, 2007):

Brainworms are usually stereotyped and invariant in character. They tend to have a certain life expectancy, going full blast for hours or days and then dying away, apart from occasional afterspurts. But even when they have apparently faded, they tend to lie in wait; a heightened sensitivity remains, so that a noise, an association, a reference to them is apt to set them off again, sometimes years later. And they are nearly always fragmentary. **THESE ARE THE QUALITIES THAT EPILEPTOLOGISTS MIGHT FIND FAMILIAR, FOR THEY ARE STRONGLY REMINISCENT OF THE BEHAVIOR OF A SMALL, SUDDEN-ONSET FOCUS, ERUPTING AND CONVULSING, THEN SUBSIDING, BUT ALWAYS READY TO IGNITE.**

The first sentence of the paragraph introduces the topic to be discussed, *brainworms*. The following two sentences describe their character and the final sentence, which is the point of the paragraph, relates the properties mentioned in the previous two to what is observed in epilepsy.

This structural analysis should not be considered as a straitjacket into which all paragraphs must fit. It is not a prescription but rather a suggestion for organizing sentences into paragraphs. It provides a useful point of reference for evaluating and appreciating how you and other writers deal with the creation of paragraphs. Unlike sentence structure, where we automatically and unconsciously distinguish what is grammatical from what is deviant, the evaluation of paragraph structure, which requires a conscious effort, does not yield a corresponding grammatical vs. deviant distinction.

5.6.1 *Making paragraphs worse*

One way to understand what makes a paragraph strong and effective is to compare it to a version which is demonstrably worse. Rewriting a strong paragraph to make it worse is easy to do, much easier than rewriting a weak paragraph to make it stronger. And the exercise can (perhaps paradoxically) provide you with an understanding of paragraphs that you can use to improve your own.

What follows are two alternative versions of the Chomsky paragraph analyzed in Section 5.6 and discussed in Chapter 3 – both of them significantly worse than Chomsky's original. There are several interesting questions that can be asked about these two revisions: (1) can one revision be argued to be worse in some well-defined sense than the other? (2) in what ways are these revised paragraphs 'worse' than the original? and (3) how well do the revisions, sentence by sentence, retain (and restate) the information contained in the original?

Words in boldface have been repositioned in the sentence and words that are underlined have been changed from the original.

Alternative 1:

*__Researchers have conducted__ the study of language – or more accurately, one substantial component of it – within a framework that understands linguistics to be a part of psychology, ultimately human biology, **for about 30 years**. This approach attempts to reintroduce several concerns **into the study of language** that **for thousands of years** have been central to Western thought, and that have **as well** deep roots in other traditions: questions about the nature and origin of knowledge in particular. **To assimilate the study of language into the main body of the natural sciences __has been the concern of__** this approach. **In the first place, __what__** this meant __was__ abandoning dogmas, **the dogmas of the several varieties of behaviorism, for example, which seek to impose a priori limits on possible theory construction, a conception that __scientists__ would properly __dismiss__** as entirely irrational in the natural sciences, that __have no place in rational inquiry__ and **that are entirely foreign to the natural sciences**. It means a frank adherence to mentalism, where we can understand talk about the mind to be talk about the brain at an abstract level at which, so we try to demonstrate, __we can formulate__ **principles** that enter into successful and insightful explanation of linguistic (and other) phenomena that **observation and experiment __provide__**. Mentalism **carries no dubious ontological burden, __having__** no taint of mysticism **in this sense**. Rather, mentalism falls strictly within the standard practice of the natural sciences and in fact, **is nothing other than the approach of the natural sciences applied to this particular domain**. This conclusion, which is the opposite of what __we__ often __assume__, becomes understandable and clear if we consider specific topics in the natural sciences: for* *example, 19th century chemistry, which sought to explain phenomena **in terms of abstract properties of then unknown, perhaps still unknown physical mechanisms – that is in terms of such abstract notions as elements, the periodic table, valence, benzene rings, and so on.** This abstract inquiry **into physical mechanisms** served as an essential preliminary and guide for the subsequent inquiry. **In approach and character to the abstract inquiry into properties of the chemical elements,** mentalistic inquiry in the brain sciences is quite similar, and that this abstract inquiry too will serve as an essential preliminary and guide for the emerging brain sciences today **may be expected by us**; the logic is quite similar.*

Alternative 2:

*The framework that understands linguistics to be a part of psychology, ultimately human biology, has been around **for about 30 years. Questions about the nature and origin of knowledge [in particular]**, which have been central to Western thought for thousands of years and [that] have deep roots in other traditions as well, were reintroduced into the study of language by **this approach. Assimilating the study of language to the main body of natural science** has also been a concern of **this approach. Abandoning dogmas that are entirely foreign to the natural sciences and that have no place in rational inquiry, the dogmas of several varieties of behaviorism, for example, which seek to impose a priori limits on possible theory construction, a conception that would properly be dismissed as entirely irrational in the natural sciences** is what **this means. A frank adherence to mentalism, where we understand talk about the mind to be talk about the brain at an abstract level at which, so we try to demonstrate, principles can be formulated that enter into successful and insightful explanation of linguistic (and other) phenomena that are provided by observation and experiment** is what **this** also **means. There is no taint of mysticism or dubious ontological burden for **mentalism in this sense. Being nothing other than the approach of the natural sciences applied to this particular domain,** mentalism falls strictly within the standard practice of the natural sciences. **If we consider specific topics in the natural sciences: for example, 19th century chemistry, which sought to explain phenomena in terms of such abstract notions as elements, the periodic table, valence, benzene rings, and so on – that is, in terms of abstract properties of then-unknown, perhaps still unknown physical mechanisms,** this conclusion, which is the opposite of what is often assumed, becomes understandable and clear. **The subsequent inquiry into physical mechanisms [served]** had, **as a guide** and **essential preliminary,** this abstract inquiry. **The abstract inquiry into the properties of the chemical elements** is quite similar in approach and character to **mentalistic inquiry in the brain sciences,** and we may expect that **the emerging brain sciences today** will also be served by **this abstract inquiry as an essential preliminary and guide; **quite similar** is **the logic.*

One important point of comparison would be the coherence of the topic strings of the three paragraphs. Another would be the formulation of the sentence that constitutes the point of the paragraph, assuming that point remains the corresponding sentence in the two alternative versions. And then it would be informative to compare each of the other nine sentences in the alternatives to those in the original paragraph.

Compare, for example, the first sentence in the original (O) and the two alternatives (A-1 and A-2):

(O)   *For about 30 years, the study of language – or more accurately, one substantial component of it – has been conducted within a framework that understands linguistics to be a part of psychology, ultimately human biology.*

(A-1)   ***Researchers have conducted*** *the study of language – or more accurately, one substantial component of it – within a framework that understands linguistics to be a part of psychology, ultimately human biology,* ***for about 30 years***.

(A-2)   *The framework that understands linguistics to be a part of psychology, ultimately human biology, has been around* ***for about 30 years***.

In contrast to the original sentence, both alternative sentences end with the prepositional phrase *for about 30 years*, thus emphasizing this duration as important information – which of course it isn't in the context of the sentence. (A-2) turns this prepositional phrase into a verb phrase *has been around for 30 years*, making this the predicate of the main clause of the sentence, which emphasizes *for 30 years* even more than (A-1) and contains the unnecessary words *has been around*. In contrast, the original highlights the infinitival subordinate clause concluding the sentence, which identifies *linguistics* as *a part of psychology, ultimately human biology* as the the most important piece of information in the sentence. The subject of main clause in (O) is *the study of language*, whereas in (A-1) it is *researchers* (forced by converting the passive *has been conducted* to the active *have conducted*), which could have been included in a *by*-phrase in (O) but isn't because *researchers* is implied and need not be specified. In (A-2) the subject of the sentence is *the framework that understands linguistics to be a part of psychology, ultimately human biology*, which stuffs all the significant information into the main clause subject, leaving the predicate to fall flat. (A-2) leaves out *the study of language*, which is identified as the general (and thus broader) topic in (O) (and in (A-1)), a topic with long intellectual history going back centuries before the advent of modern linguistics. Placing *for 30 years* at the beginning of (O) puts the information in the rest of the sentence in its historical context, whereas placing this prepositional phrase at the end of the sentence emphasizes the context, which is certainly less important than the framework that links *linguistics* to *psychology* and *human biology*.

In light of this commentary on the first sentence in (O), (A-1), and (A-2), it seems safe to conclude that (A-2) is significantly worse than (A-1), which is significantly worse than (O). The reasons in this comparison mostly involve the exclusion of crucial information (where (A-2) drops *the study of language*) and the misplacement of important (new) information in the middle of the sentence where it receives no natural emphasis. In this regard, note that (A-1) improves significantly when *for 30 years* is moved to the beginning of the sentence, as in the original.

Coda

This chapter has been devoted to an extended discussion of the phenomenon of displacement, which was first introduced in the previous chapter as part of the discussion of the syntax of relative clauses. The phenomenon of displacement concerns a single syntactic unit that is pronounced in one syntactic context, but interpreted as occupying a different one. Displacement is thus a phenomenon where a single syntactic entity occurs in more than one syntactic context, a context being defined as the sister of a syntactic unit. It involves one context for pronunciation and a different one for interpretation. This is illustrated in the chapter title, where the context of pronunciation is a syntactic subject position (the sister of a T phrase consisting of a T *is* and a predicate adjective phrase *certain to succeed*), while the context of interpretation is the covert syntactic subject position of the infinitival clause (the sister of a T phrase consisting of infinitival T *to* and the verb *succeed*).

This particular context of pronunciation (a syntactic subject) can also host a finite clause, as illustrated with certain predicate adjectives (like *certain* in the chapter title). When *certain* merges with a finite clause, it is possible, but not necessary, for that finite clause to be pronounced as the syntactic subject of a predicate phrase whose predicating element is *certain*, yielding such examples as *that Bob will succeed is certain*. This displacement, involving two contexts solely within a single clause, is intra-clausal. When *certain* merges with an infinitival clause, it is necessary that the syntactic subject of that clause be pronounced as the syntactic subject of the predicate phrase whose predicating element is also *certain*. This displacement, involving one context within a subordinate clause and another in the clause containing the subordinate clause, is inter-clausal.

Both displacement possibilities for *certain* – with noun phrases and finite clauses – also occur with certain verbs in passive voice. Intra-clausal displacement with a finite clause is possible but not necessary: *that Bob had succeeded was reported*, where the context of interpretation for the subordinate clause is main clause verb phrase. Inter-clausal displacement with the noun phrase subject of an infinitival subordinate clause is necessary: *Bob was reported to have succeeded*, where the context of interpretation would be the syntactic subject of the subordinate clause.

Inter-clausal displacement with finite clauses is also possible (but not necessary) for the subject of the verbs *seem* and *appear* – for example, *that Bob will succeed seems to be likely*. In this case the context of interpretation is the predicate adjective *likely*, where the finite clause merges with the adjective as part of the predicate of the subordinate infinitival clause. Neither verb allows simple intra-clausal displacement with a finite clause, so while *it seems* *that Bob will succeed* is perfectly acceptable English, **that Bob will succeed seems* is definitely not.

In clauses, the most ordinary examples of displacement phenomena are intra-clausal involving a single noun phrase, the passive construction. In simple passive clauses, the context of pronunciation for the noun phrase is the syntactic subject of the clause, while the context of interpretation is as the object of the main verb. And although this verb is pronounced as the passive participle, the syntactic subject of this clause is interpreted in the same way that the syntactic object of the corresponding active verb would be.

Single finite clauses can also be collapsed into a noun phrase, where the verb of the clause transforms into a noun that functions as the head of the entire noun phrase. There are two forms of nominal transformation that verbs can undergo, both involving attaching a nominal affix to a verbal root. One is both limited in the number of verbs it can affect and idiosyncratic in the correspondence between the meaning of the noun in relation to its verbal root (for example, *indict* becoming *indictment*). The other applies generally to most verbs that do not construct with subordinate clauses. The interpretation of this nominal form with respect to its corresponding verbal root generally names the action that corresponds to the verb (example, *indict* becoming *indicting*). The latter forms are called gerunds, while the former are derived nominals.

Shrinking a single finite clause into a noun phrase also applies to passive constructions, so that noun phrases too can manifest displacement. With derived nominals this occurs with such examples as *the banker's indictment by the grand jury*. With gerunds, the passive auxiliary in the corresponding clause is transformed and the passive verb remains the passive participle in the nominal: *the banker's being indicted by the grand jury*.

Generally, the subject of a sentence announces the topic that the sentence is about, while the predicate makes a comment on that topic. From this perspective displacement provides a useful tool for structuring what functions as a topic in a sentence, and the passive construction is simply one part of this tool.

However, from the beginning of the twentieth century and continuing to the present, the passive construction has been a subject of criticism, claimed to be a source of bad writing (or bad style) and proscribed in part (or completely, in the case of George Orwell). This chapter investigated various criticisms of the use of the passive (from 1906, when they apparently began, to the present century) by carefully considering the syntax of the various examples of problematic passive constructions these critics offer. In every case, it is demonstrated how the example in question is problematic for other reasons that have nothing to do with passive voice.

Displacement is also a useful tool for establishing coherence between sentences in a text, where sentences that share the same or related subjects fit together easily while those with very different subjects will seem disconnected. In this way, displacement can contribute to the coherence of paragraphs, the functional unit of written texts.

The chapter concludes with a preliminary discussion of a general analysis of paragraph structure, where coherent paragraphs can usually be divided into two parts: an issue, which introduces what the paragraph is about, and a discussion, which comments on the issue. Normally, a coherent paragraph will contain one sentence that contains the most important information, the point – organized at the end of the issue or the end of the discussion. This analysis is applied to several examples, including the paragraph by Chomsky that was first discussed in Chapter 3. The perspective on both displacement and paragraph structure developed in this chapter is used to assess the problems that occur in two revisions of Chomsky's paragraph constructed to make it worse.

6   *It is a truth universally acknowledged, that a single man in possession of a good fortune must be in want of a wife.*

The title of this chapter is the sentence that begins Jane Austen's masterpiece *Pride and Prejudice*, one of the great novels in English literature.[1] This complex sentence contains a subordinate clause *that a single man in possession of a good fortune must be in want of a wife* located at the end of sentence and separated from the rest of the sentence with a comma. The main clause consists of a syntactic subject *it* (more about this below), followed by a predicate *is a truth universally acknowledged* consisting of the finite copula *is* and a predicating noun phrase *a truth universally acknowledged*, where the phrase *universally acknowledged* modifies the noun *truth* and the adverb *universally* modifies *acknowledged*. The portion of the sentence before the comma has the following syntactic structure:

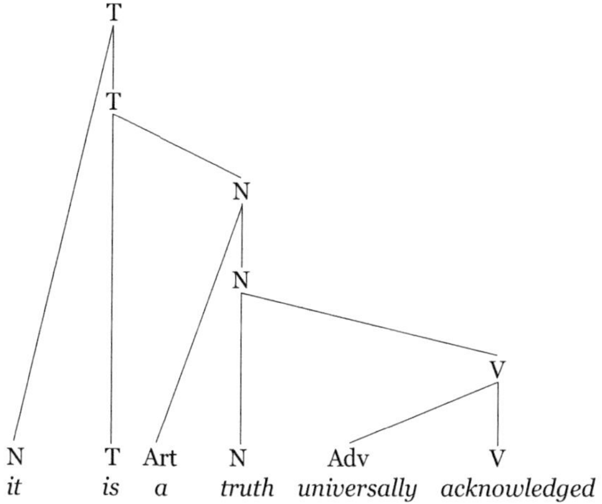

[1] We are indebted to John Logan for suggesting that I take a look at this sentence.

If *universally acknowledged* is the phonetic reduction of the relative clause *which is universally acknowledged*, then *acknowledged* is actually a passive participle in which case the structure involves displacement with a silent relative pronoun, as discussed in Chapter 4.

The subordinate finite clause that concludes the sentence consists of a subordinating particle *that* followed by a T phrase with the following syntactic structure:

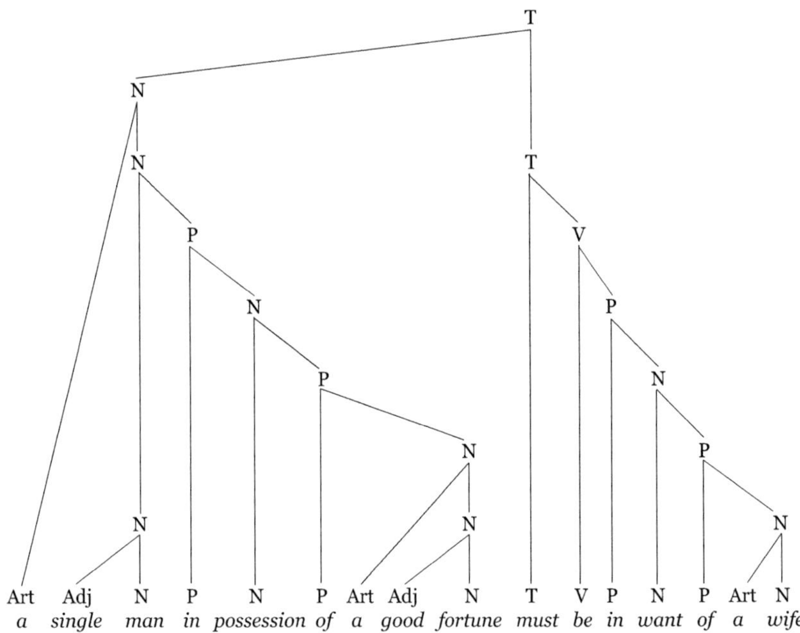

The predicate of this clause *must be in want of a wife* contains the noun *want*, which looks like a nominalization of the verb *want*.[2] The preposition *of* is the familiar semantically empty form that separates a derived nominal and its object, thus a verb phrase *wants a wife* becomes the noun phrase *want of a wife*, which is itself the object of the preposition *in*. The subject of the clause also contains a derived nominal *possession*, related to the verb *possess*, so that the verb phrase *possesses a good fortune* becomes the noun phrase *possession of a good fortune*, which is itself the object of the preposition *in*. These parallel prepositional phrases create a syntactic symmetry between the subject and the

---

[2] Whether this particular usage is the nominalization of the verb turns out to be an interesting issue. See below for discussion.

predicate of the clause, balancing each other in describing the *single man*, who the clause is about.

What remains to be determined is the syntactic connection between these structures, the main clause and the subordinate clause it contains. One clue to the syntactic structure of Austen's sentence is the comma that separates them, which indicates that the subordinate clause should not be construed as a constituent part of the predicate noun phrase *a truth universally acknowledged*.[3] If so, then the subordinate clause connects to the main clause interpretively as the antecedent of *it*. Thus *it* is designated *a truth universally acknowledged*, and so is its antecedent, the subordinate clause. If the subordinate clause replaces the pronoun (yielding *that a single man in possession of a good fortune must be in want of a wife is a truth universally acknowledged*), then *a truth universally acknowledged* describes the subordinate clause directly.

At this point, we have the tools to begin to understand the artistry of Austen's sentence. One way to gain such an understanding is to consider the other ways Austen could have formulated this sentence and to compare these to her original.

6.1   The artistry of sentence structure: an interlude with Jane Austen

We can begin by comparing Austen's sentence to the alternative mentioned above where the finite subordinate clause occurs as the syntactic subject of the main clause: *that a single man in possession of a good fortune must be in want of a wife is a truth universally acknowledged*. The 2 versions are connected by a single change to the original sentence.

Although the two sentences express the same information with virtually the same words, they nonetheless differ in discourse properties. In Austen's sentence, the subordinate clause at the end of the sentence is stressed as the most important information in the sentence, whereas in the modification this stress falls on the predicate *is a truth universally acknowledged*, which in the original is embedded in the middle, neither the syntactic subject nor the naturally highlighted final part of the sentence. Why Austen's version is

---

[3] Support for this analysis comes from substituting the noun *truth* with the adjective *true* in Austen's sentence, which would yield *it is universally acknowledged to be true that a single man in possession of a good fortune must be in want of a wife*. Separating the finite subordinate clause from the main clause with a comma won't work. The adjective *true* assigns a semantic role to subordinate clause that follows; the noun *truth* does not. The comma in Austen's sentence can also be read as an instruction to pause between the main clause and the subordinate clause, thus an annotation about phonetic form. Nonetheless, this pause is a consequence of the sentence's syntactic structure.

preferable to our alternative crucially involves the formulation of the subordinate clause, as discussed below.

Replacing *it* with the subordinate clause is only one way Austen's sentence could be rewritten. Another possibility is reversing the linear order of *universally acknowledged* to *acknowledged universally*, yielding *a truth acknowledged universally*. Because the two changes are syntactically independent,[4] the two ways of varying the sentence interact to produce 4 possible versions: Austen's original and three others – one with both changes, one with only one, and one with only the other.

In Austen's formulation, *a truth universally acknowledged*, although *truth* is adjacent to *universally* (which contains *universal* (morphologically, the adjectival root *universal* combines with the adverbial suffix *–ly* to form the adverb)), *truth* is not modified by the adverb, creating a bit of word play.[5] Thus *a truth universally acknowledged* is not necessarily *a universal truth*, as is demonstrated by the fact that *a universal truth universally acknowledged* is not redundant – in contrast to the redundant *a truth universally acknowledged by everyone*, where if the truth is *universally acknowledged* then it must be *acknowledged by everyone* and conversely. Austen could have written *a truth acknowledged universally*, which eliminates both the adjacency between *truth* and *universally* and the word play that comes with it.

The modifier *universally acknowledged* functions syntactically as a reduced relative clause and therefore could be rewritten as a full relative clause in two ways (underlined), either as *a truth <u>which is universally acknowledged</u>* or *a truth <u>that is universally acknowledged</u>*. This gives us 3 ways the modifier phrase can be realized, all of which are independent of the linear order of the adverb and passive participle. Multiplying these three variants, which includes Austen's original sentence, with the 4 variants discussed above, yields 12 ways Austen's sentence could be realized (3 × 4) including 11 ways it could be rewritten. Because the full relative clause variants also eliminate the adjacency of *truth* and *universally*, and therefore the word play in Austen's original, none are preferable. Furthermore, spelling out the relative clause merely adds additional unnecessary words.

The finite subordinate clause in Austen's sentence can also be reformulated in many different ways. Structurally, this subordinate clause consists of a

---

[4] In contrast, consider the change where *universally acknowledged* is placed in front of *truth*, yielding *a universally acknowledged truth*. In this position, the order of *universal* and *acknowledged* cannot be reversed because that produces the deviant noun phrase **an acknowledged universally truth*. This kind of change will not be considered in the discussion that follows.

[5] Regrettably, we have no way of knowing whether Austen consciously intended this effect because there are no surviving manuscripts of *Pride and Prejudice*, nor is there any discussion of this in what has survived of her correspondence. The point is that given the words themselves, including their morphological structure, these relationships exist in Austen's sentence.

subject phrase *a single man in possession of a good fortune* merged with a predicate phrase *must be in want of a wife*, where the resulting T phrase merges with the subordinating particle *that*. The subject and predicate phrases, independently, yield even more possibilities for syntactic variation than the main clause.

In the subject phrase the head *man* is modified by the indefinite article *a* followed by the adjective *single* on the left and a prepositional phrase *in possession of a good fortune* on the right. Like the modifier of *truth* in the main clause, the prepositional phrase modifier in the subject can be also be expressed in a full relative clause, either

who is in possession of a good fortune,

or

that is in possession of a good fortune

– the latter a grammatical possibility, though some speakers may find the version with the relative pronoun preferable.[6] In addition, the derived nominal *possession* can be replaced by the verb *possesses*, yielding another pair of relative clause variants:

who possesses a good fortune

---

[6] Whether Jane Austen would have used this relative clause variant to modify a noun referring to a person is open to question. While there are no instances of this with *that is* in the novel, there is the following passage in the middle of chapter 8 containing *that are*:

> *"Your list of the common extent of accomplishments," said Darcy, "has too much truth. The word is applied to many a woman who deserves it no otherwise than by netting a purse or covering a screen. But I am very far from agreeing with you in your estimation of ladies in general. I cannot boast of knowing more than half-a-dozen, in the whole range of my acquaintance, that are really accomplished."*

Note first the relative clause in the second sentence, which modifies *woman* and uses the relative pronoun *who*. This relative clause could have modified *many* instead, but then the verb of the relative clause would have been *deserve*, not *deserves*. The relative clause that ends the fourth and final sentence of this passage, *that are really accomplished*, modifies *half-a-dozen*, which itself refers to *ladies* in the previous sentence. Arguably, this relative clause establishes the usage in question.

Nonetheless, one might wonder whether Austen would have used the *that are* formulation if instead of *half-a-dozen*, the relative clause was modifying *half-a-dozen ladies*. Another question, if *who are really accomplished* would have been a possible variant for this sentence. A further issue could be separation of the relative clause from the noun it modifies by the prepositional phrase *in the whole range of my acquaintance*; that is, without it would the *that are* variant still be possible?

It may be that Austen was using this variant to make a subtle point about Darcy's general view of women, that he considered them as objects rather than persons. This line of reasoning could also apply to *a single man* in the first sentence, especially when in the second sentence of the novel it is revealed that *in the minds of the surrounding families, that he is considered as the rightful property of some one or other of their daughters.*

and

that possesses a good fortune,

though here the two versions seem equally acceptable. One further alteration converts the present tense verb *possesses* with the progressive participle *possessing*, ultimately yielding a reduced relative clause containing just the participle and its object (comparable to *written by two philosophers* in Chapter 4):

possessing a good fortune.

3 further variations unfold from replacing *possesses* and *possessing* with *has* and *having*, respectively – yielding:

who has a good fortune
that has a good fortune

and

having a good fortune.

These 3 variations can be modified to add another 3 by the addition of the perfective participle *acquired*, producing: *who has acquired a good fortune, that has acquired a good fortune,* and *having acquired a good fortune.* And finally, all of these variants can be replaced by the simple prepositional phrase *with a good fortune.* Matching these 13 variants (including the original sentence) to the 12 versions of the sentences constructed so far yields 156 ways Austen's sentence could have been written (13 x 12).

The replacement of *in possession of* with *with* may seem like a reasonable application of Strunk & White's principle *omit needless words*, but in the context of *Pride and Prejudice* Austen's choice of the noun *possession* is crucial. The subordinate clause links the nouns *man, possession,* and *wife,* subtly suggesting that like *a good fortune, a wife* would also become the possession of the single man in question. And this perspective is further supported by the second sentence of the novel, in which the relation between *a single man in possession of a good fortune* and his future wife is comically inverted and the *truth* mentioned in the first sentence is revealed as a prejudice: *However little known the feelings or views of such a man may be on his first entering a neighbourhood, this truth is so well fixed in the minds of the surrounding families, that he is considered as the rightful property of some one or other of their daughters.* Any variant that replaces the noun *possession* removes the implication, so none of the variations identified, with the possible exception of the relative clause *who is in possession of a good fortune,* are preferable to Austen's original. Further, any replacement of *possession* with a verbal form of *possess* destroys the symmetry of the prepositional phrases in the subject and the predicate of the subordinate clause. But Strunk & White's principle of omitting needless words could apply to the choice between full relative clause (*who is in possession of a good fortune*) versus just the prepositional phrase modifier. And in addition, the relative clause interferes with the symmetry of the two prepositional phrases describing the single man.

The predicate phrase of the subordinate clause *must be in want of a wife* can also be reformulated in many ways, depending on the interpretation of the words in the original, especially the noun *want* in the prepositional phrase *in want of a wife*.

In *Pride and Prejudice* the noun *want* occurs 21 times, only 2 in the collocation *in want of*. In the other 19 occurrences, *want of* can only be interpreted as 'lacking', where the object of the preposition includes *presence of mind*, *(proper) resolution*, *proper consideration*, *propriety*, *principle*, *fortune* (2×), *money*, *property*, *new clothes*, *importance in his friend's connections*, *sense*, *that cheerfulness which had been used to characterise her style*, *connection*, *discourse*, *subject*.[7] The final occurrence appears in the following wonderful sentence towards the end of the novel (the last sentence of chapter 57):

Her father had most cruelly mortified her, by what he said of Mr. Darcy's indifference, and she could do nothing but wonder at such a want of penetration, or fear that perhaps, instead of his seeing too little, she might have fancied too much.

The second occurrence of *in want of* appears at the end of chapter 31 – about halfway through the novel – in the following sentence:

He danced only four dances, though gentlemen were scarce; and, to my certain knowledge, more than one young lady was sitting down in want of a partner.

Interestingly, *in want of a partner* echoes *in want of a wife* while the situation between men and women is reversed. Here *in want of* can be interpreted as 'lacking', but it can also be interpreted as 'in need of' or 'desiring' from which lacking a partner is implied. In this way the prepositional phrase *in want of . . .* allows multiple interpretations.

Interpreting *in want of* in the novel's opening sentence as 'lacking' would be, however, implausible. The statement that a single man lacks a wife is true by definition if *single* is interpreted as 'unmarried', and thus a tautology – regardless of his financial status. Calling this statement *a truth*, let alone *a truth universally acknowledged*, would overstate the obvious. This can't be the

---

[7] The noun phrase *want of subject* occurs in the following exchange:

> *"Books – oh! no. I am sure we never read the same, or not with the same feelings."*
> *"I am sorry you think so; but if that be the case, there can at least be no want of subject. We may compare our different opinions."*

intended reading of Austen's sentence. Instead, *in want of a wife* should be interpreted as either 'in need of a wife' or 'desiring a wife'.[8]

Under the interpretation of the noun *want* as 'desire', the predicate of the subordinate clause could be reformulated with the verb *want* by using the progressive participle

must be wanting a wife

or the bare form of the verb

must want a wife

or simply the singular third person present tense of the verb

wants a wife.

Alternatively, *a wife* can be replaced by *to marry*, producing another 3 variants:

wants to marry
must want to marry
must be wanting to marry,

the last being perhaps a bit awkward, as is the variant that replaces *to marry* with the passive *to be married*:

must be wanting to be married,

in contrast to

must want to be married

and

wants to be married.

These 9 variants all refer to the feelings of the single man.

Matching these 9 variants to the 156 created so far, yields 1560 (10 × 156) possible versions of the Austen sentence.

Changing the noun *want* to any verbal form of *want* destroys the wonderful symmetry between the syntactic subject and predicate in the subordinate clause – as does changing *a wife* to either *to marry* or *to be married*, and for this reason alone none of the substitutions listed above are preferable to Austen's original formulation. This also covers the change from *possession* to either *possesses* or *possessing*. Another equally important reason for preferring Austen's formulation is the ambiguity of *be in want of* between desire and need. *A single man in possession of a good fortune* may *be in want of a wife*

---

[8] While *in need of a wife* sounds natural, *in desire of a wife* is at best stilted.

(need) without actually realizing that he wants one, as the second sentence of the novel explains. We can't normally say a single man wants (in the sense of 'desires') a wife if he is unaware that he wants one.

Interpreting *want* as *need*, changes the perspective from feelings to views, the distinction introduced in the second sentence of the novel. Replacing the noun *want* with noun *need* yields

must be in need of a wife.

Switching from the noun to the verb produces 3 additional variants, the progressive participle, the bare form of the verb and the singular third person present tense:

must be needing a wife
must need a wife
needs a wife

This shift from feelings to views raises the possibility that this view is not necessarily that of the single man in question, an interpretation that becomes clear in the second sentence of the novel. Shifting from *want* to *need* would undercut the comic force of the second sentence.

Factoring in the 4 additional variants to the 9 identified above results in 14 versions of the subordinate clause predicate. Matching these to the 96 sentences already constructed that retain Austen's formulation of the subordinate clause predicate yield a grand total of 2,184 versions (14 × 156).[9]

At this point, we can inflate the number of versions with lexical substitutions in the subject of the subordinate clause and in the main clause. To this end, *a single man* could be revised as *one man* or *an unmarried man*, given the two meanings of *single*, or the latter replace with *bachelor*.[10] Matching these 3 variants to the 2,184 possible versions, yields 8,736 versions (4 × 2184). Similarly, *a good fortune* can be reformulated as *a fortune, a great fortune, a large fortune, a substantial fortune, great wealth, substantial wealth*.[11] With these 6 variants, the total becomes 61,152 (7 × 8,736).

---

[9] Substituting *to marry* and *to be married* for *a wife* when *want* changes to *need* would create even more variants. However, some of these are highly suspect because they are extremely awkward – for example, *?must be needing to marry, ??must be needing to be married*, and **must need to marry* (which seems simply deviant). In contrast, *needs to marry* and *needs to get married* are much more natural, and *needs to be married* perhaps a little less so. Readers can factor any of these variants that seems okay to them into the calculation.

[10] Of course none of these substitutions works as well as the original. With *unmarried, wife* at the end of the sentence arrives as an anticlimax. With *bachelor*, the implication from the connection between *man – possession – wife* is lost. With *one man*, the relevant ambiguity of *single* is lost. Further, the statement is about any man who is single, not one particular man who could just as well be married because *one man* doesn't specify the man's marital status.

[11] Note that all of these words occur in *Pride and Prejudice*, in contrast, say, to substituting *substantial financial resources* for *a good fortune*. Again, none of these replacements is

With the main clause, lexical substitutions for *acknowledged* will balloon the total into the hundreds of thousands. Consider, for example, the following 6 substitutions for *acknowledged*:

understood **or** *believed* **or** *recognized* **or** *accepted* **or** *known* **or** *assumed*

Matching these 6 variants to the 61,152 sentences calculated so far yields 428,064 versions (7 × 61,152).

Again, these variants raise the question of why Austen's formulation is preferable to these other possibilities. The answer is, once again, word play. Just as *universal* constitutes a recognizable part of *universally, knowledge* constitutes a part of *acknowledged*. In this way, Austen's phrase *a truth universally acknowledged* plays with the relation between *truth* and *knowledge*.

At this point it is trivial to surpass 1,000,000 versions with further lexical substitutions for *universally*:

generally **or** *commonly* **or** *usually*

– all of which also occur in *Pride and Prejudice*. Matching these 3 variants to the 428,064 versions already constructed yields 1,712,256 sentences in addition to Austen's original (4 × 428,064 = 1,712,256). Because these substitutions eliminate the word play between *truth* and *universally*, none are preferable to Austen's original formulation.

This by no means exhausts the possibilities. Instead of *truth* Austen could have written *belief* or even *fact*, where *belief* is clearly not a synonym given that people often believe things that are not true (and therefore not facts) and where *fact* is a more rigid concept given that facts are presumably determined on the basis of straightforward evidence.[12] In contrast, a truth is something more significant than a fact – though what it is exactly is not easy to state, as the philosophical literature demonstrates. These two lexical substitutions bring the tally of sentences to 5,136,768 (3 × 1,712,256).[13]

Calling the statement *that a single man in possession of a good fortune must be in want of a wife* a belief or a fact undercuts the comic effect of the reversal that occurs in the novel's second sentence, so neither substitution would be preferable to the original.

___

preferable to Austen's original because *a good fortune* contains *good fortune*, another bit of word play to the effect that a man is fortunate (has good fortune) in having a good fortune.

[12] Actually, the situation is more complicated. What we take to be evidence often involves interpretation based on our knowledge and beliefs.

[13] And even if we eliminate what might be questionable relative clause variants (*that possesses a good fortune*, etc.), 4 in total, the number of possible versions still is more than a million (3 × 428,064) at 1,284,192.

It should be clear from the discussion in this chapter that each of the proposed changes to Austen's original sentence, although it produces perfectly grammatical sentences that are close in meaning to it, detracts significantly from the brilliance of her original, especially in the context of the sentence which follows. But the creation and examination of these weaker alternatives to Austen's original creates a powerful context that reveals the artistry of Austen's writing in a fundamental way – in terms of both lexical choice and simply sentence structure.

The ambiguity in this chapter title, which asks a question about politicians, results from the two distinct ways the adverb *instinctively* can be interpreted: either it is asking about politicians who *instinctively cheat* or politicians who *instinctively lie*; thus in this question the adverb *instinctively* is interpreted as modifying either the verb *cheats* or the verb *lie*, but not both. As will be demonstrated below, this ambiguity results from the two distinct hierarchical syntactic structures that can be assigned to the same linear string of English words. So here again we have an example that shows how interpretation is determined by covert syntactic structure.

7.1   Adverb interpretation (again[1]): hierarchical structure vs. linear order

The interpretation of this question (an INTERROGATIVE) is based on the interpretation of the corresponding statement (an INDICATIVE) in (a).

(a)   *Every politician who cheats instinctively lies.*

The main clause verb *lies* is in the third person singular form, agreeing in number and person with the main clause subject *every politician*. The verb of the relative clause is also in the third person singular form, agreeing with the subject of the relative clause, the relative pronoun *who*, which is interpreted as identical to the main clause subject and therefore also third person singular.

The interpretation of the adverb *instinctively* depends on its syntactic structure – that is, what verb it is merged with. If *instinctively* is merged with *cheats*, forming a verb phrase {*cheats, instinctively*}, this hierarchical structure can be linearized in two ways, as [*instinctively cheats*] or [*cheats*

---

[1] See Section 4.4.2 of Chapter 4, which discusses the sentence *he is planning to lie strategically*, a different syntactic construction involving a subordinated infinitival clause. The examples (a) and (p) below are based on similar examples that are briefly mentioned in *What Kind of Creatures Are We?* by Noam Chomsky (2016), p. 10.

instinctively]. The same two linearizations are possible when *instinctively* merges with *lies*. This can be represented graphically by coloring the two verbs red and blue and matching the color of the adverb to the verb it modifies. The linearization *cheats instinctively lies* corresponds to the two distinct hierarchical representation given in (b), the source of the ambiguity in (a).

(b)　　　1. *Every politician who **cheats instinctively** lies.*
　　　　　2. *Every politician who **cheats** instinctively lies.*

The hierarchical structure highlighted in (b) can be linearized with no resulting ambiguity, where (b.1) corresponds to (c.1) and (b.2) corresponds to (c.2).

(c)　　　1. *Every politician who **instinctively cheats** lies.*
　　　　　2. *Every politician who **cheats** lies instinctively.*

As illustrated, (b.1) is synonymous with (c.1), where *instinctively* modifies *cheats* in both, and (b.2) is synonymous with (c.2), where *instinctively* modifies *lies* in both. Although each pair ((b.1) & (c.1) and (b.2) & (c.2)) has a different linearization, they share the same hierarchical structure, where *cheats* and *instinctively* form a syntactic unit in (b.1) and (c.1), in contrast to (b.2) and (c.2) where *lies* and *instinctively* form a syntactic unit.

　　Another case of ambiguity in the interpretations of adverbs occurs in simple sentences whose main verb is modified by two adverbs, as illustrated in (d).

(d)　　　*Some politicians strategically lie repeatedly.*

The verb phrase in (d) consists of the string Adverb–Verb–Adverb. The computational system for English based on free Merge produces two distinct hierarchical structures for this string. If *strategically* is merged with *lie* first, then the hierarchical structure (e) is derived, but if *repeatedly* is merged with *lie* first, then (f) is derived.

(e)

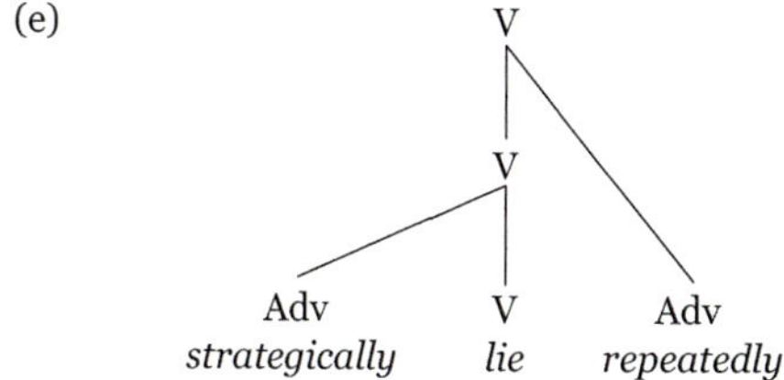

(f)

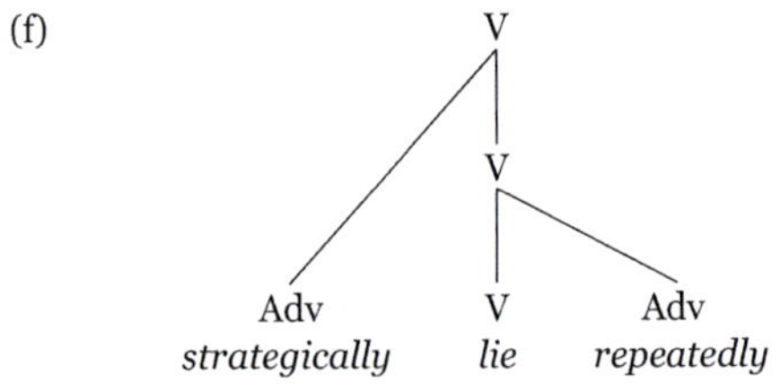

The structure in (e) correlates with the interpretation where some politicians lie strategically and do so repeatedly, whereas the structure in (f) correlates with the interpretation where some politicians lie repeatedly and do so strategically. The difference in interpretation can be described as a difference between the relative scopes of the two adverbs (recall the discussion of scope for adjectives in Chapter 2). In the interpretation that correlates with (e), *strategically* takes scope over just the verb *lie*, while *repeatedly* takes scope over the syntactic unit *strategically lie*. In the interpretation that correlates with (f), *strategically* takes scope over the syntactic unit *lie repeatedly*, while the scope of *repeatedly* is limited to just the verb *lie*.

The hierarchical structures in (e) and (f) can each be linearized in 4 different ways. With (e), for example, the following 4 representations, where the wide-scope adverb is painted red and the narrow-scope adverb, blue.

(g)
1. *strategically* lie **repeatedly**
2. lie *strategically* **repeatedly**
3. **repeatedly** lie *strategically*
4. **repeatedly** *strategically* lie

(g.1) matches the linear order given in (e). (g.3) shows that the positions of the adverbs in (g.1) can be flipped and the same scope interpretations retained. When the two adverbs are adjacent, as in (g.2), the inner adverb next to the verb can only be interpreted with narrow scope and the outer adverb will be interpreted with wide scope, modifying the verb phrase consisting of the verb and its adjacent adverb. This also applies to (g.4), where both adverbs occur in front of the verb. However, (g.4) seems somewhat awkward and distinctly less preferable to (g.2).

Given the syntactic structure of adverbs discussed above, it is possible to induce a 3-way ambiguity with 2 adverbs by reformulating the statement in (a) as (h.1), where one factor of the ambiguity concerns which verb the second adverb modifies (as illustrated in (h.2) versus (h.3)).

(h)
1. *Every politician who repeatedly cheats strategically lies.*
2. *Every politician who repeatedly cheats **strategically lies**.*
3. *Every politician who repeatedly **cheats strategically** lies.*

The analysis (h.3), where both adverbs modify *cheats*, involves a further ambiguity concerning which adverb takes scope over the other as illustrated in (e) and (f). Applying the convention in Chapter 2 where the wide-scope modifier is colored red and the narrow-scope modifier is colored blue yields two unambiguous interpretations (i), where both adverbs form a syntactic unit with *cheats* (indicated by brackets) therefore neither adverb modifies *lies*.

(i)   1. *Every politician who [**repeatedly** cheats strategically] lies.*   **W – N**
        2. *Every politician who [repeatedly cheats **strategically**] lies.*   **N – W**

The three distinct interpretations of (h.1) are summarized in table B.

Table B

	repeatedly	*strategically*
(h.2)	*cheats*	*lies*
(i.1)	*cheats –* **W**	*cheats –* N
(i.2)	*cheats –* N	*cheats –* **W**

For (h.2), politicians repeatedly cheat and strategically lie. With (i.1) strategic cheating is repeated (the politicians cheat strategically and do so repeatedly), whereas with (i.2) repeated cheating is strategic (the politicians cheat repeatedly and do so strategically).

An adverb can, under certain circumstances, occur at the beginning of a clause, as illustrated in (j), a variation based on (a) (*every politician who cheats instinctively lies*).

(j)   *Instinctively, every politician who cheats lies.*

Unlike (a) however, (j) is unambiguous. *Instinctively* in (j) can only be interpreted as modifying *lies*, not *cheats*. Thus (k.1) is a viable interpretation, whereas (k.2) is impossible.

(k)   1. ***Instinctively**, every politician who cheats **lies**.*
        2. ****Instinctively**, every politician who **cheats** lies.*

In phonetic form, the adverb at the front of the clause, which is syntactically separated from the verb it modifies, is interpreted as modifying the main verb *lies*, a relation normally expressed in terms of hierarchical structure in which the adverb forms a syntactic unit with the verb. Assuming that this relation between the verb and the adverb that modifies it exists in cognitive form leads to the conclusion that (j) constitutes another case of displacement (see Chapter 5).

Under the displacement analysis of (j), the two interpretations (one viable and the other not) that are represented in (k) would translate as (l), using brackets to indicate the relevant hierarchical structure.

(l)   1. [*Instinctively,* [[*every politician who cheats*] [~~*instinctively*~~ *lies*]]].
           2. [*Instinctively,* [[*every politician* [*who* [*cheats* ~~*instinctively*~~]]] *lies*]].

The blue boldface left brackets mark the syntactic units that contain the unpronounced counterpart of the fronted adverb under each interpretation. In terms of linear order, the adverb at the front of the clause is closer to *cheats* than to *lies*. However, in terms of hierarchical structure, the reverse is true. In (l.1) the hierarchical separation involves only 2 syntactic units, the verb phrase containing *lies* and the clause containing that verb phrase (*every politician who cheats lies*). With (l.2) the hierarchical separation involves 4 syntactic units: the verb phase containing *cheats*, the relative clause *who cheats*, the noun phrase containing the relative clause (*every politician who cheats*), and finally, the clause containing that noun phrase (*every politician who cheats lies*).

The interpretation of a displaced adverb concerns more than just the hierarchically closer verb. Further evidence for this limitation comes from sentences like (m):

(m)   *Some politicians who lie instinctively happen to be happy.*

where the adverb can be interpreted as modifying the verb of the subordinate clause (*lie*), but cannot be sensibly be interpreted as modifying either the main clause verb happen or the main clause predicate *happen to be happy* (compare #*some politicians instinctively happen to be happy*).

Displacing the adverb to the beginning of the sentence yields a deviant expression (n) that cannot be interpreted as synonymous with the only sensible reading of (m) – *instinctively lie*.

(n)   **Instinctively, some politicians who lie happen to be happy.*

Like (j) above, (n) has two possible syntactic representations, given in (o)

(o)   1. [*Instinctively,* [[*some politicians who lie*] [~~*instinctively*~~ *happen to be happy*]]].
           2. [*Instinctively,* [[*some politicians* [*who* [*lie* ~~*instinctively*~~]]] *happen to be happy*]].

Even though (o.1) represents an implausible interpretation, the interpretation represented by (o.2) remains impossible. This shows that the constraint on hierarchical distance for displacement is an absolute constraint, not one that simply chooses the hierarchically closest appropriate verb.

7.2   Displacement in questions

The syntax of questions in English also manifests displacement, as illustrated in the following comparison of the question (p) whose interpretation is based the corresponding statement (p.2) and where this displacement is explicitly represented in (p.3).

(p)   1. *Can every insect that swims fly?*
         2. *Every insect that swims can fly.*
         3. [*Can* [*every insect that swims* [~~*can*~~ *fly*]]]

(p) asks whether (p.2) is true or false, where the answer will be either *yes* (AFFIRMATIVE) or *no* (NEGATIVE). Thus (p) constitutes a *yes/no*-question, which differs syntactically from the corresponding statement in question by having the finite verbal auxiliary of the main clause verb (*can*) pronounced in clause-initial position (p.3).

Furthermore, displacement of the finite verbal auxiliary in *yes/no*-questions is constrained by the hierarchical syntactic structure in which it occurs, as illustrated by the deviance of (q.1) with the representation (q.2).

(q)   1. **Can every insect that swim flies?*
         2. [*Can* [[*every insect* [*that* [~~*can*~~ *swim*]]] [*flies*]]]

Because **can flies* is deviant – the modal auxiliary only occurs with the bare form of the following verb as discussed in Chapter 4, the only plausible interpretation of the fronted auxiliary in (q.1) would be *can swim*, questioning *swim*. However, this interpretation is blocked in (q.1), in contrast to the question *can every insect that flies swim* where *swim* can be questioned. The problem with (q.2) is that displacement of the verbal auxiliary *can* involves one position inside a relative clause and the other outside it. This is the same problem that occurs with adverb displacement (as discussed in the previous section). The absolute prohibition for the displacement of adverbs generalizes to the displacement of auxiliary verbs in *yes/no*-questions.

The clause-initial position of a finite verbal auxiliary in *yes/no*-questions can contain a modal auxiliary (*will, would, might, may, must, can, could, shall, should*), or the finite form of either aspectual auxiliary (progressive *be* and perfective *have*), or a finite passive auxiliary *be*. The corresponding *yes/no*-question for a main clause that contains a finite main verb (and therefore no auxiliary verb at all) introduces another verbal auxiliary element *do* – for example, the *does* in the chapter title. Putting aside the ethics of unfortunate politicians and the adverbial ambiguity of the chapter title, let's consider instead a simple statement about insects *every insect that swims flies* and its corresponding *yes–no* question *does every insect that swims fly?* In this question, the auxiliary *do* is inflected as singular, third person, and present tense (therefore *does*) and the main verb *fly* is the uninflected bare form.[2] In this statement/question pair it looks as if the number, person, and tense features of the verb have shifted to the clause initial position.

Another construction that requires the presence of auxiliary *do* is a negative statement, for example *every insect that swims does not fly* (compare *every insect that swims not flies* and *every insect that swims flies not*). Auxiliary *do* can also occur in affirmative statements, as in *every insect that swims does fly.* However when it does, its pronunciation is normally stressed (DOES *fly* as opposed to *does fly*), resulting in an emphatic interpretation of the main verb that is otherwise absent.

A third construction in which auxiliary *do* occurs is the so-called tag-question, examples of which are given in (r).

(r)   1. *All insects that swim fly, don't they?*
        2. *All insects that swim don't fly, do they?*

The tag-question consists of a statement followed by what looks like the beginning of the corresponding *yes/no*-question where the displaced verbal auxiliary is negative where in the statement it is positive, and positive where in the statement it is negative. In addition, the subject of the statement is reduced to a corresponding pronoun. All that's missing from this 'tag' is the verb phrase of the corresponding statement. In this way, the tag resembles an ellipsis construction where a verb phrase is understood but not pronounced, as illustrated in (s) where (s.1) is interpreted as (s.2) although the main verb in the second clausal conjunct is absent.

(s)   1. *Some insects swim and some spiders do too.*
        2. *Some insects swim and some spiders swim too.*

See the following chapter for a detailed discussion of ellipsis phenomena.

Auxiliary *do* also occurs in another question construction, examples of which are given in (u) based on the statement in (t).

(t)   *Politicians most often lie to their constituents about their intentions during townhall meetings.*

(u)   1. *Why **do** politicians most often lie to their constituents about their intentions during townhall meetings?*

---

[2] Aside from these inflectional features, the auxiliary *do* has no other semantic interpretation – in contrast to the verb *do* as in the question *did she do well in the competition?*.

2. *When **do** politicians most often lie to their constituents about their intentions?*
3. *Who **do** politicians most often lie to about their intentions? (To whom **do** politicians most often lie about their intentions?)*
4. *Where **do** politicians most often lie to their constituents about their intentions?*
5. *What **do** politicians most often lie to their constituents about during townhall meetings?*[3]
6. *How often **do** politicians lie to their constituents about their intentions during townhall meetings?*

These constructions all begin with interrogative words: *why, when, where, how*, and including the interrogative pronouns *who* and *what*. Because these words all begin with *wh-* (excepting of course *how*), these questions are referred to in linguistics as *wh*-questions.

Structurally, these *wh*-questions are similar to *yes/no*-questions in that both involve either the displacement of the finite auxiliary to a position in front of the subject or, in the case where there is no finite auxiliary, the occurrence of auxiliary *do*. This similarity was employed by the late comedian Irwin Corey, whose obituary in the *New York Times* (February 7, 2017) reports that in response to the question *why do you wear tennis shoes?*, Corey responded:

Actually, that is two questions. The first is 'Why?' This is a question that philosophers have been pondering for centuries. As for the second question, 'Do you wear tennis shoes?,' the answer is yes.

However, as every speaker of English (and no doubt every other human language) knows, *wh*-questions are never interpretable as *yes/no*-questions in spite of the structural similarity, which is why Corey's response is a joke.

Wh-questions can also occur as subordinate clauses, as in *Irwin Corey was asked why he wore tennis shoes, it was obvious why Irwin Corey wore tennis shoes*, or *historians will never know why Irwin Corey wore tennis shoes*. These subordinate clauses constitute INDIRECT QUESTIONS – in contrast to DIRECT QUESTIONS where the interrogative clause is the main clause. Indirect *wh*-questions differ from their direct counterparts in that there is no displacement

---

[3] Because the order of the prepositional phrases *to their constituents* and *about their intentions* could be reversed in the statement on which these questions are based, there are actually 12 possible *wh*-questions, including *what do politicians most often lie about to their constituents during townhall meetings?*, the variant of (u.5).

of the finite auxiliary (or occurrence of auxiliary *do*) in front of the subject. The same is true for indirect *yes/no*-questions, where the interrogative consists of a statement preceded by the question particle *whether*, which is interpreted as 'yes or no?', as in *we don't know whether we will be able to leave on time, it is unclear whether they understand our dilemma*, and *they wonder whether their strategy will solve the problem.*

7.3   The syntactic structure of questions

To understand the syntactic structure of questions, we start with the structure of indirect *yes/no*-questions, for example (v).

(v)   *They are wondering whether we will finish on time.*

The indirect *yes/no*-question *whether we will finish on time* constitutes a subordinate clause, in the same way that *that we will finish on time* is in (w).

(w)   *We believe that we will finish on time.*

The word *whether* functions as a subordinating particle in the same way *that* does. Furthermore, as the deviance of the examples in (x) shows, these two particles are not interchangeable in (v) and (w).

(x)   1. **They are wondering that we will finish on time.*
      2. **We believe whether we will finish on time.*

Given the paradigm illustrated in (v)–(x), a dependency holds between the subordinating particle and the main verb of the matrix clause containing the subordinate clause, a dependency that can be characterized as selection (see Chapter 4). The subordinating particle *whether* that marks an indirect question requires a verb that can assign a semantic role to an indirect question. *Wonder* is such a verb, *believe* is not. With the subordinating particle *that*, the converse is true.[4] Moreover, *whether* and *that* cannot occur together in the same subordinate clause: both *whether that* and *that whether* are impossible. These facts demonstrate that these particles are in complementary distribution, indicating that they are instances of a single syntactic category.

---

[4] Some verbs allow both forms of subordinate clause, as illustrated with *remember*:
    No one remembers whether Mary had finished the project on time.
    No one remembers that Mary had finished the project on time.

In Chapters 4 and 5, the subordinating particle *that* is labeled C, which would under our analysis apply to *whether* as well. Thus the structure of an indirect *yes*/*no*-question (v) would be (y).

(y)

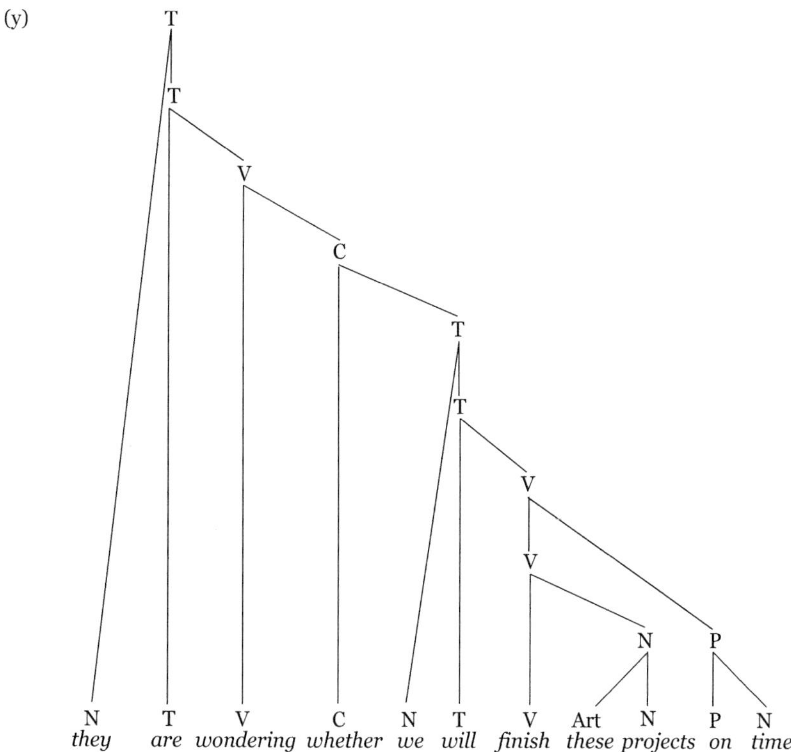

To convert the indirect *yes/no*-question *whether we will finish these projects on time* to a direct question *will we finish these projects on time*, the finite auxiliary *will* simply replaces the subordinating particle *whether*, as illustrated in (z), where ~~will~~ designates the position in which *will* is interpreted as modifying *finish*, but not pronounced there.

Given (y) and (z), *yes/no*-questions have the same syntactic structure whether they form a main clause or a subordinate clause. And to the extent that cognitive representation depends on syntactic representation, they would have the same cognitive representation, which might be rendered as a statement, a tense phrase, merged with a question operator (rendered as a question mark (?) that is interpreted as 'yes or no?'). Thus in cognitive representation all *yes/no*-questions are C phrases where C contains the question operator. In phonetic form, the question operator in indirect questions is realized as the subordinating particle *whether*, while in direct questions, it appears as a displaced finite auxiliary (or auxiliary *do* when the main clause verb is not modified by an auxiliary). The finite auxiliary is pronounced at the beginning of the clause, but is nonetheless interpreted as if it occupies the T position adjacent to the main verb.

This displacement analysis of *yes/no*-questions raises an interesting question about auxiliary *do*. Given (1) that a statement without auxiliary *do* differs in interpretation from that same statement with auxillary *do* added (*they finished those projects on time* versus *they did finish those projects on time*), and (2) that the *yes/no*-question *did they finish those projects on time* with normal sentence intonation questions the statement without the auxiliary *do*, it would appear that the cognitive form of this question would not include the auxiliary *do*. If so, then the occurrence of auxiliary *do* in *yes/no*-questions is essentially an adjustment to phonetic form. Like other finite auxiliaries, *do* in *yes/no*-questions occurs in the C position, illustrated in (z) above.[5] Thus, replacing *will* in (z) with *did* will yield the *yes/no*-question *did we finish these projects on time?*.

Because direct *wh*-questions share the displacement of the finite auxiliary that occurs in direct *yes/no*-questions, they too will contain a C phrase (as illustrated in (z)). Moreover, to convert a *yes/no*-question into a *wh*-question requires no more than substituting an interrogative word or phrase for a non-interrogative and displacing the interrogative to the front of the clause. For example, in *will we finish these projects on time*, the article *these* could be replaced by the interrogative *which*, yielding a direct *wh*-question *which projects will we finish on time?* Merging the noun phrase *which projects* with the structure (z) yields the structure (aa).

---

[5] An adjustment to the phonetic form of the *yes/no*-question would not affect the unpronounced T position, so technically there would be no displacement of auxiliary *do* involving the C and T positions, as occurs with all of the other finite auxiliaries. Instead, the inflection for tense, number, and person pronounced as part of auxiliary *do*, but interpreted as part of the main verb is what appears to be the displacement that occurs in these questions. This is essentially the analysis first proposed in Chomsky's *Syntactic Structures* (1957) but without the distinction between phonetic and cognitive form. The technical details are beyond the scope of this discussion, as is the analysis of the stressed auxiliary *does*. See Howard Lasnik's *Syntactic Structures Revisited* (MIT Press 2000) for a very clear and careful analysis of these technical details and how the analysis evolved in linguistics over the next 43 years.

(z)

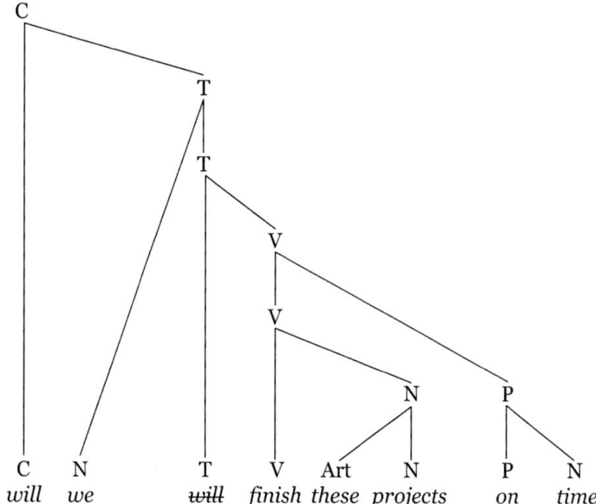

(aa)

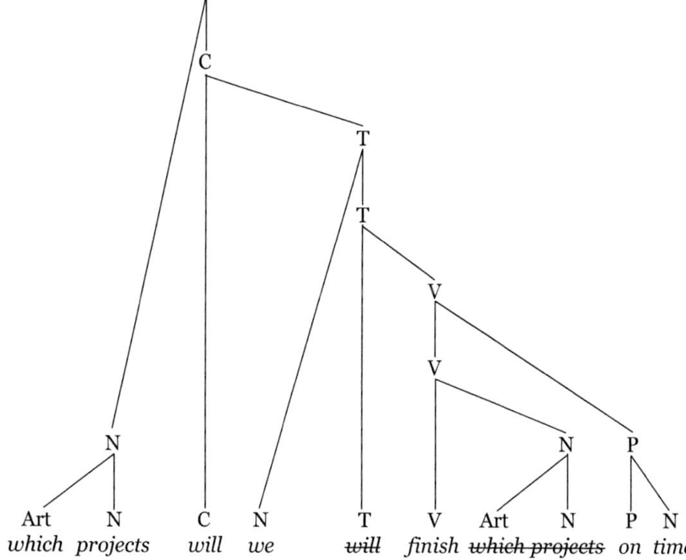

Alternatively, the prepositional phrase *on time* could be replaced by one of several interrogative phrases (*when, what time*, or *at what time*), yielding, for example, *when will we finish these projects?*. In this way, direct *wh*-questions are structurally C phrases that involve displacement with both a finite auxiliary and a *wh*-phrase, or in the case where the underlying tense phrase lacks a finite auxiliary, an auxiliary *do* in C position that carries the tense and agreement features of the main verb in the corresponding statement and leaves the main verb of the question in its bare form.

Finally, there is the *wh*-question that results from replacing the pronoun *we* with the interrogative pronoun *who*, yielding *who will finish these projects on time?* Assuming at the very least that this question is a clause and therefore has the structure of a tense phrase, there are three potential analyses: (1) like other direct *wh*-questions, this question is a C phrase involving a double displacement with *will* and *who*; or unlike other direct *wh*-questions, (2) this question involves only the displacement with *who*, or (3) it involves no displacement at all, in which case it only a tense-phrase.

The double displacement analysis (1) maintains a uniform analysis for all direct *wh*-questions – in contrast to the no-displacement analysis (3), which makes this construction a special case.

The analysis (2) where only the *wh*-phrase is displaced maintains the C-phrase structure for all direct *wh*-questions, but leaves the non-displacement of the finite auxiliary as a special case – which could be the correct analysis given that the displacement of the finite auxiliary does not occur in indirect *wh*-questions (underlined in the following examples: *they wonder <u>when we will finish these projects</u>* and *they wonder <u>which projects we will finish on time</u>*). Thus indirect *wh*-questions will be C phrases where C has no phonetic realization. And this might generalize to indirect *wh*-questions in which the subject is a *wh*-phrase, as in *we wonder <u>who will finish these projects on time</u>*. As a result, the direct *wh*-question *who will finish these projects on time?* would have the same structure as its indirect counterpart, namely (bb) where Ø designates a phonetically null C element.

(bb)

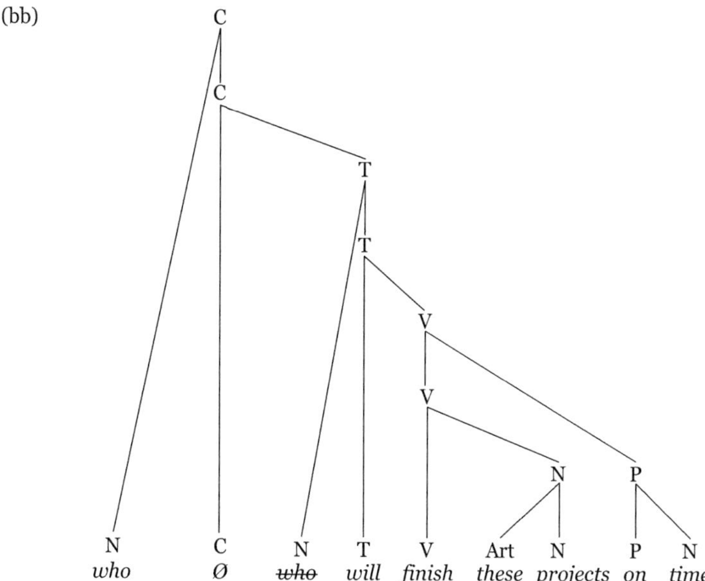

Under this analysis, all *wh*-questions are C phrases involving the displacement of the *wh*-phrase whether or not this affects word order.[6] Furthermore, perhaps surprisingly, displacement of the finite auxiliary in direct *wh*-questions must then be a special (and as yet unexplained) case, one that affects phonetic form but not cognitive form, a distinction that is now crucial for understanding English syntax.

7.4   *wh*-displacement in other constructions

The structure for indirect *wh*-questions is exactly the same structure that occurs in relative clauses with an overt relative pronoun (as first discussed in Chapter 4). Consider for example the noun phrase *students who will finish these projects on time*, where (bb) now forms a phrase with the noun *students*, in which (bb) is interpreted as a relative clause modifying *students*. Unlike the indirect *wh*-question counterpart (for example, *it is unclear who will finish these projects on time*), where *who* is interpreted as an interrogative pronoun,

---

[6] And like displacement with a finite auxiliary or adverb, *wh*-displacement can never involve a context of interpretation inside a relative clause and a context of pronunciation outside it: for example, **what did the man who bought annoy Mary?*, where *what* is interpreted as the object of *bought* in the relative clause *who bought what*.

who in the relative clause is interpreted as a relative pronoun (which is non-interrogative). In (bb), displacement with the subject relative does not affect word order, in contrast to displacement with the relative pronoun *which* in *these projects which we will finish on time*, where *which* is interpreted as the object of *finish*, but pronounced at the left edge of the relative clause.[7]

This analysis shows that relative clauses beginning with *which* are just the result of pronouncing this relative pronoun at the beginning of the clause and have no special inherently non-restrictive interpretation.[8] Therefore, relative clauses beginning with *which* should be interchangeable with those beginning with the subordinating particle *that* and therefore interpretable as restrictive relative clauses, which is easy to verify in many English texts. If so, then the relative pronoun *which* is no different from the relative pronoun *who*, which participates in both restrictive and non-restrictive relative clauses. See for example, *our friends who we invited to join our expedition to Mars* where the relative pronoun *who* is interpreted as the object of *invited*. If the relative clause is interpreted as non-restrictive, then we invited all of our friends; if restrictive, then only some of them. The non-restrictive reading can be distinguished from the restrictive reading by placing commas before and after the relative clause.

Under this analysis, *wh*-displacement is a phenomenon that generalizes across *wh*-questions and relative clauses. It is also a property of sentences like (cc), in which the underlined subordinate C phrase begins with a *wh*-word (in boldface).[9]

(cc)   *It is politicians **who** scientists are criticizing.*

The underlined segment in (cc) may look at first sight like a relative clause because it is adjacent to a noun, but, as will be discussed below, this turns out to be the wrong analysis. To determine the syntactic structure of (cc) requires answers to several questions – about the status of *it* (the syntactic subject of the

---

[7] The syntax of questions differs from that of relative clauses in that interrogative *which* also occurs as a modifier of a noun, as in the *wh*-question *which projects will they finish on time?* Displacement for this interrogative *wh*-phrase must involve the entire phrase *which projects*. If only the *wh*-element *which* is pronounced at the beginning of this *wh*-question, the result (**which we will finish projects on time*) is deviant (not English).

[8] See again the discussion in Section 4.4.3 in Chapter 4.

[9] The displacement of *who* is obvious in (cc.2), where *who* is interpreted as the object of *criticizing* but pronounced at the beginning of the C phrase, in contrast to (cc.1). Nonetheless, we assume displacement also occurs in (cc.1), where *who* is interpreted as the subject of *lying* (at the beginning of the T phrase) but also pronounced at the beginning of the C phrase (even though this has no effect on the linear order of the words). The same reasoning that applies to the case of an interrogative *wh*-phrase interpreted as the syntactic subject of a T phrase carries over to relative pronouns, which constitute another instance of *wh*-phrases in English (and other languages).

main clause), the syntactic relation between the noun *politicians* and the subordinate clause, and how these two pieces fit into the structure of the whole sentence.

Syntactically the *it* beginning the sentence functions as subject of (cc) and therefore agrees in number and gender with the following verbal element *is*. It is however non-referring, the pleonastic element encountered in Chapter 5 rather than a pronoun that would have an antecedent either in (cc) or in the discourse in which it is embedded. Given that *it* is the pleonastic element, it follows that *politicians* cannot be interpreted as a predicating noun describing the subject – as it is in *they are politicians*, in which case the subject pronoun and the predicating noun must agree in number (but do not in (cc)).

The more intricate question concerns the syntactic relationship between *politicians* and the subordinate clause that follows – and how these pieces fit into the structure of the whole sentence. This relationship depends in part on the interpretation of *who*. So far, there are two possibilities: interrogative pronoun or relative pronoun. If *who* is an interrogative pronoun, then the subordinate clause, which would be interpreted as an indirect *wh*-question, would not form a syntactic unit (a noun phrase) with *politicians*. In effect, *politicians* is an answer to the question *who are scientists criticizing?* Yet unlike interrogative pronouns in indirect *wh*-questions, which do not find antecedents in the sentences in which they occur, *politicians* in (cc) would be interpreted as the antecedent of the interrogative pronoun.

Alternatively, *who* could be analyzed as a relative pronoun with *politicians* as its antecedent. The relative clause analysis is supported by the two possible variants for (cc) given in (dd).

(dd)   1. *It is politicians that scientists are criticizing.*
          2. *It is politicians scientists are criticizing.*

In this way, the subordinate clause in this construction supports the same variation found in standard relative clauses.

Nonetheless, analyzing the subordinate clause as a relative clause modifier of *politicians*, thereby forming a syntactic unit with the noun, is not compatible with how the interpretation of these structures works. The structures in (cc) and (dd), generally referred to as CLEFT sentences, appear to result from *a proced-ure which divides a clause into two parts for information highlighting pur-poses* (Bas Aarts, *Oxford Grammar of English*, p. 331) – in essence, cleaving a clause in two. On this analysis the clause *scientists are criticizing politicians* would be divided into two pieces:

(ee)   *scientists are criticizing + politicians,*

which are reorganized so that *politicians* is foregrounded as *it is politicians*, while *scientists are criticizing* is backgrounded at the tail of the construction. A more accurate description of the process would be that *politicians* is replaced in the original clause with a *wh*-pronoun (interrogative or relative), resulting in a *wh*-displacement structure, where the pronoun is pronounced at the beginning of the clause. Further, this clause is subordinated in the predicate *is politicians*.

The backgrounded part of a cleft sentence has a special interpretation that does not occur in either the single clause from which the cleft is constructed or in a relative clause. Part of the understanding of (cc) is that scientists are criticizing someone or something whether or not it is *politicians* who are the object of their criticism. This understanding is also part of the interpretation of the negation of (cc) in (ff).

(ff)   *It isn't politicians who scientists are criticizing.*

(ff) would be seriously misleading if the writer/speaker understood that scientists aren't criticizing anyone or anything.[10] This also applies to the negation of the sentences in (dd).

That this presuppositional interpretation does not apply to a relative clause can be seen in (gg), a cleft construction which contains both a relative clause (*who deny climate change*) modifying the foregrounded *politicians* and a backgrounded subordinate clause (*who scientists are criticizing*).

(gg)   1. *It is the politicians who deny climate change who scientists are criticizing.*
         2. *It is the politicians that deny climate change that scientists are criticizing.*
         3. *It is the politicians who deny climate change that scientists are criticizing.*
         4. *It is the politicians that deny climate change who scientists are criticizing.*

As (gg) demonstrates, the two subordinate clauses may take either the pronoun *who* or the subordinating particle *that*, yielding 4 variants. In (gg.1) the first *who* is interpreted as a relative pronoun whose antecedent is *the politicians* while the second *who* is construed as the noun phrase *the politicians who deny climate change* – and similarly for the second subordinate clause in (gg.4). Given the analysis of relative clauses in Chapter 4, the clause *that deny climate change* in (gg.2) and (gg.4) contains an unpronounced relative pronoun *who* that takes *politicians* as its antecedent. In both (gg.2) and (gg.3), the second subordinate clause contains an unpronounced *wh*-pronoun which takes *politicians that deny climate change* (equivalent to *politicians who deny climate change*) as its antecedent.

---

[10] The interpretation of both (cc) and (ff) presupposes the truth of the statement 'scientists are criticizing someone/something', called in semantics a PRESUPPOSITION, a statement that must be interpreted as true regardless of whether the sentence containing the statement as a subpart is in the affirmative or the negative. Another example is the clausal object of *regret*. In both *she regrets that she arrived late* and *she doesn't regret that she arrived late*, the truth of 'she arrived late' is presupposed.

The interpretation of the two subordinate clauses in (gg) differs significantly. These sentences all carry the presupposition that scientists are criticizing someone/something, but they do not presuppose the truth of the relative clause, that someone denies climate change. Thus consider the sentences of (gg) under negation – for example, *it isn't the politicians who deny climate change who scientists are criticizing*. The presupposition holds for the backgrounded part of the cleft sentence, but not the foregrounded part, which includes the relative clause. This requires that the second subordinate clause not form a syntactic unit with foregrounded part of the cleft.[11]

At this point the question of whether *who* in the backgrounded part of the cleft sentence is a relative pronoun, an interrogative pronoun, or something else needs to be addressed. Given that the subordinate clause that it begins does not function syntactically like a normal relative clause, and also that its presuppositional interpretation is not available to regular relative clauses, designating this *who* as a relative pronoun seems difficult to maintain. The only similarity (noted above) between the backgrounded subordinate clause in cleft sentences and a relative clause is that the subordinate clause in clefts can occur without the pronoun *who*, either with the subordinating particle *that* or without it.

Designating a *who* that begins the backgrounded subordinate clause in a cleft as an interrogative pronoun entails that this subordinate clause is a form of indirect question – which are not modifiers of nouns. From this it follows that the subordinate clause in a cleft does not form a single syntactic unit with the foregrounded noun. This analysis requires that an interrogative pronoun can have an antecedent in the same sentence in which it occurs – not the usual case in indirect *wh*-questions, but with the result that what is foregrounded in a cleft construction serves as the answer to the indirect *wh*-question contained in the backgrounded part. More puzzling would be the requirement that interrogative pronouns in cleft constructions – that is, in an indirect *wh*-question – can be unpronounced in phonetic form, which is not otherwise possible. Furthermore, this analysis of the subordinate clause in clefts would require that these clauses may occur with the subordinating particle *that* unlike any other form of indirect question, which may be the hardest fact to reconcile.

---

[11] There is another syntactic analysis of (cc), not as a cleft construction, but where the subordinate clause is interpreted as a relative clause. The problem with this is that *it is (the) politicians* by itself is incomplete. It might possibly be used as an answer to a question, but it doesn't convey enough information to stand on its own. This also applies to the relative clause interpretation of the subordinate clause in (cc). It's easier to see this by reformulating the relative clause as a reduced relative clause which cannot be backgrounded in a cleft construction:

> It is politicians ~~who are~~ denying climate change.

The result *it is politicians denying climate change* has the same incomplete aura as *it is the politicians*.

Alternatively, it may be that *who* in the backgrounded subordinate clause is actually a hybrid that incorporates features of both the relative and the interrogative pronoun. It is an analysis that bows to seemingly contradictory facts. However, this seems like a makeshift answer to an interesting puzzle about English sentence structure.

In addition to cleft constructions, English also has a related construction called a PSEUDO-CLEFT SENTENCE, illustrated in (hh).

(hh)   *What they said was that cleft constructions have strange syntax.*

Like the cleft construction, the pseudo-cleft can be characterized as the result of splitting a sentence in two – in the case of (hh), as:

(ii)   *they said + that cleft constructions have strange syntax.*

More precisely, the subordinate clause is replaced by the pronoun *what*, which is pronounced at the beginning of the clause. The syntactic structure of the subject of the pseudo-cleft (hh) would involve *wh*-displacement, as illustrated in (jj).[12]

(jj)

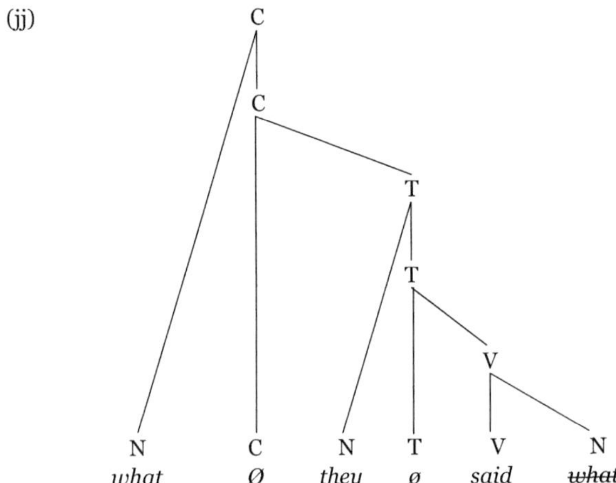

This *wh*-clause becomes the syntactic subject of a main clause and the subordinate clause of (ii) forms a predicate with the copular *be*.

With the pseudo-cleft (hh), there seems to be no motivation for analyzing the *wh*-clause as a relative clause. First, unlike the cleft, the subordinate clause requires a visible *wh*-pronoun. Second, there is no noun that this clause could

---

[12] Ø and ø indicate phonetically empty elements, Ø as the subordinating particle and ø as unpronounced T.

be said to modify. And finally, *what* in standard English is never a relative pronoun and only an interrogative pronoun; moreover, the relative pronoun corresponding to interrogative *what* is *which*.[13]

Like the cleft construction, the second piece of the 'clefted' sentence (ii) is foregrounded (in terms of information structure), while the first piece is backgrounded. And like the cleft construction, the backgrounded piece carries a presupposition – namely, that *they* said something. Yet unlike the cleft construction, the two pieces of the pseudo-cleft can switch positions, (hh) becoming (kk).

(kk)   *That cleft constructions have strange syntax was what they said.*

In (kk) the foregrounded subordinated clause functions as the syntactic subject of the pseudo-cleft while the backgrounded *wh*-clause comes at end of the sentence.

The pseudo-cleft sentences (hh) and (kk) correspond to the same complex sentence split in two in (ii). Pseudo-cleft sentences can also be constructed from simple sentences – (ll) for example, showing the sentence cleaved into two pieces

(ll)   *They recommended + the committee member with the least experience.*

There are two versions of the pseudo-cleft construction that correspond to (ll), given in (mm).

(mm)   1. *Who they recommended was the committee member with the least experience.*
         2. *The committee member with the least experience was who they recommended.*

In the subordinate *wh*-clauses in (mm) *who* functions as a pronoun whose antecedent is *the committee member with the least experience*. Changing *the committee member with the least experience* in (ll) to *the worst possible solution* yields the following pseudo-cleft constructions, where the pronoun *who* is replaced by the pronoun *what*.

(nn)   1. *What they recommended was the worst possible solution.*
         2. *The worst possible solution was what they recommended.*

In (nn), *the worst possible solution* would be interpreted as the antecedent of *what*.

If the *wh*-clauses in (hh) and (kk) can only be interpreted as indirect questions, then (barring the possibility of another analysis) the most straightforward analysis of these clauses in (mm) and (nn) would be as indirect questions as well. However, the possibility of another analysis unfolds from a consideration of another kind of *wh*-construction, illustrated in (oo).

---

[13] Thus *the book which they recommended* not **the book what they recommended*.

(oo)   *Who they recommended is unavailable.*[14]

Like the pseudo-cleft constructions discussed above, this example consists of a *wh*-clause in syntactic subject position followed by a copular *be*. Unlike pseudo-cleft constructions, copular *be* is followed by a predicate adjective instead of a noun phrase, which means that the predicate does not contain an antecedent of the *wh*-pronoun *who*. Furthermore, the predicate adjective *available* can only be interpreted as modifying an entity expressed as a noun phrase, not a question – which is clear from the paraphrase of (oo) as *the person they recommended is unavailable*. This paraphrase shows that *who* is interpreted as 'the person' and *they recommended* functions as a relative clause modifying *who*. Such constructions have been called 'headless' relative clauses, presumably because there is no overt noun for them to form a noun phrase with.

If *who they recommended* in (oo) is a noun phrase, there are potentially two ways to analyze its internal syntactic structure. Taking *who* to be a relative pronoun, *who they recommended* could be a relative clause that modifies a noun having no phonetic content. Alternatively, the pronoun *who* could be the noun modified by the relative clause *they recommended*, where both the relative pronoun and the subordinating particle are silent. If so, then this noun phrase would have the syntactic structure given in (pp).

(pp)

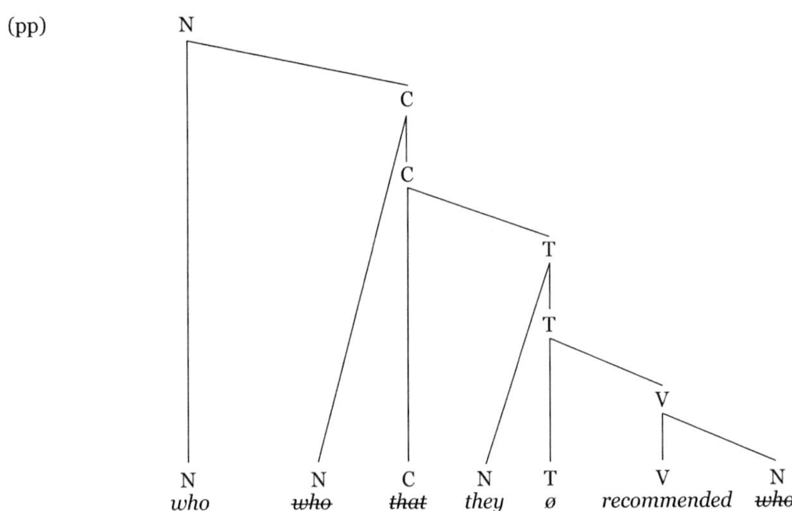

---

[14] Consider also *I like who they recommended*, where the verb *like* cannot occur with an indirect question, as in **I like whether you arrive on time*.

In this syntactic structure, the *who* that is pronounced is not an interrogative pronoun nor is it a relative pronoun, the unpronounced ~~who~~ in the relative clause.

This syntactic analysis of the headless relative clause is the only one possible for the following example.

(qq)   *What they recommended was disastrous.*

Because *what* in standard English does not function as a relative pronoun (as mentioned above), *what they recommended* could not be a relative clause. Neither can it be an indirect question given how it is interpreted. Instead, *what they recommended* would have the same hierarchical structure (pp), but with the silent relative pronoun ~~which~~ replacing ~~who~~ and *what* replacing *who* (as shown in (rr)).

(rr)

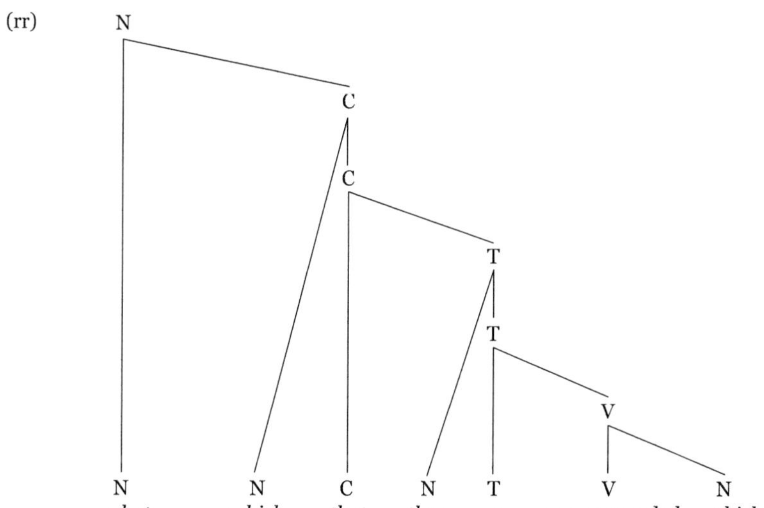

Replacing *what* in (rr) with the pronoun *that* (not to be confused with the subordinating particle *that*) would induce the pronunciation of *which* in the relative clause for the very awkward paraphrase *that which they recommended*.

This noun phrase analysis (rr) would also apply to the pseudo-cleft sentences in (nn). One reason for preferring (rr) to the indirect question analysis given in (jj) above is that *was* these pseudo-cleft sentences would be simply equational (*what they recommended = the worst possible solution*). This makes more sense than saying that *was* links an indirect question (with the syntactic structure of (jj) with the appropriate lexical substitutions) to a noun phrase. This analysis also generalizes to the pseudo-cleft sentences (mm) with *who*. The analysis of these pseudo-clefts as NP – *be* – NP explains why the two syntactic pieces on either side of *be* can occur in either order. And if *be* in the pseudo-cleft construction is equational, this would also account for the two possible linear orders when one of the pieces is a subordinate clause, as in (hh) and (kk).

Coda

The ambiguous title of this chapter triangulates the syntax of *yes/no*-questions, relative clauses, and adverbs. It begins with the intersection of relative clause and adverbial syntax, which in the chapter title creates an ambiguity because the adverb is adjacent to both the relative and main clause main verb and therefore can be interpreted as modifying either. Adding a second adverb opens the possibility for 3-way ambiguities. These ambiguities are rooted in the interaction between linear order and hierarchical structure, a central theme of this book from the second chapter on, where a single linear order yields multiple hierarchical structures.

The adverbial ambiguity of the chapter title can be eliminated in the corresponding affirmative sentence (*every politician who cheats instinctively lies*) by linearizing the adverb to eliminate its adjacency with both verbs. Alternatively, the adverb can be positioned at the front of the sentence (*instinctively every politician who cheats lies*), separated by the subject from the verb it modifies and thus another instance of displacement in syntax. In this structure, the adverb can only be interpreted as modifying the main clause verb. Displacement involving the relative clause verb phrase is simply prohibited.

This prohibition on displacement generalizes to the syntax of *yes/no*-questions, where a finite auxiliary verb is pronounced at the beginning of an interrogative sentence before the subject, but is nonetheless interpreted as modifying the main verb of the sentence. This is demonstrated by the impossibility of a *yes/no*-question in which the auxiliary at the beginning of the sentence can only be interpreted as modifying the main verb of a relative clause (**can every insect that swim flies?* – in contrast to *can every insect that swims fly?*).

The chapter title introduces a special piece of English syntax in the form of auxiliary *do*, which occurs in *yes/no*-questions when there is only a main verb in the corresponding affirmative sentence. In the interrogative, auxiliary *do* carries the tense and agreement features of the main verb in the corresponding affirmative, while the main verb in the interrogative occurs in the bare form – so that displacement in this structure seems to involve morphological features rather than a complete word. Auxiliary *do* also occurs in other constructions, including *wh*-questions, the other form of interrogative. These *wh*-questions involve displacement with both a finite auxiliary and a *wh*-interrogative pronoun (or a phrase containing one, as in *whose books did you borrow?*).

Both forms of interrogative occur as independent main clauses, direct questions, and also as subordinate clauses, indirect questions. In the syntax of indirect *yes/no*-questions, displacement with the finite auxiliary does not occur as it does with direct *yes/no*-questions. Instead, the interrogative clause contains a subordinating interrogative particle *whether*. Syntactically, indirect *yes/no*-questions are C phrases. Similarly in the syntax of indirect *wh*-questions, no displacement with a finite auxiliary occurs, nor does a visible form of a subordinating particle. Indirect *wh*-questions pattern like relative clauses that contain a visible relative pronoun, both being examples of *wh*-displacement and C phrases. They differ in that the interrogative pronoun must appear in phonetic form, whereas the relative pronoun need not.

Wh-displacement also occurs in cleft constructions, as in *it is the politicians who scientists are criticizing* where the subordinate *wh*-clause is not functioning as a relative clause. Interpretively, the subordinate *wh*-clause in these constructions functions more like an indirect *wh*-question, where the noun phrase *the politicians* following the finite verbal element *is* functions as an answer to that question. However, unlike interrogative pronouns in indirect questions, this one patterns with relative pronouns in being optional in phonetic form. And like relative clauses, this subordinate clause can also occur with a visible subordinating particle *that* – or neither particle nor *wh*-pronoun.

A cleft sentence can be thought of as the reassembly of finite clause cut in two pieces – for example, *scientists are criticizing the politicians* reassembled so that one piece shows up following *it is* and the other converted to a subordinate *wh*-clause in which the missing piece of that clause is replaced by a *wh*-pronoun. The same single clause can be reassembled another way, where the two pieces are linked by the copular *be* (one apparently the subordinate *wh*-clause that also occurs in the cleft version), yielding in this case *who the scientists are criticizing are the politicians*. In the pseudo-cleft, the two pieces of clause they reorganize can occur in either order, therefore *the politicians are who the scientist are criticizing* as well. Also unlike clefts, the *wh*-clause must express a *wh*-pronoun in the phonetic form – making the *wh*-pronoun in pseudo-clefts more like a regular interrogative pronoun and not at all like a relative pronoun.

The occurrence of *what* in pseudo-clefts (for example, *what they recommended will be the worst possible solution*) provides another factor showing that the *wh*-pronoun could not be a form of relative pronoun (which would be *which*, never *what* (in standard English)). Nonetheless, interpreting *what* as an interrogative pronoun and the *wh*-clause as an indirect question doesn't fit naturally with the interpretation of *is* as equational. An alternative analysis of these *wh*-constructions arises from a consideration of another species of English sentence involving *wh*-displacement, but clearly not a pseudo-cleft (for example, *what they recommended was disastrous*). If *what* is the head of a noun phrase modified by a relative clause with a silent subordinating particle and a silent relative pronoun (~~which~~ *that* they recommended ~~which~~), then this *wh*-construction is not some species of indirect question, but instead a noun phrase whose head is modified by a relative clause. Thus the sentence consists of a noun phrase modified by a predicate adjective. This same analysis also applies to the pseudo-cleft construction, making both pieces linked by *is* noun phrases, which should be interchangeable syntactically (as they are). However, this analysis does not extend sensibly to cleft sentences, and so reveals a fundamental difference between the two cleft constructions.

8 *Inferior defenses could then, as now, be tackled, as Vernon did at Porto Bello, Exmouth at Algiers, & Seymour at Alexandria.*

The title of this chapter returns to Henry Fowler's third example of problematic passive constructions under his entry for PASSIVE DISTURBANCES in the first edition of *A Dictionary of Modern English Usage* (1926).[1] The sentence appears to be part of a discussion about warfare, naval battles in particular.[2] It is a piece of complicated syntax involving the passive construction in the first part (*be tackled*) as well as both coordination and ellipsis in the second (*as Vernon did at Porto Bello, Exmouth at Algiers, & Seymour at Alexandria*).

The attempt to determine precisely what is wrong with Fowler's example launches us on an exploration of the syntax of ellipsis, a phenomenon in which pieces of syntax in a sentence can optionally be removed from phonetic form when they match other pieces in the sentence.[3] As will be demonstrated in this brief chapter, Fowler's sentence is astonishingly complex when we pay attention to the syntactic details. And once we do, it becomes clear that what is wrong with this sentence is not the improper use of the passive voice, but rather an improperly formed ellipsis construction. So in the end, this example of a 'bad' passive, like those discussed in Section 5.5.1 of Chapter 5, turns out to be problematic for other reasons.

Our exploration begins in Section 8.1 with a discussion of Fowler's analysis of his example, including his suggestions for transforming it into an acceptable sentence. Section 8.2 delves into the syntactic details of ellipsis by focusing on the coordination of three clauses that ends Fowler's sentence. Section 8.2.1

---

[1] The American spelling *defenses* replaces the British spelling *defences*.

[2] Vernon, Exmouth, and Seymour are all British admirals who won, respectively, famous naval battles in Portobello, Panama; Algiers, Algeria; and Alexandria, Egypt. Fowler does not identify the source of this sentence, unfortunately.

[3] Recall that ellipsis has already made an appearance in Chapter 7 in the discussion of auxiliary *do* in, where the following pair of sentences are compared:

(1)   a. *Some insects swim and some arachnids do too.*

        b. *Some insects swim and some arachnids swim too.*

(1.a) is an ellipsis construction where the verb *swim* has been removed from phonetic form in the 2nd conjunct, but is understood in the context of the 1st conjunct.

investigates the syntax the 1st conjunct in this structure, *Vernon did at Porto Bello*, and Section 8.2.2 explores the syntactic structure of the more complicated 2nd and 3rd conjuncts, *Exmouth at Algiers, & Seymour at Alexandria.*

8.1   Fowler's analysis

Fowler characterizes the problem as *active <u>do</u> after passive verb*, which he claims to be a common lapse,[4] and proposes three ways of fixing it. One involves eliminating the passive in the first part by substituting the active verb: *an admiral could then, as now, tackle inferior defenses.* This, however, changes the syntactic subject of the sentence from *inferior defenses* to *admirals*, making the sentence about *admirals* – a change that would be justified if the sentence occurs in a paragraph in which *admirals* is the topic of discussion and therefore the likely syntactic subject of the other sentences, but not if the topic of discussion is *inferior defenses* or other issues related to naval battles.

Fowler offers two other solutions that retain the passive voice in the first part. One requires that *the voice of <u>did</u> must be changed too* – to the passive as in *as was done by Vernon at Porto Bello.* This yields (a), where *done* – the verb, not the auxiliary – is understood as 'tackled inferior defenses'.

(a)   *Inferior defenses could then, as now, be tackled, as was done by Vernon at Porto Bello.*

This solution to the purported problem posed by the chapter title is not an instance of ellipsis, and therefore won't be examined further – though it does raise interesting questions of analysis.[5]

---

[4] Fowler's entry for *do* contains 9 more examples, 6 of which involve *do so*.

[5] For example, what is the internal syntactic structure of *done by Vernon at Porto Bello*? Notice that the linear order of the two prepositional phrases could be reversed, as in *done at Porto Bello by Vernon.* And what happens when the rest of the second part of the sentence is included? There is more than one possibility, as illustrated in (1):

(1)   a. *Inferior defenses could then, as now, be tackled, as was done by*
           <u>Vernon at Porto Bello, Exmouth at Algiers, & Seymour at Alexandria.</u>
       b. *Inferior defenses could then, as now, be tackled, as was done <u>by</u>*
           <u>Vernon at Porto Bello, by Exmouth at Algiers, & by Seymour at</u>
           <u>Alexandria.</u>

In (1.a) the coordinate construction (underlined) apparently involves a coordination of objects of the preposition *by* – as in *by X, Y, and Z.* Under this interpretation, *Vernon at Porto Bello* is a noun phrase with *at Porto Bello* modifying *Vernon*, not *tackled.* (1.a) therefore does not involve ellipsis. In (1.b) *at Porto Bello* can be interpreted as modifying the verb *done*, but it can also be interpreted as modifying *Vernon* as in (1.a).

Switching the order of the prepositional phrases in (1) produces the following two examples, where (2.a) corresponding to (1.a) results in deviance. [footnote continues on the following page]

Fowler's second solution substitutes *they were* for *was done*, producing *as they were by Vernon at Porto Bello*, where *inferior defenses* in the main clause is interpreted as the antecedent of *they*. This solution is clearly a phonetic reduction of the alternative where the full passive predicate occurs: *as they were ~~tackled~~ by Vernon at Porto Bello* (the strikethrough indicating the phonetic reduction). In this way, Fowler's second solution involves the deletion of the passive verb *tackled*, which removes it from the representation of phonetic form, producing an ellipsis construction. This reduction is possible because the deleted material matches syntactic material elsewhere in the sentence that acts as an antecedent for material missing in phonetic form, thereby making the deletion 'recoverable'.[6]

Extending Fowler's ellipsis solution to his full sentence produces several possible variants, 2 of which are given in (b).[7]

(b)　　　1. *Inferior defenses could then, as now, be tackled, as they were by Vernon at Porto Bello, by Exmouth at Algiers, & by Seymour at Alexandria.*

(2)　　a. **Inferior defenses could then, as now, be tackled, as was done at Porto Bello by Vernon, Algiers by Exmouth, & Alexandria by Seymour.*
　　　　b. *Inferior defenses could then, as now, be tackled, as was done <u>at Porto Bello by Vernon, at Algiers by Exmouth, & at Alexandria by Seymour</u>.*

The deviance in (2.a) comes from the impossible reading where for example the prepositional phrase *by Exmouth* modifies *Algiers* – which is the only possible interpretation of (2.a) given its syntactic structure, where *at* locks the *by*-phrases in the 2nd and 3rd conjuncts into the noun phrases headed by *Algiers* and *Alexandria*.

With (2.b) this impossible interpretation can be ignored because the two prepositional phrases in the 1st conjunct have a viable interpretation where they modify the verb *done*, forming a verb phrase. In the 2nd and 3rd conjuncts, the two prepositional phrases are also interpreted as modifying *done*. Syntactically, the three conjuncts form a coordination of predicate phrases in which the verbs of the 2nd and 3rd conjuncts are silent. Therefore (2.b) is an instance of ellipsis, as illustrated in (3).

(3)　　*Inferior defenses could then, as now, be tackled, as was done <u>at Porto Bello by Vernon</u>, ~~was done~~ <u>at Algiers by Exmouth</u>, & ~~was done~~ <u>at Alexandria by Seymour</u>.*

Because the two prepositional phrases do not form a single syntactic unit, (2.b) cannot be interpreted as a coordinate structure each of whose conjuncts contains the two separate prepositional phrases. The entire analysis generalizes to (1.b) when the two prepositional phrases are interpreted as modifying the verb *done*. Stylistically, the repetition of *was done* in the 2nd and 3rd conjuncts in phonetic form would be problematic. However, as will be demonstrated in what follows, the majority of cases of ellipsis in English are optional variants of a non-elided sentence.

[6] How matching applies will be spelled out in more detail as we consider more examples of ellipsis.
[7] Spelling out *as they were* in all three conjuncts at the end of the sentence seems extremely awkward:

??*Inferior defenses could then, as now, be tackled, as they were <u>by Vernon at Porto Bello</u>, as they were <u>by Exmouth at Algiers</u>, & as they were <u>by Seymour at Alexandria</u>.*

> 2. *Inferior defenses could then, as now, be tackled, as they were by*
> *Vernon at Porto Bello, Exmouth at Algiers, & Seymour at Alexandria.*

(b.1) can actually be interpreted in two different ways, each correlating with a distinct syntactic structure. The difference concerns the interpretation of the prepositional phrases with *at*.

On one interpretation of (b.1) each *at*-phrase modifies the adjacent noun. For example, *at Algiers* modifies *Exmouth*, and so the prepositional phrase and the noun combine into a larger noun phrase *Exmouth at Algiers* (where the prepositional phrase can be understood as part of a reduced relative clause: ~~who was~~ *at Algiers*). Under this analysis, the second part of (b.1) coordinates three prepositional *by*-phrases. Furthermore, this coordinate prepositional phrase modifies the missing passive verb *tackled* that follows *as they were*. (b.2) has essentially the same interpretation, but with a slightly different structure. In (b.2) the coordinate structure contains the three noun phrase objects of *by*. Once again, each *at*-phrase modifies the name of an admiral, while the one *by*-phrase with three coordinated objects modifies the missing *tackled*.

On the other interpretation of (b.1), the prepositional phrases with *at* modify the verb, the passive participle *tackled*. Therefore the *at*-phrase is not contained inside the *by*-phrase as must be the case for (b.2). For the syntax to render this explicitly, *tackled* must be present in the 2nd and 3rd conjuncts of the coordinate structure that ends the sentence – in which case the interpretation involves a coordination of predicate phrases (including *were tackled by Exmouth at Algiers* and *were tackled by Seymour at Alexandria*). The difference between the structure underlying this interpretation and that of the other two can be represented concretely by showing the deleted verbs with strikethroughs in red boldface, and bracketing the three conjuncts in blue. This is illustrated in (c).

(c)   1. *Inferior defenses could then, as now, be tackled, as they were* ~~**tackled**~~ [
           by Vernon at Porto Bello],[*by Exmouth at Algiers*], & [*by Seymour at*
           Alexandria].
           2. *Inferior defenses could then, as now, be tackled, as they* [*were* ~~**tackled**~~ *by*
           Vernon at Porto Bello], [~~**were tackled**~~ *by Exmouth at Algiers*], & [~~**were**~~
           ~~**tackled**~~ *by Seymour at Alexandria*].
           3. *Inferior defenses could then, as now, be tackled, as they were* ~~**tackled**~~ *by* [
           Vernon at Porto Bello],[*Exmouth at Algiers*], & [*Seymour at*
           Alexandria].

(c.1) represents the interpretation of (b.1) where the *at*-phrases do not modify the verb *tackled*, while (c.2) represents the interpretation of (b.1) where they do.[8] (c.3) has essentially the same interpretation as (c.1), where each *at*-phrase modifies the name of an admiral.

---

[8] To be completely explicit, (c.2) would have to show the verb phrase bracketing as (1), where one prepositional phrase with its left and right boundaries is painted red, and the other is painted blue. [footnote continues on the following page]

In (c.1) and (c.3), *tackled* in *be tackled* serves as the antecedent for the ellipsis because it matches the passive participle in *were tackled*. In (c.2), *were tackled* in the 1st conjunct serves as the antecedent for the ellipsis of *were tackled* in the 2nd and 3rd conjuncts. The antecedent for the ellipsis of *tackled* in the 1st conjunct of (c.2) is, as in (c.1) and (c.3), the *tackled* in *be tackled*. It looks like two separate operations apply in (c.2) to produce (b.1) with this interpretation. If the deletion of *tackled* in the 1st conjunct applies before the deletion of *were tackled* in the 2nd and 3rd conjuncts, we might wonder how a deleted piece of syntax could function as part of the antecedent in an ellipsis construction. But we don't have to answer this question if the deletions of *were tackled* apply before the deletion of *tackled* in the 1st conjunct. When these deletions apply, the antecedent that makes them possible functions as it would if no deletion affected it.[9]

This analysis once again shows how the computation of syntactic structure relies on elements that do not show up in phonetic form. It raises the question of how ellipsis constructions are formed from corresponding sentences that have none, a question that will be answered by the end of the chapter.

Applying Fowler's solution *as they were* to his original sentence has revealed both an ambiguity of the result as well as the complexity that results from the interaction of coordination and ellipsis in the second part. With this understanding, we are ready to tackle the syntax of our chapter title in order to explain how it works and what is actually wrong with it.

(1)   [[*tackled* [*by Vernon*]] [*at Porto Bello*]].

(1) shows that the second prepositional phrase is not contained in the first, as occurs in (c.1) and (c.3). This structure also applies to the 2nd and 3rd conjuncts in (c.2).

   It is worth noting that (1), and therefore (c.2) is the only viable representation when the linear order of the two prepositional phrases is reversed, yielding (2).

(2)   *Inferior defenses could then, as now, be tackled, as they were at Porto*
             Bello by Vernon, at Algiers by Exmouth, & at Alexandria by Seymour.

There is no plausible interpretation in which these *by*-phrases could modify the name of a city. This can be demonstrated with the bizarre (3), the counterpart to (b.2), where the three conjuncts are interpreted as objects of a preposition (*by* in (b.2) and *at* in (3)).

(3)   **Inferior defenses could then, as now, be tackled, as they were at Porto*
             Bello by Vernon, Algiers by Exmouth, & Alexandria by Seymour.

The source of the deviance in (3) is more a matter of semantics than syntax.

[9] Suppose that none of the deletions indicated in (c) apply. The resulting phonetic form for (c.2) would contain two additional instances of *were tackled* in the latter two conjuncts, and another *tackled* in the first. This repetition would be stylistically problematic. In contrast, the phonetic forms for (c.1) and (c.3) would contain only one additional *tackled*. The resulting sentences seem natural by comparison.

8.2   A syntactic analysis of ellipsis

As the discussion of Fowler's solutions to the problem posed by the chapter title demonstrates, the syntax of this sentence turns out to be more complicated than Fowler's brief comments suggest. To understand the complexity of Fowler's example, we can start by undoing the ellipsis in it, making visible the various parts that are unpronounced and unwritten. The coordinate structure *Vernon did at Porto Bello, Exmouth at Algiers, & Seymour at Alexandria* coordinates three syntactic units, indicated in (d).

(d)   [[*Vernon did at Porto Bello*] [*Exmouth at Algiers*] & [*Seymour at Alexandria*]]

One alternative to the title sentence would be (e), where the additions to the original sentence are highlighted in boldface.

(e)   *Inferior defenses could then, as now, be tackled, as Vernon did at Porto Bello, Exmouth **did** at Algiers, & Seymour **did** at Alexandria.*

Given that the chapter title and (e) have the same interpretation, they will have the same cognitive representation and are, therefore, simply alternative ways of assigning a phonetic form to this single cognitive representation. The two sentences are related by a deletion operation that adjusts the phonetic form (e) by eliminating the two boldface instances of *did*, producing the chapter title.[10] In this way, the first instance of *did* functions as the antecedent for the deleted elements in the 2nd and 3rd conjuncts, as illustrated in (f).

(f)   *Inferior defenses could then, as now, be tackled, as Vernon ~~did~~ at Porto Bello, Exmouth ~~did~~ at Algiers, & Seymour ~~did~~ at Alexandria.*

But this gives only one piece of the analysis of the chapter title, the other being the connection between the conjuncts in the second part of the sentence and the passive construction in the first part.

8.2.1   as Vernon did at Porto Bello

One possible analysis of this relation takes *did* to be the third person singular of the main verb *do*, where *did* is understood as 'tackled inferior defenses' (Fowler's analysis mentioned above). The problem with this, as Fowler notes, is that past tense *did* in the active does not match the passive *be tackled*, a problem with parallelism.

There is, however, another analysis where the phrase *Vernon did at Porto Bello* itself results from ellipsis that relates to the alternative sentence (g).

---

[10] Minimally, deletion would involve the erasure of the phonetic content of the lexical elements deleted.

(g)   *Inferior defenses could then, as now, be tackled, as Vernon **tackled inferior defenses** at Porto Bello.*

An ellipsis analysis would involve deleting the *tackle inferior defenses* but leaving behind the past tense as manifested in the auxiliary *did*, which can be represented as (h).

(h)   *Inferior defenses could then, as now, be tackled, as Vernon did ~~tackle inferior defenses~~ at Porto Bello.*

Given that the past tense of *tackled* (a verb form which doesn't occur in (h)) shows up in phonetic form as *did* under ellipsis, the elided form of *tackle* cannot also be inflected for past tense.

The trouble with (h) is that there appears to be no matching antecedent phrase in the first part of the sentence that governs the ellipsis of *tackle inferior defenses* in the 1st conjunct of the second part. However, under the displacement analysis of passive constructions presented in Chapter 5, *tackled inferior defenses* would occur as a phrase in the cognitive representation of the main clause, as indicated in (i) where the occurrence of *inferior defenses* in braces is silent in phonetic form.

(i)   *Inferior defenses could then, as now, be <u>tackled {~~inferior defenses~~}</u>, as Vernon did ~~tackle inferior defenses~~ at Porto Bello.*

If the unpronounced *inferior defenses* in braces in this representation of the first part of the sentence can function as part of the antecedent phrase that governs the ellipsis, then the only problem with Fowler's example is the phonetic and morphological mismatch between the passive participle *tackled* and the active bare verb *tackle*.

The partially invisible phrase *tackled {~~inferior defenses~~}* in (i) is a verb phrase, as is the elided phrase *~~tackle inferior defenses~~*. Moreover, the elided verb phrase is actually a subpart of a larger verb phrase that includes the prepositional phrase *at Porto Bello*, illustrated in (j).

(j)

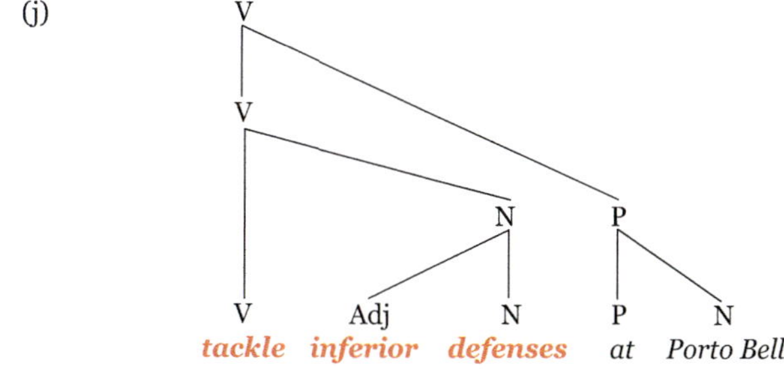

And this phrase merges with the tensed element *did*, and then the subject of *tackle (Vernon)* to form a full clause, a T phrase as shown in (k).

(k)

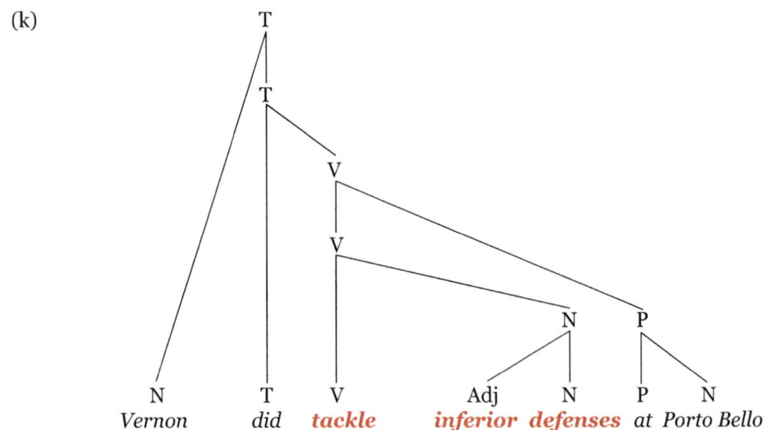

Thus, the chapter title ends with a coordination of clauses, which give greater syntactic weight to this sentence than the alternatives given in (c), which coordinate smaller syntactic units.

The awkwardness in the chapter title – which led Fowler to characterize it as a 'passive disturbance' – results in part from the phonetic mismatch between the passive *tackled* and the bare form *tackle*. This mismatch can be eliminated by replacing *did* with perfective auxiliary *had*, where the passive participle and the perfective participle have the same phonetic form *tackled*. Under this replacement, the chapter title with just the first 1st conjunct would be rendered as (l.1), with the ellipsis analysis (l.2).

(l)   1. *Inferior defenses could then, as now, be tackled, as Vernon had at Porto Bello.*
          2. *Inferior defenses could then, as now, be* tackled {inferior defenses}, *as Vernon had* tackled inferior defenses *at Porto Bello.*

If anything, the phonetic match between the elided phrase and its antecedent makes (l.1) a more acceptable sentence than the chapter title. Furthermore, both forms share the same grammatical status as participles. The only mismatch remaining is that *tackled* in the antecedent is the passive participle whereas in the elided phrase it is the perfective participle, a mismatch of voice between passive and active. The question that remains is whether eliminating this mismatch improves the sentence: that is, does eliminating the passive in the first part of the sentence, as in (m.1) with the analysis (m.2), result in a noticeably better-sounding sentence?

(m)   1. *Admirals could then, as now, have tackled inferior defenses, as Vernon had at Porto Bello.*
          2. *Admirals could then, as now, have **tackled inferior defenses**, as Vernon had **tackled inferior defenses** at Porto Bello.*

The answer seems to be *no*.

The foregoing analysis shows that the chapter title violates conditions that govern ellipsis – in particular, the matching condition on the relation between the ellipsis site (containing what is deleted from phonetic form) and its antecedent. From this perspective, the chapter title could be just as well be claimed as a misuse of the active voice, rather than a misuse of the passive.

Extending (l.1), where *had* replaces *did*, to include the 2nd and 3rd conjuncts in the chapter title yields (n.1) with the ellipsis analysis (n.2).

(n)   1. *Inferior defenses could then, as now, be tackled, as Vernon had at Porto Bello, Exmouth had at Algiers, & Seymour had at Alexandria.*
          2. *Inferior defenses could then, as now, be **tackled {inferior defenses}**, as Vernon had **tackled inferior defenses** at Porto Bello, Exmouth had **tackled inferior defenses** at Algiers, & Seymour had **tackled inferior defenses** at Alexandria.*

The coordinate structure in the second part of (n.1) thus involves three instances of verb phrase ellipsis, which is optional for each conjunct. As a result, there are 8 distinct variants for the phonetic form of this sentence, including the one where ellipsis affects all three conjuncts and the one where none of the conjuncts are elided. This can be graphically represented without spelling out every variant by assigning numbers to the three conjuncts:

1 = *Vernon had tackled inferior defenses at Porto Bello*
2 = *Exmouth had tackled inferior defenses at Algiers*
3 = *Seymour had tackled inferior defenses at Alexandria*

and then color-coding the numbers, where **red** indicates ellipsis and blue no ellipsis. Of the 8 possible variants, 4 are perfectly ordinary

1 2 3 [maximum ellipsis]
1 **2 3**
1 2 **3**
1 2 3 [no ellipsis]

but the other 4

1 2 3
1 2 3

1 **2** 3
1 2 **3**

seem distinctly clumsy. Compare, for example, the second pattern in the list above (o.1) to the sixth (o.2).

(o)   1. *Inferior defenses could then, as now, be tackled, as Vernon had tackled them at Porto Bello, Exmouth had at Algiers, & Seymour had at Alexandria.*
         2. *?Inferior defenses could then, as now, be tackled, as Vernon had at Porto Bello, Exmouth had tackled them at Algiers, & Seymour had tackled them at Alexandria.*

The clumsiness of (o.2) resulting from a non-elided conjunct following an elided one (a property that each member of the second group of 4 variants shares) is plausibly a question of style rather than an instance of grammatical deviance –mostly a matter of taste.[11]

These 8 variants can be expanded to 16 by repositioning *as Vernon had* … *at Alexandria* at the beginning of the sentence, as in (p) for example.

(p)   *As Vernon had tackled inferior defenses at Porto Bello, Exmouth had at Algiers, & Seymour had at Alexandria, inferior defenses could then, as now, be tackled.*

One problem with (p) is that second part of the sentence is mostly redundant, making it anticlimactic. The version with verb phrase ellipsis in all three conjuncts fares better; thus compare (p) with (q.1) or better (q.2), which eliminates an awkwardness created by *could then, as now*.

(q)   1. *As Vernon had at Porto Bello, Exmouth had at Algiers, & Seymour had at Alexandria, inferior defenses could then, as now, be tackled.*
         2. *As Vernon had at Porto Bello, Exmouth had at Algiers, & Seymour had at Alexandria, inferior defenses could again be tackled.*

---

[11] In this regard, it is worth considering whether Strunk & White's dictum *omit needless words* should apply to ellipsis constructions. In virtually every case of ellipsis in English, the corresponding sentence without ellipsis is nonetheless a legitimate sentence. As a grammatical process, ellipsis is entirely optional. Whether ellipsis in general is better writing style, is pretty much a matter of taste. Consider for example what you think of *as Vernon had at Porto Bello, Exmouth had at Algiers, & Seymour had at Alexandria* compared to *as Vernon had at Porto Bello, Exmouth at Algiers, & Seymour at Alexandria*. The repetition of *had* in the 2nd and 3rd conjunct seems negligible, especially compared to the repetition of *tackled inferior defenses* in *as Vernon had tackled inferior defenses at Porto Bello, Exmouth had tackled inferior defenses at Algiers, & Seymour had tackled inferior defenses at Alexandria*. Repetition, unless it is done for emphasis, is generally weak writing style.

(q.2) still involves the voice mismatch between *had tackled* and *be tackled*, as well as the potential problem of an antecedent for ellipsis that comes at the very end of a complicated sentence.

8.2.2   Exmouth at Algiers, & Seymour at Alexandria

These 16 variations can be further extended given the option of deleting the finite auxiliary in the 2nd and 3rd conjuncts of the coordinate structure. Applying deletion to (r.1) as indicated in (r.2) yields the ellipsis in (r.3).

(r)   1. *Inferior defenses could then, as now, be tackled, as Vernon had at*
                Porto Bello, Exmouth had at Algiers, & Seymour had at Alexandria.
             2. *Inferior defenses could then, as now, be tackled, as Vernon* **had** *at*
                Porto Bello, Exmouth **had** *at Algiers, & Seymour* **had** *at Alexandria.*
             3. *Inferior defenses could then, as now, be tackled, as Vernon had at*
                Porto Bello, Exmouth at Algiers, & Seymour at Alexandria.

Each conjunct in (r.1) is already an instance of verb phrase ellipsis, where *tackled inferior defenses* has been deleted from the predicate of each conjunct. Because ellipsis of the finite auxiliary is an option for the 2nd and 3rd conjuncts, the pattern of ellipsis **1–2–3** above (where all three conjuncts show verb phrase ellipsis) has 3 additional variants. The full pattern is given below with the deletion of the finite auxiliary indicated by an asterisk.

1 2   3
1 2   3*
1 2*   3*   [maximum ellipsis]
1 2*   3

The 4th possibility **1 – 2* – 3**, spelled out in (s), is stylistically odd – again because a conjunct with ellipsis is followed by one without the same ellipsis, in contrast to (r).

(s)   *Inferior defenses could then, as now, be tackled, as Vernon had at Porto*
             Bello, Exmouth at Algiers, & Seymour had at Alexandria.

Adhering to this stylistic restriction, there are 10 possible variants for the first four patterns of verb phrase ellipsis given above. What further variants are stylistically viable when the coordinate structure is positioned at the beginning of the sentence is left for the reader to decide.

   The pattern of maximum ellipsis **1 – 2* – 3*** involves the deletion of both the finite auxiliary *had* and the verb phrase *tackled inferior defenses* in the 2nd and 3rd conjuncts. In addition, there are corresponding legitimate sentences with verb phrase ellipsis only (**1 – 2 – 3**) or with no ellipsis (1 – 2 – 3), variants spelled out in (t).

(t)   1. *Inferior defenses could then, as now, be tackled, as Vernon had tackled inferior defenses at Porto Bello, Exmouth had tackled them at Algiers, & Seymour had tackled them at Alexandria.*
                 (1 − 2 − 3 = no ellipsis)
              2. *Inferior defenses could then, as now, be tackled, as Vernon had at Porto Bello, Exmouth had at Algiers, & Seymour had at Alexandria.*
                 (**1 − 2 − 3** = verb phrase ellipsis only)
              3. *Inferior defenses could then, as now, be tackled, as Vernon had at Porto Bello, Exmouth at Algiers, & Seymour at Alexandria.*
                 (**1 − 2* − 3*** = maximum ellipsis)

The use of the pronoun *them* in (t.1) avoids the infelicitous repetition of *inferior defenses* in the 2nd and 3rd conjuncts.

One way to consider the relation between these three options is as a process (t.1) > (t.2) > (t.3), where verb phrase ellipsis (deletion of *tackled inferior defenses*) is a separate operation that precedes finite auxiliary ellipsis (deletion of *had*). The other would involve a process (t.1) > (t.3), where (t.2) is not an intermediate step and thus the ellipsis in (t.3) results directly from the deletion of *had tackled inferior defenses.*

Whether there is an ellipsis operation that deletes just the finite auxiliary, as opposed to the maximally identical T + verb phrase, needs to be established independently of the examples under discussion. To this end, consider the simpler coordinate constructions in (u), where deletion of *should* applies to (u.1), illustrated in (u.2), producing (u.3).

(u)   1. *Bill should buy a used car, and Mary should lease a new one.*
              2. *Bill **should** buy a used car, and Mary, ~~should~~ lease a new one.*
              3. *Bill should buy a used car, and Mary, lease a new one.*

Not all English speakers find (u.3) acceptable. The unacceptability of (u.3) constitutes evidence against ellipsis in English involving just the finite auxiliary; whereas, in contrast, the acceptability of (u.3) constitutes evidence that supports such ellipsis.

Nonetheless, speakers of English generally accept ellipsis involving the finite auxiliary plus the following main verb, as illustrated in (v), where (v.1) is converted to (v.3).

(v)   1. *Bill should buy a new car and Mary should buy a new bicycle.*
              2. *Bill **should buy** a new car and Mary ~~should buy~~ a new bicycle.*
              3. *Bill should buy a new car and Mary, a new bicycle.*

And when the main verb is finite, then it appears as if the ellipsis involves just the finite verb, as in (w).

(w)   1. *Bill bought a new car and Mary bought a new bicycle.*
              2. *Bill **bought** a new car and Mary ~~bought~~ a new bicycle.*
              3. *Bill bought a new car and Mary, a new bicycle.*

However, given the analysis of clauses in the Chapters 4–6, the 2nd conjunct in (w.2) would have cognitive representation (x).

(x)

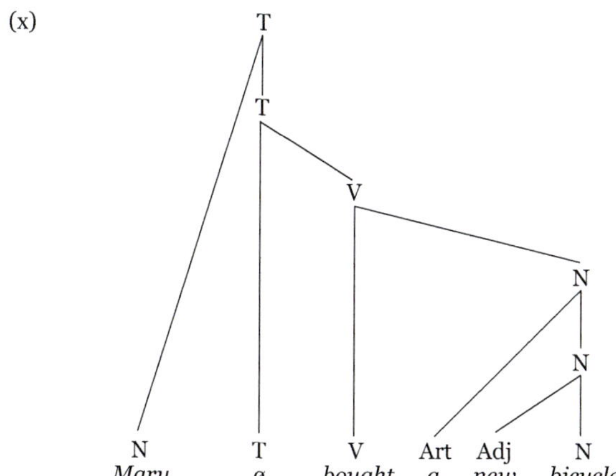

The ellipsis in (w) could then be analyzed as deletion of T plus the verb, where finite T (ø) is invisible when the main verb is finite. Thus the deletion of T in this case would be vacuous, having no phonetic effect.

T plus verb ellipsis also occurs in the quotation from Francis Bacon in the Preface where that quotation is part of the full sentence *Reading maketh a full man; conference a ready man; and writing an exact man.* Bacon's sentence coordinates three clauses: *reading maketh a full man, conference [maketh] a ready man,* and *writing [maketh] an exact man.* The word *maketh* is an archaic form of modern English *makes.* The word *conference* was probably intended by Bacon as a nominalization of the verb *confer* with the interpretation 'conversation' or 'speaking'; whereas in Modern English *conference* has a more limited interpretation. According to the *Oxford English Dictionary,* the word *ready* in this sentence means *quick and lively in speech, discourse, or writing; eloquent.* The 2nd and 3rd clausal conjuncts elide the finite verb.

So far, we seem to have two distinct forms of ellipsis, one involving just a verb phrase (illustrated in (n) – repeated below) and another involving finite T plus the verb (T+V).

(n)   1. *Inferior defenses could then, as now, be tackled, as Vernon had at*
             Porto Bello, Exmouth had at Algiers, & Seymour had at Alexandria.
         2. *Inferior defenses could then, as now, be* *tackled* ~~*inferior defenses*~~*, as*

> *Vernon had ~~tackled inferior defenses~~ at Porto Bello, Exmouth had ~~tackled inferior defenses~~ at Algiers, & Seymour had ~~tackled inferior defenses~~ at Alexandria.*

In general, both ellipsis operations are optional as all of the examples cited above demonstrate. Furthermore, there is good evidence for distinguishing these two ellipsis operations: T+V ellipsis cannot apply in some syntactic configurations that verb phrase ellipsis can. Consider the following variations on (v).

(y)   1. *Bill should buy a new car and Susan said that Mary should buy a new bicycle.*
      2. *Bill **should buy** a new car and Susan said that Mary ~~should buy~~ a new bicycle.*
      3. **Bill should buy a new car and Susan said that Mary, a new bicycle.*

(z)   1. *Fred said that Bill should buy a new car and Susan said that Mary should buy a new bicycle.*
      2. *Fred said that Bill **should buy** a new car and Susan said that Mary ~~should buy~~ a new bicycle.*
      3. **Fred said that Bill should buy a new car and Susan said that Mary, a new bicycle.*

(y) and (z) compared to (v) show that T+V ellipsis is not possible when the clause that contains the antecedent of the ellipsis site is not coordinated with the smallest clause containing the ellipsis site.

In stark contrast, verb phrase ellipsis is completely acceptable in these same configurations. (aa) shows that verb phrase ellipsis occurs in the same configuration as T+V ellipsis, and (bb) and (cc) show that the verb phrase ellipsis is possible where T+V ellipsis is not.

(aa)   1. *Bill should buy a new car and Mary should buy a new car too.*
       2. *Bill should **buy a new car** and Mary should ~~buy a new car~~ too.*
       3. *Bill should buy a new car and Mary should too.*

(bb)   1. *Bill should buy a new car and Susan said that Mary should buy a new car too.*
       2. *Bill should **buy a new car** and Susan said that Mary should ~~buy a new car~~ too.*
       3. *Bill should buy a new car and Susan said that Mary should too.*

(cc)   1. *Fred said that Bill should buy a new car and Susan said that Mary should buy a new car too.*
       2. *Fred said that Bill should **buy a new car** and Susan said that Mary should ~~buy a new car~~ too.*
       3. *Fred said that Bill should buy a new car and Susan said that Mary should too.*

But even this difference does not rule out the possibility that *Exmouth at Algiers* could be derived by a single ellipsis operation that deletes the maximally identical string *had tackled inferior defenses*, which might be a form of T+V ellipsis.

That T+V ellipsis must apply to the corresponding main verb when possible – hence to the maximally identical T + verb – is supported by the impossibility of interpreting *tackled* in the 2nd and 3rd conjuncts of (dd) as the perfective participle.

(dd)   *As Vernon had tackled inferior defenses at Porto Bello, Exmouth tackled inferior defenses at Algiers, & Seymour tackled inferior defenses at Alexandria.*

Under this impossible interpretation, the second two conjuncts would involve deletion of just the perfective auxiliary *had*. The only possible interpretation for (dd) is where *tackled* in the latter two conjuncts is understood as the past tense of *tackle*, not the perfective participle. Because of the repetition, (dd) is stylistically problematic – a problem that is mitigated by replacing *inferior defenses* with *them* in the two conjuncts: *As Vernon had tackled inferior defenses at Porto Bello, Exmouth tackled them at Algiers, & Seymour tackled them at Alexandria.*

Applying this constraint on T+V ellipsis to Fowler's example creates a potential paradox for the analysis in which *Exmouth at Algiers* and *Seymour at Alexandria* result from the operation of both verb phrase ellipsis and T+V ellipsis. If T+V ellipsis applies first, then the result is acceptable English but only if the prepositional phrases *at Porto Bello*, *at Algiers*, and *at Alexandria* are interpreted as modifying *inferior defenses* and therefore is part of noun phrase headed by *defenses*.

(ee)   1. *... as Vernon had tackled inferior defenses at Porto Bello, Exmouth had tackled inferior defenses at Algiers, & Seymour has tackled inferior defenses at Alexandria.*
         2. *... as Vernon had tackled inferior defenses at Porto Bello, Exmouth had tackled inferior defenses at Algiers, & Seymour had tackled inferior defenses at Alexandria.*
         3. *... as Vernon had tackled inferior defenses at Porto Bello, Exmouth, inferior defenses at Algiers, & Seymour, inferior defenses at Alexandria.*

If verb phrase ellipsis applies first, then (ff) results.

(ff)   1. *... as Vernon had tackled inferior defenses at Porto Bello, Exmouth had tackled inferior defenses at Algiers, & Seymour has tackled inferior defenses at Alexandria.*
         2. *... as Vernon had tackled inferior defenses at Porto Bello, Exmouth had tackled inferior defenses at Algiers, & Seymour had tackled inferior defenses at Algiers.*

> 3. … *as Vernon had tackled inferior defenses at Porto Bello, Exmouth*
>   *had at Algiers, & Seymour had at Alexandria.*

However, unlike the analysis for (ee), the prepositional phrases *at Porto Bello* and *at Algiers* must be interpreted as modifying the verb *tackled* (and not the noun *defenses*).

Neither derivation in (ee) or (ff) yields Fowler's *Exmouth at Algiers, & Seymour at Alexandria* with the interpretation 'Exmouth tackled inferior defenses at Algiers, & Seymour tackled inferior defenses at Alexandria' in which *at Algiers* and *at Alexandria* both modify *tackled*. To derive this construction with (ee), it would appear that T+V ellipsis must be able to apply to just the finite auxiliary – which is not possible for those speakers of English who find *Bill should buy a used car, and Mary, lease a new one* ((u.2) above) unacceptable. But this conclusion is based on an assumption that an ellipsis operation is in fact a deletion operation that immediately removes phonetic features from a phonetic representation, making them inaccessible to further ellipsis operations. This is not a necessary assumption however.

Suppose instead that an ellipsis operation only marks the phonetic features in a structure as destined to be removed from phonetic representation. Under this assumption, even if one ellipsis operation marks the main verb for eventual deletion from phonetic form, it will still be possible for another ellipsis operation to mark the same main verb for future removal as well. Consider the case under discussion, *Exmouth at Algiers* derived from *Exmouth had tackled inferior defenses at Algiers*. T+V ellipsis yields (gg.1), where the material to be removed from phonetic form is marked in non-italic strike-through small caps, and verb phrase ellipsis yields (gg.2), where the material to be removed is marked in strike-through bold italics.

(gg)   1. *Exmouth* ~~HAD TACKLED~~ *inferior defenses at Algiers*

        2. *Exmouth had* ~~**tackled inferior defenses**~~ *at Algiers*

Overlaying (gg.1) and (gg.2) would yield (hh), where ~~*tackled*~~ shows up in both boldface italics (via verb phrase ellipsis) and small caps (via T+V ellipsis).

(hh)   *Exmouth* ~~HAD **TACKLED inferior defenses**~~ *at Algiers*

Of course, all that is relevant for the determination of phonetic form is whether certain phonetic material has been marked as destined for removal from phonetic representation. The fact that two distinct ellipsis processes mark the same phonetic material for deletion more than once has no special meaning for phonetic form. Once marked for deletion, phonetic material will be removed at some later stage in the derivation of phonetic representation.

Under this analysis, the existence of an idiolect of English in which finite T ellipsis cannot apply to just a finite auxiliary poses no problem for deriving

Exmouth at Algiers, where the prepositional phrase *at Algiers* is interpreted as modifying the verb *tackled*. Furthermore, either order of ellipsis operations, T+V > verb phrase or verb phrase > T+V, yields the same result. And if this is the correct analysis for how the computational system for human language operates in the generation of ellipsis constructions in English (and presumably other languages), then this small investigation into one surprisingly rich and revealing example of English (our chapter title) has once again revealed something of the hidden depth and abstract nature of our knowledge of the language we speak.

Coda

This chapter has explored the syntax of Henry Fowler's example that titles it, which he cites as an improper use of the passive voice. On closer inspection, we find that it is a complicated piece of English syntax involving not only the passive voice, but also coordination and ellipsis.

Fowler makes three suggestions for improving the acceptability of the sentence, two of which retain the passive construction in the first part. Fowler's suggestion to replace *as Vernon did* with *as they were by Vernon*, which isn't applied to the remainder of the sentence, can be realized in two ways: as coordinating the three objects of a single *by*-phrases, where the following *at*-phrase can only be interpreted as modifying the name of an admiral, or as a coordination of predicates *were tackled* where both of the following prepositional phrases modify the elided passive participle *tackled* in each conjunct. In the third alternative, the preposition *by* is not repeated in the 2nd and 3rd conjuncts, making this coordinate structure a coordination of noun phrase objects of a single *by*-phrase. For this case too, the three *at*-phrases can only modify the names of the admirals.

But when the linear order of the two prepositional phrases is reversed (for example *at Porto Bello by Vernon*), because the *by*-phrase cannot be sensibly construed as a modifier of a place, the only possible construal of the coordinate structure is as a coordination of predicates, not a coordination of *at*-phrases. Under this construal, both prepositional phrases modify the elided *tackled*.

All of these examples involve the same instance of ellipsis, where *as they were* is understood as 'as they were tackled', *they* standing in for *inferior defenses*. Given that ellipsis requires a matching antecedent elsewhere in the sentence, it appears that *tackled* in *be tackled*, functions as the antecedent of the missing passive participle in *were tackled*. And on the interpretation of the coordinate structure as a coordination of predicates, then *were tackled* in the first conjunct functions as the antecedent of the ellipsis in the second two conjuncts. Given the conclusion at the end of this chapter that the operation leading to the reduction of phonetic form only marks syntactic material for deletion at a later stage, then it won't matter which operation applies first.

Therefore an ellipsis site can still function as an antecedent for ellipsis elsewhere, even though syntactic material of the antecedent won't show up in the phonetic form of the sentence.

Fowler's original sentence, unlike his proposals for fixing it, can only be interpreted as ending with a coordination of clauses, where each admiral is the subject of a conjunct and each *at*-phrase is part of the predicate of that clausal conjunct. Fowler wants to pin the trouble with the sentence on the mismatch between the passive voice in the first part and the active voice in the second, interpreting *did* as the past tense of the main verb *do*. And clearly, he is right that something is wrong with this ostensible failure of parallelism between the two parts – but what exactly? The first conjunct, on this analysis, involves no ellipsis.

Alternatively, *did* can be interpreted as the auxiliary *do*, in which case the first clausal conjunct is an instance of ellipsis where part of the verb phrase of the predicate (*tackle inferior defenses*) has been elided. This raises the question of what the antecedent for this ellipsis in the first part of the sentence could be. The answer is provided by the displacement analysis of passive constructions where the object of the verb, which is pronounced as the syntactic subject of the clause, nonetheless occurs in the verb phrase as the object of the verb (its semantic interpretation). In this way, *tackled inferior defenses* also occurs in the first part – just not in its phonetic form – and could serve as the antecedent of the ellipsis in the first clausal conjunct. However, this antecedent doesn't match what is elided, phonetically or morphologically: *tackled* being a participle in contrast to the active verb *tackle*.

That the problem with Fowler's sentence probably isn't the mismatch between passive and active is demonstrated by replacing *did* with *had*, which appears to eliminate the problem while maintaining the voice mismatch between the two parts of the sentence. In the revised sentence, *tackled inferior defenses* in the first part matches what is elided in the second part, phonetically and also morphologically to the extent that both verbs are participles. The difference in voice seems to have no significant effect.

How ellipsis works in the last two conjuncts involves two distinct, but overlapping, processes: the verb phrase ellipsis that functions in the 1st conjunct and another operation that elides a T element and its adjacent main verb (T+V). These two processes are distinct because only VP ellipsis can apply in a subordinate clause where the antecedent of the ellipsis occurs in a clause that contains this subordinate clause. Both result in the ellipsis of the main verb.

The 2nd and 3rd conjuncts in our revision of Fowler's sentence demonstrate that both can apply to the same clause. This would be paradoxical if each operation affects an immediate reduction in phonetic form. Applying one before the other would eliminate a piece of syntax required for the operation of the other. The paradox is resolved if these operations merely mark phonetic material destined for elimination from phonetic form, where the phonetic reduction happens at a later stage. A main verb can only be eliminated from phonetic form once, so it won't matter if it is twice marked for reduction by different processes.

The analysis of ellipsis in Fowler's sentence once again reveals something of the abstract nature and hidden depth that are involved in the computation of English sentence structure. It also shows how syntactic structure plays a central role in this computation.

Concluding comment

Having followed the preceding chapters to this point, you now have a basic understanding of English sentence structure that you can use in your writing and reading. Aside from its intrinsic interest as an insight into a part of human cognition that defines us as a species and because of the fundamental usefulness of this understanding, a basic knowledge of English sentence structure should figure in an English speaker's basic education. This point is made by Noam Chomsky in a 1984 letter to an English teacher:

I don't see how any person can truly be called "educated" who doesn't know the elements of sentence structure, or who doesn't understand the nature of a relative clause, a passive construction, and so on. Furthermore, if one is going to discuss literature, including here what students write themselves, and to come to understand how it is written and why, these conceptual tools are indispensable.[12]

Incorporating these indispensable conceptual tools into the curricula of high school English classes and college writing courses would enrich and enliven the work of both teachers and students significantly.

Compared to the 1860 pages of the *Cambridge Grammar of the English Language*, this book provides only a brief sketch of the vast territory of English syntax, but one that lays a solid foundation for further exploration. If it is successful, it will serve as a demonstration that the structure of language is endlessly fascinating when you pay attention.

---

[12] "Letter about the teaching of grammar (March 4, 1984)" in Noam Chomsky, *Chomsky on Democracy and Education* (2003), p. 355.

Glossary

---

active voice: (see *passive voice*)

affirmative: (see negative)

anaphoric relation: A word–word relation where a word (for example, a pronoun) may stand in for another word or phrase. For example, the relative pronoun *which* stands in for *books* in *books which have been written by philosophers*, or for *those new books* in *those new books which were written by philosophers*.

antecedent of a relative pronoun: The noun modified by a relative clause where the relative pronoun stands in for that noun.

asyndetic coordination: A coordinate structure without a visible conjunction, where a comma stands in for *and*, including before the final conjunct.

bare infinitival clause: An infinitival clause that lacks a visible subject.

cognitive form: The syntactic representation of a linguistic expression represents the explicit interpretation of the expression, including its invisible hierarchical structure and labeling.

complementary distribution: A relation between linguistic elements such that two or more elements occur in the same context(s) but can never occur together, for example, modal auxiliaries and auxiliary *do*.

coordinate structure: Two or more syntactic units joined together with a coordinating conjunction (*and*, *or*), where the units constitute conjuncts of the coordinate structure.

Deletion: An operation that results in the removal of pieces of phonetic form from phonetic representations.

displacement: A phenomenon in syntax where a syntactic unit is pronounced in one context and interpreted as if it occupies a different context.

ellipsis: The syntactic phenomenon involving the optional removal from phonetic form of pieces of syntax in a linguistic expression, which are nonetheless interpreted as if they existed where they are missing.

gerund: A form of noun, constructed from a verbal root plus a nominalizing suffix –*ing* (not to be confused with the verbal inflectional suffix –*ing* on progressive participles).

grammar: A computational system plus a lexicon that together accounts for the linguistic expressions in a language.

head: The lexical item in a syntactic unit whose category label labels the syntactic unit. In the case of a prepositional phrase, for example, the preposition labels the syntactic unit consisting of the preposition and its object.

head-to-head dependence: A requirement imposed by the head of a syntactic unit on a lexical item it merges with, where this lexical item becomes the head of the syntactic unit created. For example, verb phrase headed by a passive participle can only merge with some form of the passive auxiliary *be*. And if that form of the passive auxiliary is not finite (not T), then it will determine what further verbal T element that syntactic unit can merge with.

hierarchical structure:
: The structure in which words are grouped together to form distinct syntactic units.

indicative:
: The form of a clause that indicates a statement.

indirect question:
: A subordinate interrogative clause (contrast with an interrogative main clause, a direct question).

interrogative:
: The form of a clause that indicates a question.

Label:
: The operation that determines the category label of a syntactic unit created by Merge.

layered coordination:
: A coordinate structure in which a coordination with one conjunction forms a conjunct for a coordinate structure involving another conjunction.

lexicon:
: Roughly, the words of a language.

Linearize:
: The operation that assigns linear order to hierarchical structure.

main clause:
: A non-subordinate clause.

Merge:
: An operation that combines two syntactic units (minimally words in the lexicon) to form a new syntactic unit. Merge creates the hierarchical structure of syntactic representations.

morphology:
: The internal structure of words, where words are composed of a root plus one or more affixes. Compare the verb *indicts* to the noun *indictments*. The verb consists of a root *indict* plus an inflectional suffix *–s* that adds number, person, and tense information: singular, third, and present to the verbal meaning of root, which does not express this information. The noun *indictments* contains the same verbal root indict to which is added the nominalizing suffix *–ment* that changes the category of the resulting form to noun and also changes its

	interpretation. To this is added an inflectional suffix *–s* that indicates the noun is a plural.
morphosyntax:	The intersection of syntax and morphology.
negative:	A clause whose verbal elements are negated by *not* (contrasts with an affirmative clause, which does not contain *not*).
non-restrictive relative clause:	(see restrictive relative clause)
noun phrase:	A syntactic unit whose head is a noun.
passive voice:	A verb form that is phonetically identical to the perfective participle, but must occur with an auxiliary form of *be*. In simple sentences containing the passive verb, the semantic object of the verb appears as the syntactic subject of the clause and the semantic subject will appear as the object of agentive *by* in the predicate. With all other (active) forms of the verb, the agent of the verb occurs in the subject position.
phonetic form:	The representation of linguistic expressions in terms of their phonetic features, their pronunciation or written form.
predicate:	The part of a clause that predicates something about the subject. Syntactically, this includes the main verb, its auxiliary modifiers, adverbial and prepositional phrase modifiers, and its objects (nominal or clausal).
preposition stranding:	A phenomenon where the object of a preposition is not pronounced adjacent to its preposition, leaving the preposition 'stranded' in phonetic form.
prepositional phrase:	A syntactic unit consisting of a preposition and a noun phrase object.
progressive aspect:	A participial form of a verb or auxiliary that expresses ongoing action: *fooling*

	in *they were fooling us* and *being* in *they were being fooled.*
relative clause:	A clause that modifies a noun.
restrictive relative clause:	A relative clause that characterizes a subset of the entities named by noun it modifies. In contrast, a non-restrictive relative clause characterizes all the entities named by the noun it modifies.
selection:	A head-to-head dependency relation.
simple sentence:	A clause that contains no subordinate clause and can occur as an independent sentence.
singular:	For countable nouns, indicating just 1, whereas plural indicates more than 1. With verbs the distinction applies with respect to whether a finite verb agrees with a singular or plural subject.
sister:	The relation between two syntactic units combined by Merge.
subordinate clause:	A clause that forms a subpart of a larger linguistic expression.
syntax:	How the elements of sentence structure (including words) fit together; in linguistics, the study of the principles and processes by which sentences are constructed in particular languages.
tree diagram:	A graphic representation of hierarchical sentence structure.

References

Aarts, Bas. 2011. *Oxford Modern English Grammar*. Oxford: Oxford University Press.
The American Heritage Dictionary of the English Language (2000), 4th edition.
    Boston: Houghton Mifflin Co.
Angell, Roger. 2015. Foreword to the 4th edition of *Elements of Style*. In *This Old Man:
    Roger Angell All in Pieces* (ed.). New York: Doubleday.
Bernstein, Theodore. 1965. *The Careful Writer: A Modern Guide to English Usage*.
    New York: Atheneum.
Berwick, Robert & Noam Chomsky. 2016. *Why Only Us: Language and Evolution*.
    Cambridge, MA: MIT Press.
Brooks, Cleanth & Robert Penn Warren. 1958. *Modern Rhetoric*, 2nd edition. New
    York: Harcourt, Brace & World.
Burchfield, R.W. 2000. *The New Fowler's Modern English Usage*, 3rd revised edition.
    Oxford: Oxford University Press.
Chomsky, Noam. 1957. *Syntactic Structures*. The Hague: Mouton.
    1987. *Generative Grammar: Its Basis, Development and Prospects*, published as a
        special issue of *Studies in English Linguistics and Literature*. Kyoto: Kyoto
        University of Foreign Studies.
    1993. *Language and Thought*. Wakefield, RI: Moyer Bell.
    2003. *Chomsky on Democracy and Education*. Carlos Otero (ed.). New York:
        RoutledgeFalmer.
    2009a. *Language and Mind*, 3rd edition. Cambridge, UK: Cambridge University
        Press.
    2009b. *Cartesian Linguistics: A Chapter in the History of Rationalist Thought*, 3rd
        edition. Cambridge, UK: Cambridge University Press.
    2016. *What Kind of Creatures Are We?* New York: Columbia University Press.
Crews, Frederick. 1977. *The Random House Handbook*, 2nd edition. New York:
    Random House.
Crystal, David. 2008. *Dictionary of Linguistics and Phonetics*, 6th edition. Oxford:
    Blackwell Publishers.
Cusack, John & Arundhati Roy. 2016. *Things that Can and Cannot Be Said: Essays
    and Conversations*. Chicago: Haymarket Books.
Dryden, John. 1672. "Defence of the Epilogue." In *Essays of John Dryden*. W.P. Ker
    (ed.). Oxford: The Clarendon Press (1900).
Foerster, Norman & J.M. Steadman Jr. 1923. *Sentences and Thinking: A Handbook of
    Composition and Revision*. Boston: Houghton Mifflin Co.

Fowler, Henry W. 1906. *Sentence Analysis for the Lower Forms of Public Schools.* Oxford: The Clarendon Press.

 1926. *A Dictionary of Modern English Usage.* Oxford: The Clarendon Press.

Fowler, Henry W. & Francis G. Fowler. 1906. *The King's English.* Oxford: The Clarendon Press.

Freidin, Robert. 2012. *Syntax: Basic Concepts and Applications.* Cambridge, UK: Cambridge University Press.

Haussamen, Brock. 2003. *Grammar Alive!: A Guide for Teachers.* Urbana, IL: National Council of Teachers of English.

Huddleston, Rodney & Geoffrey K. Pullum, 2002. *Cambridge Grammar of the English Language.* Cambridge, UK: Cambridge University Press.

Kolln, Martha & Craig Hancock. 2005. "The Story of English Grammar in United States Schools," *English Teaching: Practice and Critique,* 4.3: 11–31.

Kolln, Martha, Loretta Gray, & Joseph Salvatore. 2016. *Understanding English Grammar,* 10th edition. Boston: Pearson.

Krantz, Steven G. 1997. *A Primer of Mathematical Writing: Being a Disquisition on Having Your Ideas Recorded, Typeset, Published, Read & Appreciated.* Providence, RI: American Mathematical Society.

Le Guin, Ursula. 1998. *Steering the Craft: Exercises and Discussions on Story Writing for the Lone Navigator or the Mutinous Crew.* Portland, OR: The Eight Mountain Press.

Liberman, Mark. 2013. "A Decline in *which*-hunting?" (http://languagelog.ldc.upenn.edu/nll/?p=5479)

Lowth, Robert. 1775. *A Short Introduction to English Grammar with Critical Notes.* London: J. Dodsley & T. Cadell.

Martin, Andy. 2015. *Reacher Said Nothing: Lee Child and the Making of <u>Make Me</u>.* New York: Bantam Books.

Mortimer, John. 2002. *Rumpole Rests His Case.* New York: Viking.

Murray, Lindley. 1908. *English Grammar.* New York: Collins & Perkins.

Nunberg, Geoffrey. 2009. "Our Friend the Passive Voice" (http://people.ischool.berkeley.edu/~nunberg/passive.html)

Orwell, George. 1946. "Politics and the English Language," In *A Collection of Essays.* Garden City, NY: Doubleday (1954).

Pinker, Steven. 1994. *The Language Instinct: How the Mind Creates Language.* New York: W. Morrow and Co.

 2014. *The Sense of Style: The Thinking Person's Guide to Writing in the 21st Century.* New York: Viking Adult.

Prose, Francine. 2006. *Reading Like a Writer.* New York: HarperCollins.

Pullum, Geoffrey K. 2012. "A Rule Which Will Live in Infamy," *The Chronicle of Higher Education.* December 7, 2012.

 2014. "Fear and Loathing of the English Passive," *Language & Communication,* 37: 60–74.

 2015. "On the Myth that Passives are Wordy" (www.sense-online.nl/files/jubilee-conference/jubilee-public/674-esensemagazine-issue-37-april-2015-gk-pullum-on-myths-about-passives/file)

Reed, Alonzo & Brainerd Kellogg. 1878. *Graded Lessons in English.* New York: Clark & Maynard.

Sacks, Oliver. 2007. *Musicophilia*. New York: Alfred A. Knopf.

Sistrunk, Walter. 2012. *"The Syntax of Zero in African American Relative Clauses."* PhD dissertation, Michigan State University.

Solan, Lawrence M. 1993. *The Language of Judges*. Chicago: University of Chicago Press.

Strunk, William & E.B. White. 1959. *The Elements of Style*. New York: Macmillan.

Tattersall, Ian. 2012. *Masters of the Planet*. New York: Palgrave Macmillan.

Truss, Lynne. 2004. *Eats, Shoots & Leaves: The Zero Tolerance Approach to Punctuation*. New York: Gotham Books.

Vidal, Gore. 1993. *United States: Essays 1952–1992*. New York: Random House.

Williams, Joseph M. 1991. *Style: Towards Clarity and Grace*. Chicago: University of Chicago Press.

Woolley, Edwin C. 1907. *Handbook of Composition: A Compendium of Rules Regarding Good English, Grammar, Sentence Structure, Paragraphing, Manuscript Arrangement, Punctuation, Spelling, Essay Writing, and Letter Writing*. Boston: D.C. Heath & Co.

Zinn, Howard. 2002. Letter, in James L. Harmon (ed.), *Take My Advice: Letters to the Next Generation from People Who Know a Thing or Two*. New York: Simon & Schuster.

Index